T0207178

Lecture Notes of the Institute for Computer Sciences, Social Informatics and Telecommunications Engineering 430

More information about this series at https://link.springer.com/bookseries/8197

Mohammad R. Khosravi · Qiang He ·
Haipeng Dai (Eds.)

Cloud Computing

11th EAI International Conference, CloudComp 2021
Virtual Event, December 9–10, 2021
Proceedings

 Springer

Editors
Mohammad R. Khosravi ⓘ
Persian Gulf University
Bushehr, Iran

Qiang He
Swinburne University of Technology
Hawthorn, VIC, Australia

Haipeng Dai ⓘ
Nanjing University
Nanjing, China

ISSN 1867-8211   ISSN 1867-822X (electronic)
Lecture Notes of the Institute for Computer Sciences, Social Informatics
and Telecommunications Engineering
ISBN 978-3-030-99190-6   ISBN 978-3-030-99191-3 (eBook)
https://doi.org/10.1007/978-3-030-99191-3

This Springer imprint is published by the registered company Springer Nature Switzerland AG
The registered company address is: Gewerbestrasse 11, 6330 Cham, Switzerland

Preface

We are delighted to introduce the proceedings of the 11th edition of the European Alliance for Innovation (EAI) International Conference on Cloud Computing (CloudComp 2021). This conference brought together researchers, developers, and practitioners around the world who are leveraging and developing cloud computing technologies for efficient and intelligent computing in secure and smart environments with distributed devices. The theme of CloudComp 2021 was "Cloud Computing for Secure and Smart Applications".

The technical program of CloudComp 2021 consisted of 17 papers, comprising three review papers and 14 original research papers, presented at the main conference tracks. The conference proceedings has been organized into three general sections in this book: Data Analytics for Cloud Systems with Distributed Applications, Cloud Architecture and Challenges in Real-World Use, and Security in Cloud/Edge Platforms. In the first section, seven papers around the importance of intelligent computing, efficient processing, and machine leaning (specifically deep learning) with applications to traditional and distributed cloud systems are presented. In the second section, there are five papers with a serious focus on architecture and challenges of cloud systems for realizing cloud-based services. And finally, the last section introduces the five remaining papers focused on different aspects of security for cloud- and internet of things (IoT)-based applications.

We deeply thank all of our Technical Program Committee members and reviewers who helped us to organize the conference under the difficult circumstances of the COVID-19 pandemic. Also, the contribution of our participants is highly appreciated and we hope to have all of them at the next meeting of CloudComp. Finally, a great thanks to all the EAI staff and managers for their constant support is needed. We strongly believe that CloudComp 2021 provided a good forum for all researchers, developers, and practitioners to discuss all scientific and technological aspects that are relevant to cloud systems and cloud/edge computing applications.

December 2021

Mohammad R. Khosravi
Qiang He
Haipeng Dai
Shangguang Wang
Jun Shen
Lianyong Qi

Organization

Steering Committee

Imrich Chlamtac (Chair)   University of Trento, Italy
Xuyun Zhang   Macquarie University, Australia
Guanfeng Liu   Macquarie University, Australia

Organizing Committee

General Chairs

Qiang He   Swinburne University of Technology, Australia
Yun Yang   Swinburne University of Technology, Australia
Haipeng Dai   Nanjing University, China
Yuan Yuan   Michigan State University, USA

Technical Program Committee Chairs

Shangguang Wang   Beijing University of Posts and
                                   Telecommunications, China
Jun Shen   University of Wollongong, Australia
Lianyong Qi   Qufu Normal University, China
Mohammad R. Khosravi   Persian Gulf University, Iran

Sponsorship and Exhibit Chairs

Dong Yuan   University of Sydney, Australia
Xiaokang Zhou   Shiga University, Japan
Dharavath Ramesh   Indian Institute of Technology (ISM) Dhanbad,
                                   India

Local Chairs

Hai Dong   RMIT University, Australia
Fei Dai   Southwest Forestry University, China
Keshav Sood   Deakin University, Australia

Workshops Chairs

Prem Prakash Jayaraman	Swinburne University of Technology, Australia
Varun G. Menon	SCMS School of Engineering and Technology, India
Xiaokang Wang	St. Francis Xavier University, Canada

Publicity and Social Media Chairs

Xiaolong Xu	Nanjing University of Information Science and Technology, China
Mehdi Elahi	University of Bergen, Norway
Maqbool Khan	Sino-Pak Center for Artificial Intelligence, PAF-IAST, Pakistan

Publications Chairs

Mohammad R. Khosravi	Persian Gulf University, Iran
Yiwen Zhang	Anhui University, China
Xuyun Zhang	Macquarie University, Australia

Web Chairs

Deze Zeng	China University of Geosciences, China
Shancang Li	University of the West of England, UK
Alireza Jolfaei	Macquarie University, Australia

Technical Program Committee

Fiza Abdul Rahim	Universiti Tenaga Nasional, Malaysia
Liangyi Gong	Tsinghua University, China
Zhifeng Bao	Royal Melbourne Institute of Technology University, Australia
Maria Dolores Cano	Universidad Politecnica de Cartagena, Spain
Lianhua Chi	La Trobe University, Australia
Guangming Cui	Swinburne University of Technology, Australia
Wenwen Gong	China Agricultural University, China
Qiang He	Swinburne University, Australia
Md. Kafiul Islam	Independent University, Bangladesh
Wenmin Lin	Hangzhou Normal University, China
Guanfeng Liu	Macquarie University, Australia
Mahesh Maddumala	University of Missouri, USA
Tamim Al Mahmud	Aston University, UK
Yiping Wen	Hunan University of Science and Technology, China

Syeda Naqvi	University of Engineering and Technology Taxila, Pakistan
Manik Sharma	DAV University, India
Patrick Siarry	Université Paris-Est Créteil, France
Daniel Sun	CSIRO, Australia
Wenda Tang	Lancaster University, UK
Khosro Rezaee	Meybod University, Iran

Contents

Security in Cloud/Edge Platforms

Data Analytics for Cloud Systems with Distributed Applications

Load Quality Analysis and Forecasting for Power Data Set on Cloud Platform

Jixiang Gan, Qi Liu[✉], and Jing Zhang

School of Computer and Software, Engineering Research Center of Digital Forensics,
Ministry of Education, Nanjing University of Information Science
and Technology, Nanjing 210044, China
{20201249454,qi.liu,20191221030}@nuist.edu.cn

Abstract. In the era of big data, The prediction management system combined with cloud computing platform can start from massive structured, semi-structured and unstructured data, which has a positive impact on improving the compliance quality analysis and prediction of power data sets. This paper focuses on the characteristics of all kinds of data sets needed in the research of power demand side business process of cloud platform at home and abroad, and analyzes, compares and summarizes all kinds of data sets. First, this paper analyzes the problems existing in various common data sets, and expounds the methods to improve the quality of data sets from two aspects of data cleaning and data preprocessing. Secondly, the LSTM prediction model and ARIMA prediction model are used to predict and analyze the collected power data to judge whether the data set has obvious defects in advance. Finally, through the experimental comparison of the two models, a more efficient prediction model is analyzed.

Keywords: Data quality · Load forecasting · Data cleaning · Cloud platform

1 Introduction

Under the background of "energy Internet plus new electricity reform", the power technology represented by smart grid is constantly integrating with information technology represented by cloud computing and big data, changing the way of production and operation of power enterprises [1, 2]. Through the combination of "cloud platform + big data". On the one hand, the established big data management system can not only coordinate the data management within the enterprise, but also make use of the existing data processing technology to clean and preprocess the relevant data, ensure the quality of data, and improve the efficiency of data utilization. On the other hand, cloud platform technology can be used to share various data and improve data utilization [3].

Cloud is what we usually call network or Internet, and cloud platform is a space for data storage and operation (such as network disk, micro disk, etc.) with the help of network or Internet. It is abbreviated as CMP (cloud management platform), which is a third-party platform derived from the development of cloud computing. Using the convenient and fast characteristics of the cloud platform, the staff can use their own files in

M. R. Khosravi et al. (Eds.): CloudComp 2021, LNICST 430, pp. 3–16, 2022.
https://doi.org/10.1007/978-3-030-99191-3_1

different network environments or different computers, providing convenient channels and space for enterprises. Since the development trend of cloud platform application technology in China [4]. The data quality in the big data management system established by "cloud platform + big data" has become a key and difficult point. Improving the quality of process data can improve the value of data in use, reduce the cost and risk in the later stage of the project, and improve the accuracy of real-time information analysis [5]. At the same time, the cloud platform can further concentrate on information processing, transmission, storage and other links, improve the speed, and make it more convenient to access resources. Therefore, the factors affecting data quality in cloud platform big data have become one of the concerns of major enterprises to improve big data management system.

With the continuous development of smart grid construction, as an important way of power consumption information acquisition and control, power consumption information acquisition system produces more and more big data. In the face of massive power consumption data, how to ensure the quality of data and how to improve the quality of relevant power data in the cloud platform big data management system has become the current research hotspot [6]. For example, in the process of power data collection, through the use of intelligent terminal devices such as smart meters, the operation data of the whole power system can be collected, so as to realize the authenticity and accuracy in the data collection stage, and then the collected power big data can be processed and analyzed systematically, so as to realize the timeliness of data. Finally, combined with big data analysis and power system model, it can diagnose, optimize and forecast the operation of power grid, and provide guarantee for safe, reliable, economic and efficient operation of power grid [7–9]. Therefore, to achieve reasonable business process management, we need to have enough perfect data sets to improve the quality of process data.

In order to obtain accurate and perfect data sets, in the power business process management of cloud platform big data management system, each scholar collected and established different power data sets. In "Non-intrusive load monitoring and load disaggregation using transient data analysis" by Sachin Kumar Jain in 2018, the author collected the power consumption data of 20 types and 8 different appliances in the campus through the sensor acquisition device, with the sampling frequency of 12800 Hz and the duration of about 5 h each time, After noise removal and unified data format preprocessing, it is used as the experimental data set [10]. Meanwhile, in 2020, Seongbae Kong and others developed a set of power data acquisition system in "home appliance load disaggregation using cepstrum-smoothing based method", which is used to obtain the characteristic signals of electrical appliances [11]. But whether it is sensor acquisition device or power data acquisition system, compared with the existing public data set, although the data they collected is more targeted than the public data set, their sampling accuracy and duration are not perfect, and for the existing monitoring model, it is not as universal as the current public data set.

2 Analysis and Improvement of Power Data

2.1 Classification and Comparison of Common Power Data Sets

With the improvement of smart meters and the popularity of data management system, a large number of power data acquisition, storage and management have been realized. At the same time, with the mature application of big data analysis, machine learning and other technologies, the information value contained in smart meters can be better mined. The authenticity, accuracy and integrity of power data set are guaranteed. At present, the more popular power data sets mainly include REDD data set, BLUED data set and UK-DALE data set [12]. The detailed information table of REDD data set, BLUED data set and UK-DALE data set is shown in Table 1.

REDD Data Set. REDD data set contains data of six American families in different time periods. REDD data set provides both high and low frequency household power data. The main advantage of REDD data set is that its data volume is rich enough to adapt to the large network training model [13]. REDD data set is relatively clean compared with other data sets, and good results can be achieved without post-processing [14].

BLUED Data Set. The BLUED data set contains data collected by an American family in about 8 days. The BLUED data set provides high-frequency household electric power data with a frequency of 12 kHz. The data set also provides an event list when the household appliance changes state [15]. The advantage of BLUED data set is that it provides equipment power data with time axis, which is conducive to use in evaluation algorithm to confirm decomposition results [16]. The main disadvantage of BLUED data set is the high redundancy of high frequency data.

UK-DALE Data Set. The UK-DALE data set contains two to four years' electricity data of six UK households. UK-DALE data set provides both high-frequency household power data with sampling frequency of 16 kHz and an independent low-frequency household power data [17]. The main advantage of UK-DALE data set is that it can provide a long duration of data and meet the needs of monitoring at different times of the year. The main disadvantage of UK-DALE dataset is that due to the large number of data samples in UK-DALE dataset, the data classification is unbalanced. Finally, the accuracy of the experiment is affected.

The analysis shows that REDD data set, BLUED data set and UK-DALE data set have obvious differences in collection area, data duration, collection frequency and data volume. According to these different attributes, the application scenarios of different data sets are also different. However, due to the reasonable collection time and diverse collection frequency of REDD data set, REDD data set has gradually become the standard data set for benchmark test of decomposition prediction algorithm [18]. At the same time, REDD data set, blue data set and UK-DALE data set play an important role in the implementation and management of power business process.

2.2 The Function of Electric Power Data Set

A reasonable power data set can not only analyze in the power data system of cloud platform and formulate a reasonable management process, but also predict and plan the

Table 1. Detailed information of REDD data set, BLUED data set and UK-DALE data set

Dataset name	Acquisition frequency	Collection area	Duration	Collection of house types	Number of equipment
REDD dataset	16500 Hz/1 Hz	America	A few months	Residential district	6 houses
BLUED dataset	12000 Hz	America	8 days	Residential district	1 house
UK-DALE dataset	16000 Hz/1 Hz	Britain	2–4 years	Residential district	6 houses

future schedule, resource allocation and process management. In the whole life cycle of business process management, reasonable data sets play different roles in different stages. In the business process evaluation stage, the appropriate business process is defined by analyzing the data set. In the business process design and analysis stage, based on the actual data set, using the defined business process, the business process content is modeled and the modeling model is verified and analyzed. In the business process configuration stage, the real data set is used to configure the analyzed business process and deploy the related process. In the business process implementation stage, the configured business process is properly implemented and monitored with effective data set [19–23]. Business process management flow chart, as shown in Fig. 1. Therefore, in order to improve the efficiency of business process management, it is essential to improve the data quality of relevant data.

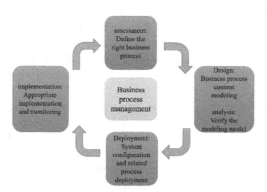

Fig. 1. Business process management flow chart

2.3 Methods of Improving Data Quality

After big data construction, most enterprises have achieved good data construction results and accumulated considerable amount of data. However, it is a great risk to use these data directly. Therefore, it is necessary to analyze the data before processing to improve the data quality [24]. There are many ways to improve the quality of data, and the academia generally starts to consider data cleaning and data preprocessing [25]. From the perspective of data cleaning, improving the quality of data mainly from three perspectives: box method, clustering method and regression method. From the perspective of data preprocessing, there are two ways to improve data quality: standardization and normalization.

Data Cleaning. There are three methods for data cleaning, which are box division, clustering and regression [26].

(1) *Separate Box Method*. Due to the complex characteristics of data quality management, the data to be processed is put into the box according to certain rules, and then the data in each box is tested. also, the data is processed by means of the actual situation of each box in the data.
(2) *Clustering*. It is to group abstract objects into different sets, find unexpected outliers in the collection, which are noise. This allows you to detect noise directly and then clear it.
(3) *Regression Method*. Data regression method is to use the data of the function to draw the image, and then smooth the image. There are two regression methods, one is single linear regression, the other is multiple linear regression. Single linear regression is to find out the best line of two attributes, which can predict another attribute from one. Multilinear regression is to find many attributes, and then fit the data to a multi-dimensional surface, which can eliminate the noise.

Data Preprocessing. Data preprocessing is mainly divided into normalization and standardization. Normalization is to change the number into a decimal between (0, 1), which is mainly proposed for the convenience of data processing. It is more rapid and convenient to map the data to the range of 0–1. Standardization is to scale data to a specific range. Standardized data is more conducive to the use of the properties of standard normal distribution. The common methods of standardization and normalization are z-sorce (zero mean) method and min max method [27].

(1) *Z-sorce*. Zero mean normalization is also called standard deviation normalization. The mean value of processed data is 0 and the standard deviation is 1. The formula is as follows: Where, $\bar{x}$ is the mean value of the original data, σ is the standard deviation of the original data.

$$x^* = \frac{x - \bar{x}}{\sigma} \tag{1}$$

(2) *Min-Max*. Min max normalization, also known as discrete normalization, is a linear transformation of the original data, mapping the data values between [0, 1]. The formula is as follows:

$$x^* = \frac{x - min}{max - min} \tag{2}$$

Discrete standardization retains the relationship existing in the original data, and is the simplest method to eliminate the influence of dimension and data value range. The disadvantage of this method is that if the values are concentrated and a certain value is large, the normalized values are close to 0.

3   Data Prediction

In practical application, it is very important to ensure the data quality of the application system and to supervise and predict the data quality of the future period. The premise of the guarantee is the accurate prediction and evaluation of the time series data. According to the historical series data of the time series data, the series value of the future period can be predicted. We can learn from the common time series prediction methods and models. ARIMA model (autoregressive integrated moving average model) and LSTM model (long short term memory) have good case results in forecasting [28–30]. This paper also uses the above models to forecast and analyze the load power data, and reviews whether the data set meets the data requirements of the application system through the predicted data, Judge whether the quality of follow-up data is qualified.

3.1   ARIMA Model

Arima is a typical time series model, which consists of three parts: AR model (autoregressive model), MA model (moving average model), and difference method. Therefore, ARIMA (p, d, q) is called autoregressive moving average model [31].

Autoregressive Model (AR). The autoregressive model describes the relationship between the current value and the historical value, and forecasts itself with the historical time data of the variable itself. In the autoregressive model, the order P should be determined first, which means that the current value can be predicted by the historical value of several periods. The formula of p-order autoregressive model is defined as:

$$y_t = \mu + \sum_{i=1}^{p} \gamma_i y_{t-i} + \epsilon_t \tag{3}$$

Moving Average Model (MA). The moving average model focuses on the accumulation of error terms in the autoregression model. The formula of q-order autoregression process is defined as follows:

$$y_t = \mu + \sum_{i=1}^{q} \theta_i \epsilon_{t-i} + \epsilon_t \tag{4}$$

By combining autoregressive model, moving average model and difference method, ARIMA (p, d, q) is obtained, where D is the order of data difference.

Determine the Parameters of ARIMA Model. The identification and order determination of the model are mainly to determine the three parameters p, d and q. the order D of the difference is generally obtained by observing the graph. The determination of P and Q is mainly obtained by autocorrelation function ACF (auto correlation function) and partial autocorrelation function PACF (partial auto correlation function).

Autocorrelation Function (ACF). Correlation: compared with the ordered random variable sequence, the autocorrelation function reflects the correlation of its own data in the same sequence in different time series. The formula of autocorrelation function is as follows:

$$ACF(k) = \rho_k = \frac{Cov(y_t, y_{t-k})}{Var(y_t)} \tag{5}$$

Autocorrelation function $ACF(k) = \rho_k$ The value range of K is $[-1, 1]$. The definition of this value range is as follows, -1 is negative correlation, $+1$ is positive correlation and 0 is no correlation.

Partial Autocorrelation Function (PACF). The partial autocorrelation function is used to measure the effect of temporary adjustment of all other short lag terms ($y_t - 1, y_t - 2, ...,$ $y_t - k - 1$). In time series, K time units (y_t and $y_t - k$). It is the linear correlation between the time series observations and the expected past observations given the intermediate observations.

ARIMA Model Overall Process

- Check the data for stability, and if it is not stable, carry out differential processing
- White noise test of stationary post sequence
- ACF function and PACF function are used to determine the order of sequence meeting the requirements
- Test the accuracy of the model
- Using model prediction to forecast and analyze data

3.2 LSTM Model

LSTM network is a special type of RNN, which can learn long-term dependent information. Of course, LSTM and baseline RNN are not very different in structure, but they use different functions to calculate the "hidden" state. LSTM can avoid the problem of long-term dependence, and the central idea is cell state. The network consists of various gates. Through the sigmoid function and point multiplication operation to complete the creation of a door. RNN is a repetitive single neural network layer, while the repetitive module in LSTM contains four interactive layers, three sigmoid layers and one tanh layer, and interacts in a very special way [32–34]. The network structure of LSTM is shown in Fig. 2.

Forgetting Gate. LSTM decides which part of the original cell state to delete. The decision is made through a structure called the forgetting gate. The forgetting gate reads the last output h_{t-1} and the current input x_t. Do a sigmoid nonlinear mapping, and then output a vector f_t. The value of each dimension of the vector is between 0 and 1. 0 means to give up completely and 1 means to keep. Finally, it is related to cell state C_{t-1}. The screening formula of forgetting gate is as follows:

$$f_t = \sigma\left(W_f \cdot [h_{t-1}, x_t] + b_f\right) \tag{6}$$

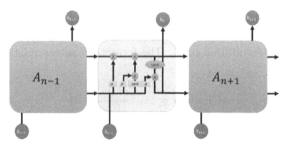

Fig. 2. Network structure of LSTM

Among them, σ Is the sigmoid function, W_f is the parameter of linear relation coefficient, b_f is the bias parameter.

Input Gate. In order to determine the required information of the cell state, firstly, the input information needs to be filtered by sigmoid function, and then the new update state is created by tanh function $\widetilde{C}_t$. The update formula of the input door is:

$$i_t = \sigma\left(W_i \cdot \left[h_{t-1}, x_t\right] + b_i\right) \tag{7}$$

$$\widetilde{C}_t = \tanh\left(W_c \cdot \left[h_{t-1}, x_t\right] + b_c\right) \tag{8}$$

Cellular State. Cell state is to update the old cell state, discard part of the old cell information and add new information. C_{t-1} to C_t. New state C_t is from the old state C_{t-1} and f produced by forgetting gate f_t to determine the information to be updated, and then add the product of the parameters generated by the input gate: $i_t * \widetilde{C}_t$. The change formula of cell state is as follows:

$$C_t = f_t * C_{t-1} + i_t * \widetilde{C}_t \tag{9}$$

Output Gate. The final output is achieved by fitting sigmoid function and tanh function. A sigmoid function to determine which part of the cell's state will be output. Then, the cell state is processed through the tanh layer (a value between -1 and 1 is obtained) and multiplied by the output of the sigmoid function to determine the part of the output. The related formula of output gate is as follows:

$$o_t = \sigma\left(W_o \cdot \left[h_{t-1}, x_t\right] + b_o\right) \tag{10}$$

$$h_t = o_t * \tanh(C_t) \tag{11}$$

3.3 Experimental Results and Evaluation

Dataset Description. The data set used to verify the data quality is the power data of a room in October, and the sampling rate is one hour. ARIMA model and LSTM model were established respectively. The two models established in this paper are implemented in Python language, and the pandas, numpy, statsmodel and Matplotlib libraries are downloaded for use. Table 2 shows the partial power data of a single room in October 2020.

Table 2. Partial power data of single room in October 2020.

Time	Power consumption (KWH)	Time	Power consumption (KWH)	Time	Power consumption (KWH)
2020100100	670718	2020100110	608067	2020100120	568008
2020100101	648975	2020100111	639951	2020100121	354354
2020100102	635599	2020100112	663172	2020100122	435257
2020100103	536269	2020100113	669666	2020100123	360796
2020100104	356870	2020100114	674347	2020100200	674078
2020100105	395430	2020100115	683242	2020100201	652474
2020100106	420034	2020100116	692810	2020100202	643138
2020100107	477297	2020100117	711472	2020100203	536794
2020100108	528439	2020100118	757839	2020100204	383872
2020100109	573939	2020100119	783315	2020100205	389773

Time Series Power Data Prediction Based on ARIMA Model. After the ADF stationarity test and judging whether the sequence is a stationary sequence, the p-value of the sequence is $6.356402463960776 * 10^{(-14)} < 0.05$, and the stationary sequence is obtained. The white noise test of the stationary sequence shows that $0.0027 < 0.05$ is a non white noise sequence. The order of ARIMA model is determined by observing the autocorrelation diagram and partial autocorrelation diagram of the stationary sequence, as shown in Fig. 3. Finally, the values of P and Q are 2 and 4 respectively, which are determined as ARIMA (2, 1, 4) according to the rule of thumb.

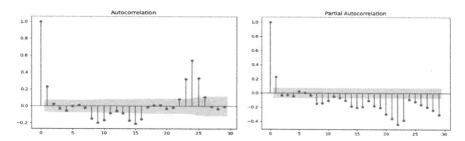

Fig. 3. Autocorrelation graph and partial autocorrelation graph

Through data validation, this paper establishes ARIMA (2, 1, 4) time series model as a model of load forecasting power data. After the model is determined, the data in the next 250 days are predicted. The prediction results are shown in Fig. 4.

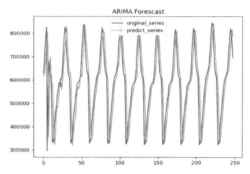

Fig. 4. Data prediction results of ARIMA model in the next 250 days

Time Series Power Data Prediction Based on LSTM Model. Due to the small amount of data, the number of iterations epochs is set to 50, batch_size is 1. In order to further prevent over fitting, dropout technique is used in model training [35]. The loss rate of the experimental model is set to 0.2, that is, 20% of the nodes are discarded in each round of weight update. The loss function is MSE, the activation function is sigmoid, and the optimizer parameter is Adam. The input data also use ADF stationary test and white noise test. Finally, the data of the next 250 days are also predicted, and the prediction results are shown in Fig. 5.

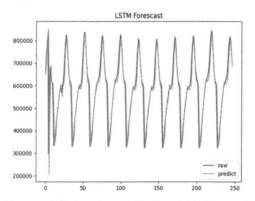

Fig. 5. Data prediction results of LSTM model in the next 250 days

Comparison of Prediction Results of Different Models. Through the comparison of the prediction results in Fig. 4 and Fig. 5, we can intuitively see the effect comparison of the two models, in which the abscissa is hour and the ordinate is kilowatt hour. It can be seen from Fig. 4 that the lag of ARIMA model is serious, and the prediction offset is large in the first 50 h, while the LSTM model shown in Fig. 5 has no serious lag, and the offset is small in the first 50 h. This also illustrates the outstanding performance of LSTM model in single prediction model.

This paper also uses two representative evaluation error standards to evaluate the accuracy of prediction, namely root mean square error (RMSE) and mean absolute deviation (MAE). Their mathematical expressions are as follows:

$$MSE = \sqrt{\frac{1}{n} \times \sum_{i=1}^{n} (F_i - R_i)^2} \tag{12}$$

$$MAE = \sum_{i=1}^{n} \frac{|F_i - R_i|}{n} \tag{13}$$

Among them, F_i is the i-th predicted value, R_i is the ith real value, and N is the sequence length (number of sample points). The smaller the RMSE and Mae, the smaller the prediction error and the higher the accuracy of the model, the better the fitting ability of the model. Table 3 shows the RMSE and Mae values of the prediction results of each model. It can be seen from Table 3 that LSTM model is lower than ARIMA model in all indexes, and the difference is large. LSTM model performs better than ARIMA model in time series prediction.

Therefore, LSTM model has the highest prediction accuracy and the best performance, and can be better applied to the prediction and analysis of data quality.

Table 3. Comparison of prediction results of different models

Model	RMSE	MAE
ARIMA	0.96154	0.74402
LSTM	0.59511	0.32526

4 Conclusion

The load data quality analysis of cloud platform big data can be divided into process evaluation, process design and analysis, process deployment and process implementation. This paper starts with the process implementation, analyzes the process data quality related problems in process implementation management and the ways to improve the data quality. Taking the power business process execution management as an example, the paper analyzes the shortcomings of the existing power data sets: (1) In terms of data scale, the mainstream data sets can provide large-scale household power data, but in large-scale data, the data classification is very unbalanced, which will seriously lead to the accuracy of the experiment. (2) In terms of data frequency, high frequency data is prone to redundant data, while low frequency data has a long sampling period and data collection is slow. (3) In terms of data duration and distribution, they are different, and the big data sets are not unified. These aspects seriously affect the quality of process data in the implementation and management of power process. In view of this kind of problem, and summarized the methods to improve the data quality. From the load data itself, the paper respectively improves the final data quality from two methods: data cleaning and data preprocessing. Finally, there are common methods of data prediction, and compare them on the data set collected by ourselves. The advantages and disadvantages of the prediction model are compared through experiments. The results of future prediction are analyzed, and the advantages and disadvantages of data sets are compared. Thus, the quality problems of the dataset can be predicted in advance and the business risks caused by the data quality will be reduced. In cloud platform data management, data quality is an important part. Therefore, how to efficiently process the data sets to be used in business processes and how to improve the data quality of these data still need to be explored and discovered constantly.

Acknowledgements. This work has received funding from the Key Laboratory Foundation of National Defence Technology under Grant 61424010208, National Natural Science Foundation of China (No. 41911530242 and 41975142), 5150 Spring Specialists (05492018012 and 05762018039), Major Program of the National Social Science Fund of China (Grant No. 17ZDA092), 333 High-Level Talent Cultivation Project of Jiangsu Province (BRA2018332), Royal Society of Edinburgh, UK and China Natural Science Foundation Council (RSE Reference: 62967_Liu_2018_2) under their Joint International Projects funding scheme and basic Research Programs (Natural Science Foundation) of Jiangsu Province (BK20191398 and BK20180794).

References

1. Hengjing, H., Wei, Z., Songling, H., et al.: Research on the application of cloud computing in power user electric energy data acquisition system. Electr. Measur. Instrum. **53**(1), 1–7 (2016)
2. Junwei, C., Zhongda, Y., Yangyang, M., et al.: Survey of big data analysis technology for energy internet. South. Power Syst. Technol. **9**(11), 1–2 (2015)
3. Yao, Y.: The construction of comprehensive budget management in Colleges and Universities under the environment of "big data + cloud platform" – Taking D University as an example. Friends Acc. **01**, 119–124 (2020)
4. Xiao, B., Wang, Z., Liu, Q., Liu, X.: SMK-means: an improved mini batch K-means algorithm based on Mapreduce with big data. Comput. Mater. Continua **56**(3), 365–379 (2018)
5. Neubauer, T., Stummer, C.: Extending business process management to determine efficient IT investments. In: Proceedings of the 2007 ACM symposium on Applied computing (SAC 2007), pp. 1250–1256. Association for Computing Machinery, New York (2007)
6. Huang, A.Q., Crow, M.L., Heydt, G.T., et al.: The future renewable electric energy delivery and management (FREEDM) system: the energy internet. Proc. IEEE **99**(1), 133–148 (2010)
7. Wang, Y., Chen, Q.X., Hong, T., Kang, C.Q., et al.: Review of smart meter data analytics: applications, methodologies, and challenges. IEEE Trans. Smart Grid **10**(3), 3125–3148 (2019)
8. Wang, K., Xu, C., Zhang, Y., Guo, S., Zomaya, A.Y., et al.: Robust big data analytics for electricity price forecasting in the smart grid. IEEE Trans. Big Data **5**(1), 34–45 (2017)
9. Tao, W., Xiaolei, W., Rui, Y., et al.: Research on power energy big data acquisition and application based on big data cloud platform. Electron. World **15**, 155–156 (2020)
10. Zhang, J., Liu, Q., Chen, L., Tian, Y., Wang, J., et al.: Non-intrusive load management based on distributed edge and secure key agreement. Wirel. Commun. Mob. Comput. (WCMC) (2021)
11. Liu, Q., Kamoto, K.M., Liu, X., Sun, M., Linge, N., et al.: Low-complexity non-intrusive load monitoring using unsupervised learning and generalized appliance models. IEEE Trans. Consum. Electron. **65**(1), 28–37 (2019)

12. Dash, S., Sodhi, R., Sodhi, B., et al.: An appliance load disaggregation scheme using automatic state detection enabled enhanced integer-programming. IEEE Trans. Ind. Inf. **17**, 1176–1185 (2020)

13. Kolter, Z.J., Redd, J.M.J., et al.: A public data set for energy disaggregation research. In: Proceedings of the in Workshop on Data Mining Applications in Sustainability (SIGKDD), pp. 59–62, San Diego, CA, USA (2007)

14. Liu, Q., Lu, M., Liu, X., Linge, N., et al.: Non-intrusive load monitoring and its challenges in a NILM system framework. Int. J. High Perform. Comput. Netw. **14**(1), 102–111 (2019)

15. Anderson, K., Ocneanu, A., Benitez, D., Carlson, D., Rowe, A., Berges, M.: BLUED: a fully labeled public dataset for event-based non-intrusive load monitoring research. In: Proceedings of the 2nd KDD Workshop on Data Mining Applications in Sustainability (SustKDD), Beijing, China (2012). Young, M.: The Technical Writer's Handbook. University Science, Mill Valley (1989)

16. Liu, Q., Li, S., Liu, X., Linge, N.: A method for electric load data verification and repair in a home energy management environment. Int. J. Embed. Syst. **10**(3), 248–256 (2018). https://doi.org/10.1504/IJES.2018.091788

17. Kelly, J., Knottenbelt, W.: The UK-DALE dataset, domestic appliance-level electricity demand and whole-house demand from five UK homes. Sci. Data **2**, 1–14 (2015). https://doi.org/10.1038/sdata.2015.7.150007

18. Dumas, M., La Rosa, M., Mendling, J., Reijers, H.A., et al.: Fundamentals of Business Process Management (2013)

19. Mathias, W.: Business Process Management. Springer, Heidelberg (2012). https://doi.org/10.1007/978-3-642-28616-2

20. Jeston, J., Nelis, J., et al.: Business Process Management: Practical Guidelines to Successful Implementation. Routledge, London (2008)

21. Becker, J., Kugeler, M., Rosemann, M., et al.: Process management: a guide for the design of business processes. Springer Publishing Company, Heidelberg (2011). https://doi.org/10.1007/978-1-4302-3645-0_15

22. Rosemann, M., Brocke, J., et al.: The six core elements of business process management. Handbook on Business Process Management, vol. 1, pp. 107–122 (2010). https://doi.org/10.1007/978-3-642-00416-2

23. Ahmad, T., Looy, A.V., et al.: Business process management and digital innovations: a systematic literature review. Sustainability **12**(17), 6827 (2020). https://doi.org/10.3390/su12176827

24. Pipino, L.L., Lee, Y.W., Wang, R.Y., et al.: Data quality assessment. Commun. ACM **45**(4), 211–218 (2002). https://doi.org/10.1145/505248.506010

25. Jingyu, H., Lizhen, X., Yisheng, D., et al.: Review of data quality research. Comput. Sci. **02**, 1–5+12 (2008)

26. Ilyas, I.F., Chu, X.: Data Cleaning. Association for Computing Machinery, New York (2019)

27. Gupta, V., Hewett, R.: Adaptive normalization in streaming data. In: Proceedings of the 2019 3rd International Conference on Big Data Research (ICBDR 2019), pp. 12–17. Association for Computing Machinery, New York (2019). https://doi.org/10.1145/3372454.3372466

28. Shiguang, P., Xianhui, G., et al.: Prediction of China's soybean import volume and import volume based on ARIMA and GM (1, 1) models. Soybean Sci. **39**(4), 626–632 (2020)

29. Yurou, C.: Short term prediction of China's core CPI based on ARIMA model. Time Honor. Brand Mark. **7**, 37–38 (2020)

30. Zijian, H., Yuanhua, L., et al.: Application of long-term and short-term memory model in stock price trend prediction. Prod. Res. **1**, 36–39 (2020)

31. Box, G.E.P., Pierce, D.A., et al.: Distribution of residual autocorrelations in autoregressive-integrated moving average time series models. J. Am. Stat. Assoc. **65**(332), 1509–1526 (1970)

32. D'Informatique, D.E., Ese, N., Esent, P., et al.: Long short-term memory in recurrent neural networks. EPFL (2001)

33. Yamak, P.T., Li, Y., Gadosey, P.K.: A comparison between ARIMA, LSTM, and GRU for time series forecasting. In: ACAI 2019: 2019 2nd International Conference on Algorithms, Computing and Artificial Intelligence 92019)

34. Wang Xin, W., Ji, L., et al.: Fault time series prediction based on LSTM recurrent neural network. J. Beijing Univ. Aeronaut. Astronaut. **44**(4), 772–784 (2018)

35. Srivastava, N., Hinton, G., Krizhevsky, A., et al.: Dropout: a simple way to prevent neural networks from overfitting. J. Mach. Learn. Res. **15**(1), 1929–1958 (2014)

A Survey of Traffic Prediction Based on Deep Neural Network: Data, Methods and Challenges

Pengfei Cao⬤, Fei Dai⬤, Guozhi Liu⬤, Jinmei Yang⬤, and Bi Huang$^{(\boxtimes)}$

Big Data and Intelligent Engineering College, Southwest Forestry University, Kunming 650224, China
2955663264@qq.com

Abstract. Traffic prediction plays an important role in the intelligent transportation system (ITS), because it can increase people's travel convenience. Despite the deep neural network has been widely used in the field of traffic prediction, literature surveys of such methods and data categories are rare. In this paper, we have a summary of traffic forecasting from data, methods and challenges. Firstly, we are according to the difference of in spatio-temporal dimensions, divide the data into three types, including the spatio-temporal static data, spatial static time dynamic data, and spatio-temporal dynamic data. Secondly, we explore three significant neural networks of deep learning in traffic prediction, including the convolutional neural network (CNN), the recurrent neural network (RNN), and the hybrid neural networks models. These methods are used in many aspects of traffic prediction, including road traffic accidents forecast, road traffic flow prediction, road traffic speed forecast, and road traffic congestion forecast introduced. Finally, we provide a discussion of some current challenges and development prospects.

Keywords: Deep neural network · Traffic forecasting · Spatio-temporal data

1 Introduction

Since the 21st century, most cities have generally entered a period of rapid urbanization. With the continuous improvement of the urbanization process, the resulting huge traffic demand has caused a lot of pressure on urban traffic. The traffic conditions became very terrible in many big cities, which directly affects the development and environment of a city. In addition, the demand of urban traffic management can no longer be met solely by relying on manpower, so the application and development of traffic prediction are particularly important. In order to solve the problem of people's transportation demand, the intelligent transportation system (ITS) is getting better development gradually, which include electronic sensor technology, data transmission technology, intelligent control technology, and advanced technology into transportation system structures. The purpose of ITS is to provide better service for drivers and passengers, in the context of increasingly serious environmental pollution, more accurate control of traffic conditions can reduce some unnecessary exhaust emissions and provide better channels for energy conservation and environmental protection.

M. R. Khosravi et al. (Eds.): CloudComp 2021, LNICST 430, pp. 17–29, 2022.
https://doi.org/10.1007/978-3-030-99191-3_2

In the process of traffic prediction is used to meet people's needs, researchers use a variety of data, most of which come from road sensors, road reflectors, camera images, aerial photos, remote sensing images, etc. With the development of ITS, more and more data to be used in traffic prediction, the traditional data analysis method is hard to figure out such a huge data in the traffic field, so we need to use deep learning as an important means of the big data analysis methods in traffic prediction, it can be predicted from the following several aspects to traffic development benefits.

1. Vast amounts of diverse and complex data generated in the traffic forecast can be handled by deep learning.
2. Deep learning can improve the validity and accuracy of traffic forecasts. Through fast data collection and analysis of current and historical massive traffic data, the traffic management department can predict traffic conditions in real-time.
3. Deep learning in the data analysis can improve people's travel safety level. Through deep learning analytics, we can effectively predict the occurrence of traffic accidents and congestion.

The overview of traffic prediction in this paper is shown in Fig. 1. The rest of the paper is organized as follows. The architecture of traffic forecasting based on deep learning is discussed in Sect. 2. Section 3 summarizes the data source and collection methods. Deep learning analytics methods are discussed in Sect. 4. Some open challenges of using deep learning in ITS are discussed in Sect. 4. Finally, we conclude the paper in Sect. 5.

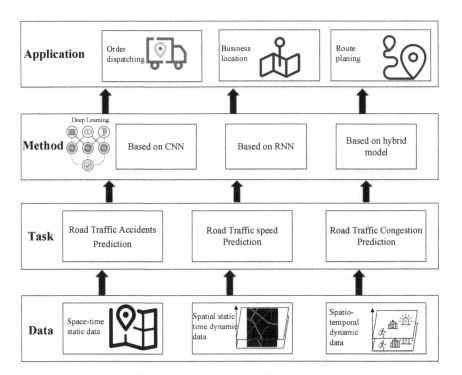

Fig. 1. The overview of traffic prediction

2   Classification of Traffic Data

In this section, we will summarize 56 literature and the methodologies used to predict traffic. We only consider recent papers from 2014 to 2021, which provided sufficiently novel methods and contributions to the field.

In our lives, we unconsciously participate in the collection, transmission and application of big data. With the increase of people's attention to travel conditions, the complexity and diversity of data are an improvement. According to different sources of data in ITS, traffic data are classified into the following categories from the perspective of time and space: spatio-temporal static data, spatial static temporal dynamic data, spatio-temporal dynamic data, point data, network data. The collected data are shown in Table 1. In this table, the STSDS stands for spatio-temporal static data, the SSTDD stands for spatial static temporal dynamic data, the STDD stands for spatio-temporal dynamic data, the PD stands for point-data, and the ND stands for network data.

Table 1. Data statistics for different types

Tasks	Techniques	Example	STSD	SSTDD	STDD	PD	ND
Flow	CNN	[1–3]	×	×	√	×	√
		[4, 5]	×	×	√	√	√
		[6, 7]	×	√	×	×	√
	RNN	[8–10]	×	√	×	×	√
		[11–16]	×	×	√	√	√
	Hybrid model	[17, 18]	×	√	×	√	√
		[19–22]	×	√	×	×	√
		[23–28]	×	×	√	√	√
Speed	CNN	[29, 30]	×	√	×	×	√
	RNN	[31]	×	×	√	×	√
		[32–36]	×	√	×	×	√
	Hybrid model	[37, 38]	×	×	√	√	√
		[39, 40]	×	×	√	×	√
		[41, 42]	×	√	×	×	√
Accident	CNN	[43]	×	×	√	√	√
	RNN	[44–46]	×	×	√	√	√
	Hybrid model	[47]	×	×	√	√	√
Congestion	CNN	[48]	×	×	√	×	√
	RNN	[49, 50]	×	√	×	×	√
		[31, 51–53]	×	×	√	×	√
	Hybrid model	[54–56]	×	×	√	×	√

2.1   Spatial Static Time Dynamic Data

Compared with the space-time static data, with the change of the time dimension, the spatial static time dynamic data will produce. For example, sensors are placed on the fixed points to collect the passing vehicle information. The spatial dimension is stationary, but each point's time is changing. These data are widely used in traffic forecasting, such as traffic flow forecast, traffic speed forecast, traffic congestion forecast, and traffic demand forecast, and so on.

Many studies use spatial static time dynamic data from different sources to collect. For example, Ma et al. [32] in the process of using the deep learning method of LSTM NN for traffic speed prediction, use travel speed data from traffic microwave detectors in Beijing. Zhao et al. [24] propose the EnLSTM-WPEO, which uses the six traffic flow data sets from the highways of Seattle, includes the traffic flow from north to south, west to east, south to north, and east to west. In [57] the built model is based on the traffic flow dataset extracted from the Wisconsin Traffic Operation and Safety Laboratory at the University of Wisconsin Madison. All available data came from the locations of nine detectors in this study.

In these works, the spatial static time dynamic data of Beijing by remote traffic microwave sensors is relatively more popular. We summarize the top-3 most popular main datasets in Table 2, which include 40% of the literature works we surveyed.

Table 2. Popular spatial static temporal dynamic data

Main dataset	Task	References
Beijing dataset	Flow, Speed, Accident, Congestion	[3, 23, 41, 42, 58]
PEMS dataset	Flow, Speed, Accident, Congestion	[12, 28, 40, 52]
Spain dataset	Flow, Speed	[34, 59, 60]

2.2   Spatio-Temporal Dynamic Data

Time and space dimensions are changing constantly, which constitute the spatio-temporal dynamic data, and belongs to the point data of space and time change too. Spatio-temporal dynamic data is the main research hot spot of traffic prediction from the present to the future. With the rise of "sharing", people always unconsciously participate in the collection of spatio-temporal data. In short, many people using Mobike at the same time in different places, or there are different people in the same place using Mobike.

According to current studies, most models are build based on a dataset of PeMS, which is collected from the transportation system of England. PeMS is a typical spatio-temporal dynamic data. In this paper, we explore 60 papers, this dataset is used the ten of them. For example, the most cited papers in this field through the PeMS [27], which include 2501 traffic roads of England. In many papers, traffic forecasting is dependent on external factors, such as weather, holidays, policies and so on. All in all, spatio-temporal dynamic data is the most widely used data type in traffic forecasting. The

Table 3. Popular spatio-temporal dynamic data

Main dataset	Task	References
PEMS dataset	Flow, Speed, Accident, Congestion	[11, 13, 23, 27, 58]
Beijing dataset	Flow, Speed, Accident, Congestion	[2, 20, 31, 44]
Another dataset	Flow, Speed, Congestion	[4, 8]

spatio-temporal dynamic data are shown in Table 3, which includes 35% of the literary works we surveyed.

In addition to the above two kinds of data, spatio-temporal data also includes spatio-temporal static data. In the process of traffic prediction, the spatio-temporal static data plays a very important role as the foundation of in the whole traffic big data. In ITS, spatio-temporal static data (or point data) is fixed and immobile from the beginning of construction, such as building position, floor area, floor height and so on.

3   Deep Neural Networks for Traffic Prediction

With the rapid development of ITS, a large number of deep learning models have been adopted to traffic forecasting recently. Deep learning plays an important role in ITS, which becoming more and more popular in many tasks of traffic forecasting. The main function of deep learning methods is modeling for a large amount of traffic data, then providing the right decisions for people's travel. Since 2014, deep learning is beginning to be used in traffic prediction by Lv et al. [59], which usually use a separate method to predict traffic condition in the future. In 2016, Fu et al. [28] proposed the hybrid deep learning methods to model traffic data jointly. Until 2018, many scholars have been involved in the research of deep learning on traffic prediction, and then in many papers have explored and supplement. The development process of deep learning applied to traffic prediction is shown in Fig. 2.

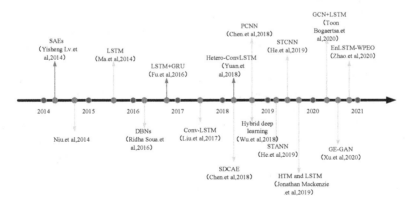

Fig. 2. The development of traffic prediction based on deep learning.

According to the main research methods of current traffic forecast, which can be divided into three types: CNN-based, RNN-based and hybrid model-based. In the following subsections, we will discuss different deep learning methods of traffic prediction.

3.1   A Traffic Forecasting Method Based on CNN

In deep learning, the convolutional neural network (CNN, or ConvNet) is a class of deep neural network, most commonly applied to analyze visual imagery [3]. A CNN consists of several "convolution" and "pooling" layers. Convolution's purpose is to extract features from the input, whereas pooling's purpose is to reduce the dimensionality of each feature map and preserve the most important information. Typical CNN architecture is shown in Fig. 3.

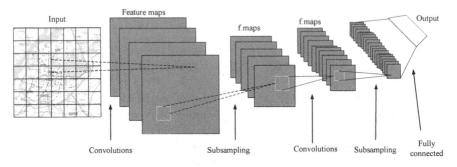

Fig. 3. Typical CNN architecture.

Therefore, many researchers in the domain of traffic forecasting try to take advantage of CNN techniques to solve related to images problems. According to [59], a classic road traffic flow prediction model using deep learning analytics is shown in Fig. 4, this is the first time that a deep architecture model using auto-encoders as building blocks to predict the traffic flow features. It is currently the most cited paper in the field of traffic forecasting. The original traffic data is preprocessed in the first, then we can get the usable data set. Using the deep learning method, which considers the spatial and temporal correlations inherently. Using a stacked autoencoder model to learn usual traffic flow features, and it is trained in a greedy layerwise fashion.

Many scholars have studied traffic flow prediction using deep learning. For example, Chen et al. [1] use 3D CNNs to abstract the spatio-temporal correlation features jointly from low-level to high-level layers for traffic data. Similarly, Chen et al. [4] propose novel spatio-temporal CNNs to extract spatio-temporal features simultaneously from low-level to high-level layers, and propose a novel gated scheme to control the spatio-temporal features that should be propagated through the hierarchy of layers. Deng et al. [6] try to transform the spatio-temporal traffic data analysis problem into the task of image-like analysis, for jointly exploring spatio-temporal relations. To traffic speed prediction, Byeonghyeop Yu et al. [29] adopt the graph convolution models in the field of traffic forecasting, which improve the forecasting accuracy and saved more training time. To

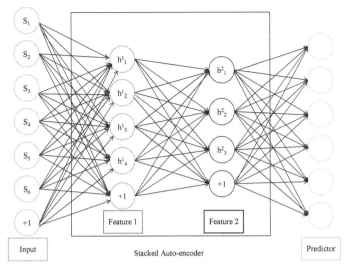

Fig. 4. A typical traffic flow prediction model [59].

traffic accident prediction, Zheng et al. [43] propose the feature matrix to gray image (FM2GI) algorithm, which strengthens the traffic accident severity performance. Chen et al. [48] propose a novel method based on a deep convolutional neural network named PCNN, which models periodic traffic data for short-term traffic congestion prediction.

In the application of traffic prediction, CNN is often as a component in a hybrid deep neural network, whose main task is to capture the spatial aspect of traffic data.

3.2 A Traffic Forecasting Method Based on RNN

Recurrent Neural Networks (RNN) is commonly applied to sequence data because their memorization capability, which learns the sequence of both long and short-term dependencies. In the process of working, the Feedforward Neural Network is based on only the current input, however, the RNN takes decisions based on current and previous inputs [4]. This visualization can be seen in Fig. 5.

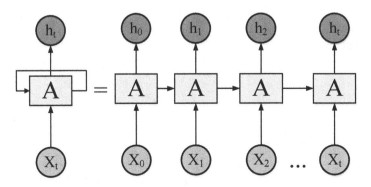

Fig. 5. A recurrent neural network [4].

Additionally, RNN is able to scale to longer sequences compared to other network architectures. Its unique capability makes it as one of the most popular deep neural networks. For example, Mou et al. [10] propose a piece of temporal information enhancing LSTM (T-LSTM) to predict traffic flow of a single road section, the model can improve prediction accuracy by capturing the intrinsic correlation between traffic flow and temporal information. Moreover, Ma et al. [32] propose Long Short-Term Neural Network (LSTM NN) captures nonlinear traffic dynamics in an effective manner. The LSTM NN can overcome the issue of back-propagated error decay by memory blocks. For traffic prediction of different tasks, RNN is beneficial to extract temporal correlation of spatio-temporal data.

3.3 A Traffic Forecasting Method Based on the Hybrid Model

Because the traffic data have the following three complex features: temporal correlations, spatial correlations, and diversity of spatio-temporal (ST) correlations. Traffic predicting accurately and timely is a challenging problem in ITS. However, Modeling for these various types of ST correlations is very difficult, so many of these existing works taken attention to the diversity of ST correlations through the hybrid model [23], details are shown in Fig. 6.

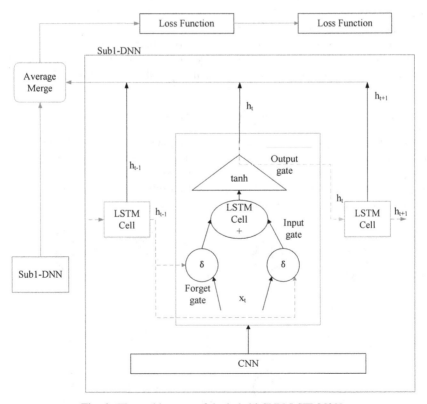

Fig. 6. The architecture of the hybrid CNN-LSTM [23].

Therefore, many researchers propose a traffic forecasting method based on the hybrid model. For example, Zhang et al. [40] propose Spatial-Temporal Graph Attention Networks (ST-GAT). The graph attention mechanism extracts the spatial dependencies and introduces an LSTM network to extract temporal domain features, this approach is able to capture dynamic spatial dependencies of traffic networks. Duan et al. [26] propose a hybrid neural network to predict urban flow which is made up of CNN and LSTM. The CNN can statically extract the potential spatial features and the LSTM to dynamically abstract the short term and long term temporal features of urban traffic data.

In the field of traffic prediction, the forecasting method based on the hybrid model is commonly used as a component spatio-temporal data analysis of ITS. Its task is to capture the spatio-temporal patterns of traffic data.

4 Challenges

Although deep learning has made great achievements in traffic prediction, there are still many challenges have not been fully studied. We need to solve these questions in future works. This section introduces the main challenges of traffic forecasting based on deep learning as follows.

1) Traffic data characteristic and complexity: traffic data belongs to spatio-temporal data, which has spatial correlation, temporal correlation and heterogeneity. However, in most of the existing studies only extracting spatio-temporal correlation, the heterogeneity of the correlations contribution takes into account is very rarely [60]. Furthermore, we also need to solve the many external factors in the complex urban environment, such as social media data, weather data, accidents data and so on. How to improve the accuracy of traffic prediction when we consider to add the weather conditions and holidays? Or considering other types of traffic data like a truck, bus and metro, and personal phone signals data simultaneously to get better deep learning models. And then most of the existing traffic prediction data is collected by equipment such as an annular coil detector or ultrasonic sensor. These data are often missing, invalid and uncertain due to weather, sensor failure, traffic control and other reasons. This will increase the difficulty of data preprocessing.

2) The performance capacity of the model: the short-term traffic prediction works well, but with the increase of prediction time, the error gets bigger, and the accuracy of long-term prediction will become worse. With the continuous expansion of the road network, the number of intersections and sensors will increase, the road network topology will become more complex, the amount of historical traffic data will become larger, and the performance of the model will be lower. Besides, due to the limited available traffic sensors in urban areas, limiting the traffic data availability, we need to take into account the dependency of different sensors. In this case, how to effectively improve the accuracy of the long-term forecasts is a challenging and very difficult task.

3) Application of actual traffic scenarios: most of the existing traffic prediction models are based on data sets to train and test, but the application of models is extremely scarce in real scenarios. However, accurate traffic prediction of actual traffic scenarios can bring many benefits: provide convenience for traffic managers and travelers,

reduce traffic jams, realize intelligent transportation. In practical application, traffic data around the selected scene is first collected for traffic prediction, and then the predicted traffic data is used to plan travel roads and design automatic control of traffic lights.

With the rapid development of the 6G network [61], future research should focus on how to apply traffic prediction to actual scenarios, which will help traffic managers to control traffic and bring convenience to people's travel. Accurate traffic prediction is the most important part of the traffic information service system, which is beneficial to alleviate traffic congestion and reduce the occurrence of traffic accidents. In the future, various types of data can be combined with each other for better depicting the hourly traffic information and human mobility in urban areas and generating a better prediction.

5 Conclusions

Ever since IBM came up with the concept of Smarter Earth in 2018, intelligence has become the main goal of today's society development, such as intelligent transportation, intelligent medical, intelligent currency, and so on. In short, traffic forecasting is able to provide useful information use the past and present traffic data, then achieve a vision of traffic conditions in the future. However, due to the various characteristics of traffic data and the complexity of traffic networks in different regions, it is still a big challenge to achieve an accurate assessment of future traffic forecasts.

We hope the traffic prediction field will inspire more scholars to study, which can directly contribute to the improvement of traffic conditions. Deep learning will have profound impacts on the traffic forecast.

References

1. An, J., Fu, L., Hu, M., Chen, W., Zhan, J.: A novel fuzzy-based convolutional neural network method to traffic flow prediction with uncertain traffic accident information. IEEE Access 7, 20708–20722 (2019)
2. Chen, C., et al.: Exploiting spatio-temporal correlations with multiple 3D convolutional neural networks for citywide vehicle flow prediction, pp. 893–898 (2018)
3. Peng, H., et al.: Spatial temporal incidence dynamic graph neural networks for traffic flow forecasting. Inf. Sci. 521, 277–290 (2020)
4. Chen, C., Li, K., Teo, S.G., Zou, X., Li, K., Zeng, Z.: Citywide traffic flow prediction based on multiple gated spatio-temporal convolutional neural networks. ACM Trans. Knowl. Discov. Data 14(4), 1–23 (2020)
5. Zhang, D., Kabuka, M.R.: Combining weather condition data to predict traffic flow: a GRU based deep learning approach. IET Intell. Transp. Syst. 12(7), 578–585 (2018)
6. Deng, S., Jia, S., Chen, J.: Exploring spatial–temporal relations via deep convolutional neural networks for traffic flow prediction with incomplete data. Appl. Soft Comput. 78, 712–721 (2019)
7. Wang, X., et al.: Traffic flow prediction via spatial temporal graph neural network, pp. 1082–1092 (2020)
8. Zhang, C., Patras, P.: Long-term mobile traffic forecasting using deep spatio-tem poral neural networks, pp. 231–240 (2018)

9. Ma, Y., Zhang, Z., Ihler, A.: Multi-lane short-term traffic forecasting with convolutional LSTM network. IEEE Access **8**, 34629–34643 (2020)
10. Mou, L., Zhao, P., Xie, H., Chen, Y.: T-LSTM: a long short-term memory neural network enhanced by temporal information for traffic flow prediction. IEEE Access **7**, 98053–98060 (2019)
11. Ryu, U., Wang, J., Kim, T., Kwak, S., U, J.: Construction of traffic state vector using mutual information for short-term traffic flow prediction. Transp. Res. Part C Emerg. Technol. **96**, 55–71 (2018)
12. Liu, Y., Zheng, H., Feng, X., Chen, Z.: Short-term traffic flow prediction with conv-LSTM. In: 2017 9th International Conference on Wireless Communications and Signal Processing (WCSP), pp. 1–6. IEEE
13. Kang, D., Lv, Y., Chen, Y.Y.: Short-term traffic flow prediction with LSTM recurrent neural network. In: 2017 IEEE 20th International Conference on Intelligent Transportation Systems (ITSC), pp. 1–6. IEEE
14. He, Z., Chow, C.Y., Zhang, J.D.: STANN: a spatio–temporal attentive neural network for traffic prediction. IEEE Access **7**, 4795–4806 (2019)
15. Shao, H., Soong, B.H.: Traffic flow prediction with long short-term memory networks (LSTMs). In: 2016 IEEE Region 10 Conference (TENCON), pp. 2986–2989. IEEE
16. Hua, Y., Zhao, Z., Liu, Z., Chen, X., Li, R., Zhang, H.: Traffic prediction based on random connectivity in deep learning with long short-term memory. In: 2018 IEEE 88th Vehicular Technology Conference (VTC-Fall), pp. 1–6. IEEE
17. Polson, N.G., Sokolov, V.O.: Deep learning for short-term traffic flow prediction. Transp. Res. Part C: Emerg. Technol. **79**, 1–17 (2017)
18. Koesdwiady, A., Soua, R., Karray, F.: Improving traffic flow prediction with weather information in connected cars: a deep learning approach. IEEE Trans. Veh. Technol. **65**(12), 9508–9517 (2016)
19. Mackenzie, J., Roddick, J.F., Zito, R.: An evaluation of HTM and LSTM for short-term arterial traffic flow prediction. IEEE Trans. Intell. Transp. Syst. **20**(5), 1847–1857 (2019). https://doi.org/10.1109/tits.2018.2843349
20. Gu, Y., Lu, W., Xu, X., Qin, L., Shao, Z., Zhang, H.: An improved Bayesian combination model for short-term traffic prediction with deep learning. IEEE Trans. Intell. Transp. Syst. **21**(3), 1332–1342 (2020)
21. Wu, Y., Tan, H., Qin, L., Ran, B., Jiang, Z.: A hybrid deep learning based traffic flow prediction method and its understanding. Transp. Res. Part C Emerg. Technol. **90**, 166–180 (2018)
22. Pan, Z., Liang, Y., Wang, W., Yu, Y., Zheng, Y., Zhang, J.: Urban traffic prediction from spatio-temporal data using deep meta learning, pp. 1720–1730 (2019)
23. Guo, S., Lin, Y., Li, S., Chen, Z., Wan, H.: Deep spatial–temporal 3D convolutional neural networks for traffic data forecasting. IEEE Trans. Intell. Transp. Syst. **20**(10), 3913–3926 (2019)
24. Zhao, F., Zeng, G.Q., Lu, K.D.: EnLSTM-WEPO: short-term traffic flow prediction by ensemble LSTM, NNCT weight integration, and population extremal optimization. IEEE Trans. Veh. Technol. **69**(1), 101–113 (2020)
25. Zheng, H., Lin, F., Feng, X., Chen, Y.: A hybrid deep learning model with attention-based conv-LSTM networks for short-term traffic flow prediction. IEEE Trans. Intell. Transp. Syst. **22**, 1–11 (2020)
26. Duan, Z., Yang, Y., Zhang, K., Ni, Y., Bajgain, S.: Improved deep hybrid networks for urban traffic flow prediction using trajectory data. IEEE Access **6**, 31820–31827 (2018)
27. Chen, Y., Shu, L., Wang, L.: Traffic flow prediction with big data: a deep learning based time series model. In: 2017 IEEE Conference on Computer Communications Workshops (INFOCOM WKSHPS), pp. 1010–1011. IEEE

28. Fu, R., Zhang, Z., Li, L.: Using LSTM and GRU neural network methods for traffic flow prediction. In: 2016 31st Youth Academic Annual Conference of Chinese Association of Automation (YAC), pp. 324–328. IEEE

29. Yu, B., Lee, Y., Sohn, K.: Forecasting road traffic speeds by considering areawide spatio-temporal dependencies based on a graph convolutional neural network (GCN). Transp. Res. Part C Emerg. Technol. **114**, 189–204 (2020)

30. Guo, G., Yuan, W.: Short-term traffic speed forecasting based on graph attention temporal convolutional networks. Neurocomputing **410**, 387–393 (2020)

31. Wang, J., Gu, Q., Wu, J., Liu, G., Xiong, Z.: Traffic speed prediction and congestion source exploration: A deep learning method. In: 2016 IEEE 16th International Conference on Data Mining (ICDM), pp. 499–508. IEEE

32. Ma, X., Tao, Z., Wang, Y., Yu, H., Wang, Y.: Long short-term memory neural network for traffic speed prediction using remote microwave sensor data. Transp. Res. Part C Emerg. Technol. **54**, 187–197 (2015)

33. Zang, D., Ling, J., Wei, Z., Tang, K., Cheng, J.: Long-term traffic speed prediction based on multiscale spatio-temporal feature learning network. IEEE Trans. Intell. Transp. Syst. **20**(10), 3700–3709 (2019)

34. Kim, Y., Wang, P., Mihaylova, L.: Structural recurrent neural network for traffic speed prediction. In: ICASSP 2019–2019 IEEE International Conference on Acoustics, Speech and Signal Processing (ICASSP), pp. 5207–5211. IEEE

35. Wang, J., Chen, R., He, Z.: Traffic speed prediction for urban transportation network: A path based deep learning approach. Transp. Res. Part C Emerg. Technol. **100**, 372–385 (2019)

36. Zheng, Z., Wang, D., Pei, J., Yuan, Y., Fan, C., Xiao, F.: Urban traffic prediction through the second use of inexpensive big data from buildings, pp. 1363–1372 (2016)

37. Cheng, Z., Chow, M.Y., Jung, D., Jeon, J.: A big data based deep learning approach for vehicle speed prediction. In: 2017 IEEE 26th International Symposium on Industrial Electronics (ISIE), pp. 389–394. IEEE

38. Essien, A., Petrounias, I., Sampaio, P., Sampaio, S.: Improving urban traffic speed prediction using data source fusion and deep learning. In: 2019 IEEE International Conference on Big Data and Smart Computing (BigComp), pp. 1–8. IEEE

39. Zhang, Z., Li, M., Lin, X., Wang, Y., He, F.: Multistep speed prediction on traffic networks: A deep learning approach considering spatio-temporal dependencies. Transp. Res. Part C Emerg. Technol. **105**, 297–322 (2019)

40. Zhang, C., Yu, J.J.Q., Liu, Y.: Spatial-temporal graph attention networks: a deep learning approach for traffic forecasting. IEEE Access **7**, 166246–166256 (2019)

41. Ma, X., Zhong, H., Li, Y., Ma, J., Cui, Z., Wang, Y.: Forecasting transportation network speed using deep capsule networks with nested lstm models. IEEE Trans. Intell. Transp. Syst. **22**, 1–12 (2020)

42. Gu, Y., Lu, W., Qin, L., Li, M., Shao, Z.: Short-term prediction of lane-level traffic speeds: a fusion deep learning model. Transp. Res. Part C Emerg. Technol. **106**, 1–16 (2019). https://doi.org/10.1016/j.trc.2019.07.003

43. Zheng, M., et al.: Traffic accident's severity prediction: a deep-learning approach-based CNN network. IEEE Access **7**, 39897–39910 (2019). https://doi.org/10.1109/access.2019.2903319

44. Ren, H., Song, Y., Wang, J., Hu, Y., Lei, J.: A deep learning approach to the citywide traffic accident risk prediction. In: 2018 21st International Conference on Intelligent Transportation Systems (ITSC), pp. 3346–3351. IEEE

45. Yuan, Z., Zhou, X., Yang, T.: Hetero-ConvLSTM: a deep learning approach to traffic accident prediction on heterogeneous spatio-temporal data. In: Proceedings of the 24th ACM SIGKDD International Conference on Knowledge Discovery Data Mining, pp. 984–992

46. Bao, J., Liu, P., Ukkusuri, S.V.: A spatiotemporal deep learning approach for citywide short-term crash risk prediction with multi-source data. Accid. Anal. Prev. **122**, 239–254 (2019)

47. Chen, C., Fan, X., Zheng, C., Xiao, L., Cheng, M., Wang, C.: SDCAE: stack denoising convolutional autoencoder model for accident risk prediction via traffic big datapp, pp. 328–333 (2018)
48. Chen, M., Yu, X., Liu, Y.: PCNN: deep convolutional networks for short-term traffic congestion prediction. IEEE Trans. Intell. Transp. Syst. **19**(11), 3550–3559 (2018)
49. Majumdar, S., Subhani, M.M., Roullier, B., Anjum, A., Zhu, R.: Congestion prediction for smart sustainable cities using IoT and machine learning approaches. Sustain. Cities Soc. **64**, 102500 (2021)
50. Di, X., Xiao, Y., Zhu, C., Deng, Y., Zhao, Q., Rao, W.: Traffic congestion prediction by spatiotemporal propagation patterns, pp. 298–303 (2019)
51. Choi, S., Kim, J., Yeo, H.: Attention-based recurrent neural network for urban vehicle trajectory prediction. Procedia Comput. Sci. **151**, 327–334 (2019)
52. Kong, F., Li, J., Lv, Z.: Construction of intelligent traffic information recommendation system based on long short-term memory. J. Comput. Sci. **26**, 78–86 (2018)
53. Chen, Y.Y., Lv, Y., Li, Z., Wang, F.Y.: Long short-term memory model for traffic congestion prediction with online open data. In: 2016 IEEE 19th International Conference on Intelligent Transportation Systems (ITSC), pp. 132–137. IEEE
54. Zhu, J., Huang, C., Yang, M., Fung, G.P.C.: Context-based prediction for road traffic state using trajectory pattern mining and recurrent convolutional neural networks. Inf. Sci. **473**, 190–201 (2019)
55. Bogaerts, T., Masegosa, A.D., Angarita-Zapata, J.S., Onieva, E., Hellinckx, P.: A graph CNN-LSTM neural network for short and long-term traffic forecasting based on trajectory data. Transp. Res. Part C Emerg. Technol. **112**, 62–77 (2020)
56. Hassija, V., Gupta, V., Garg, S., Chamola, V.: Traffic jam probability estimation based on blockchain and deep neural networks. IEEE Trans. Intell. Transp. Syst. **22**, 1–10 (2020)
57. Li, L., Qin, L., Qu, X., Zhang, J., Wang, Y., Ran, B.: Day-ahead traffic flow forecasting based on a deep belief network optimized by the multi objective particle swarm algorithm. Knowl.-Based Syst. **172**, 1–14 (2019)
58. Arif, M., Wang, G., Chen, S.: Deep learning with non-parametric regression model for traffic flow prediction, pp. 681–688 (2018)
59. Kim, Y., Wang, P., Zhu, Y., Mihaylova, L.: A capsule network for traffic speed prediction in complex road networks. In: 2018 Sensor Data Fusion: Trends, Solutions, Applications (SDF), pp. 1–6. IEEE
60. Lv, Y., Duan, Y., Kang, W., Li, Z., Wang, F.Y.: Traffic flow prediction with big data: a deep learning approach. IEEE Trans. Intell. Transp. Syst. **16**, 1–9 (2014)
61. Zhou, Y.Q., Liu, L., Wang, L.: Service-aware 6G: an intelligent and open network based on the convergence of communication. Digit. Commun. Netw. **6**, 253–260 (2020)

A Dynamic Gesture Recognition Control File Method Based on Deep Learning

Fumin Liu, Yuezhong Wu, Falong Xiao, and Qiang Liu[✉]

Hunan University of Technology, Zhuzhou 412000, Hunan, China
liuqiang@hut.edu.cn

Abstract. In order to realize the remote control of the meeting documents in progress, the traditional method uses infrared remote control or 2.4 GHz wireless remote control. However, the shortcomings of carrying and storing the remote control, the infrared itself cannot pass through obstacles or the remote control of the device from a large angle, the 2.4 GHz cost is slightly higher, etc., this article introduces the use of PyTorch model and YOLO network gesture control to facilitate this practical problem. The plan proposes to use the PyTorch model to establish a neural network, train to achieve the purpose of classifying gestures, and use the YOLO network to cooperate with the corresponding control algorithm to achieve the purpose of controlling conference documents. The experimental results show that the proposed scheme is feasible and complete to achieve the required functions.

Keywords: Deep learning · Gesture recognition · Control algorithm

1 Introduction

With the development of artificial intelligence, the United States, Japan, South Korea and other countries have formulated their own strategic plans for the development of artificial intelligence in their respective countries. my country also mentioned "intelligent manufacturing engineering" in the five major projects in "Made in China 2025". One of the two main lines in "Made in China 2025" is "the main line of digital networked intelligent manufacturing that reflects the deep integration of information technology and manufacturing technology" [1]. The formulation of these guidelines clearly defines the need to bring intelligence to all aspects of our lives. In this process, good human-computer interaction is an important foundation of "human-machine co-prosperity" and "human-machine collaboration". Among them, human-computer interaction includes three types: human-computer interaction (HCI), human-machine interaction (HMI), and human-robot interaction (HRI) [2]. This has gone through a long period of development, from people using binary codes to control computers to Today's voice or gesture control machines, scientists have gone through unremitting efforts [3].

Gesture is an important way of non-verbal communication between people and an important way of interaction between humans and machines. But before implementing

M. R. Khosravi et al. (Eds.): CloudComp 2021, LNICST 430, pp. 30–39, 2022.
https://doi.org/10.1007/978-3-030-99191-3_3

gesture control, define what a gesture is. In 1990, Eric Hulteen and Gord Kurtenbach published an article entitled Gestures in Human-Computer Interaction, which defined the question of what gestures are. The core is that gestures can be used to communicate, and the meaning of gestures lies in telling rather than executing. After clarifying the definition of gestures, gesture recognition also has different implementation methods. It is roughly divided into two categories according to whether the gesture recognition device is in contact with the body: contact gesture recognition and non-contact gesture recognition. Among them, contact gesture recognition is the most widely known. For example, the release of the first iPhone in 2007 is also praised by many as the creation of the era of smart phones. Among them, gesture taps account for a large proportion of the smart word. Non-contact gesture recognition, for example, references the Kinect3D somatosensory camera, the BMW iDrive system that introduces the gesture recognition function, etc. [4].

In the early stage of gesture development, people mainly used external auxiliary tools, such as a large number of sensors, to realize gesture recognition. Its advantage is that the recognition accuracy is high, but it needs the assistance of a large number of sensors, which is relatively cumbersome to implement and cannot be achieved by simply using a computer. Non-contact gesture recognition is mainly based on the feature extraction of gestures, using skin color, shape and other features to segment the gestures, and then using support vector machine (SVM) and other classification algorithms for recognition. The difficulty of this method is how to extract and segment the gestures from the environment. If the extraction algorithm is not perfect or the model training set is insufficient, the accuracy of gesture recognition is not high. After a long period of development, Grobel et al. used Hidden Markov Model to complete gesture recognition with an accuracy of 94%. Although the recognition effect is gratifying, it still needs to use an external sensor to obtain the tester's hand skin color to distinguish it. Popularize this method on a large scale [5]. The gesture recognition method based on Kinect depth information proposed by Dominio et al. has great accuracy and can reach 99.5% of recognition accuracy, but its algorithm is relatively complex and requires high equipment implementation [6]. The deep learning method proposed by Wang Xiaohua can better obtain the high-level and multi-dimensional features of past images, and can realize detection and recognition in complex environments. And the algorithm complexity is not high, but the detection speed is not high. Liu Zhijia et al. proposed a method that can use infrared image detection to improve the accuracy of gesture recognition, but infrared photoelectric technology is needed to detect the heat radiation signal of an object, which still has relative limitations.

After several years of initial development, non-contact gesture recognition has become the mainstream, and the direction of researchers has gradually changed to the realization and optimization of non-contact gesture recognition in different categories and in different situations. In 2014, Yu Jing et al. proposed a fast dynamic recognition algorithm based on the depth information of the Kinect sensor. The depth image was acquired through the Kinect depth camera, the depth image was preprocessed by the threshold segmentation method, and the foreground was extracted by the OpenCV function library [7]. In 2015, Zhao Feifei and others used the Kinect camera to design a set of gesture recognition algorithms to obtain bone information. The algorithm detects the start and end points of the gesture, then intercepts and pushes to extract the gesture features, and finally uses the distance-weighted dynamic time warping algorithm to calculate the test samples, Get the recognition result [8]. At the same time, Redmon et al. proposed a detection YOLO algorithm at the 2016 CVPR conference, which greatly shortened the detection time. In 2018, Wu Xiaofeng and others proposed a gesture recognition algorithm based on Faster R-CNN, and modified the key parameters of the Faster R-CNN framework to achieve the purpose of detecting and recognizing gestures at the same time [9].

2   Construction of PyTorch Model, YOLOv4 and Realization of Control Algorithm

2.1   PyTorch Model

PyTorch is a Python-based scientific computing package, originally developed by the Facebook artificial intelligence research team, and its underlying layer is implemented in C++. PyTorch has two major features [10], one can use tensor calculations similar to Numpy, and GPU or CPU can be used to accelerate the speed of the training set [11]. And the common graphics card NVIDIA configures the corresponding CUDA for the graphics card after MX150 so that researchers can use GPU acceleration [12]. Then it is a deep neural network with an automatic differentiation system, which can quickly build a neural network and has a rich API interface for researchers to use [13].

Using PyTorch to build a neural network can be achieved by using the torch.nn package. Each nn.Module contains various layers and a forward (input) method, which returns output. The realization of a simple digital classification neural network is shown in Fig. 1.

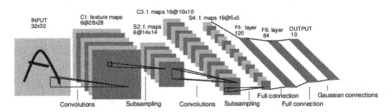

Fig. 1. Implementation diagram of digital classification neural network

On the basis of this example, the image, text, audio or video data we need to process is loaded into a numpy array using the Python standard library before building a neural network, and then the array is converted to torch.*Tensor. For pictures, Pillow or OpenCV can be used for processing [14].

2.2   Introduction to YOLO

The YOLO algorithm was published "You Only Look Once: Unified, Real-Time Object Detection" by Joseph Redmon in CVPR2016. As the name suggests, the author emphasizes the single-stage model, as shown in Fig. 2.

Fig. 2. Single-stage model diagram of YOLOv1 algorithm

After three iterations of YOLOv1, YOLOv2 and YOLOv3, the YOLO algorithm has matured. The structure of YOLOv1 is to add 4 convolutional layers and 2 fully connected layers on the 20 layers of the GoogleNet network [16]. Divide each image into 7×7 grids. When an object in the image exists in one of the grids, a single grid is responsible for judging the object. Each grid is assigned 2 bounding boxes, and finally a $7 \times 7 \times 30$ tensor is output. The number of channels 30 is the number of channels, including 5 coordinate information of 2 bounding boxes [15]. Its confidence is shown in Eq. 1.

$$c_c = p(*)U_t^p \tag{1}$$

Where P(*) indicates whether there is an object center in the grid, if it exists, it is 1, otherwise it is 0. U indicates the intersection ratio of the predicted frame and the real frame. The calculation formula is shown in formula 2.

$$U = \frac{B_T \cap B_P}{B_T \cup B_P} \tag{2}$$

The YOLOv2 algorithm is improved on the basis of YOLOv1. Using the structure of Darknet19, using a small convolution kernel operation. And YOLOv2 draws on the Faster R-CNN algorithm and uses anchor boxes to generate more detection boxes for each small table that is segmented [17]. And in the selection of the anchor point frame, the k-means clustering algorithm is used to select the anchor point frame closer to the detected object, which makes the network bracelet faster and easier to learn [18]. The calculation formula is shown in formula 3

$$d(b, c) = 1 - U(b, c) \tag{3}$$

C is the cluster center; U(b,c) is the intersection ratio of the center box and the ground truth box. YOLOv2 also uses batch normalization to process the input of each layer, which greatly improves the training speed and prevents overfitting.

YOLOv3 uses a new convolutional network Darknet-53 on the basis of YOLOv2 to extract features of target detection objects, and uses multi-scale features to detect target detection objects. While ensuring the detection speed of YOLOv2, the accuracy of predicting objects is improved. The new Darknet-53 network has 53 convolutional layers in order to have more accurate small grid segmentation [19]. Correspondingly, a 1 × 1 convolution kernel is also used to reduce the number of feature channels. As shown in Fig. 3.

	Type	Filters	Size	Output
	Convolutional	32	3×3	256×256
	Convolutional	64	3×3/2	128×128
1	Convolutional	32	1×1	
	Convolutional	64	3×3	
	Resnet unit			
	Convolutional	128	3×3/2	64×64
2	Convolutional	64	1×1	
	Convolutional	128	3×3	
	Resnet unit			
	Convolutional	256	3×3/2	32×32
8	Convolutional	128	1×1	
	Convolutional	256	3×3	
	Resnet unit			
	Convolutional	512	3×3/2	16×16
8	Convolutional	256	1×1	
	Convolutional	512	3×3	
	Resnet unit			
	Convolutional	1 024	3×3/2	8×8
4	Convolutional	512	1×1	
	Convolutional	1 024	3×3	
	Resnet unit			
	Avgpool		Global	
	Connected		1 000	
	Softmax			

Fig. 3. Darknet-53 network diagram

In Fig. 3: Type is the type; Filters is the number of convolutions; Size is the size; Output is the output; Convonlutional is the convolution; Resnet unit is the Resnet residual unit; Avgpool is the average pooling; Global is the global; Connected is the full connection; Softmax is a Softmax classifier.

Compared with YOLOv3's Darknet-53, YOLOv4 uses CSPDarknet-53, and introduces the SPP-Net structure, so that the YOLOv4 network can adapt to different sizes of input. At the same time, PANet is also introduced, making full use of feature fusion. And YOLOv4 has also been improved on the input end of the training model, mainly using Mosaic, cmBN, and SAT self-adversarial training, with Mosaic being the focus [20]. Figure 3 describes the architecture of the YOLOv4 algorithm in detail. The CSP-DarkNet53 network structure, which is the most obvious improvement over YOLOv3, is shown in Fig. 4.

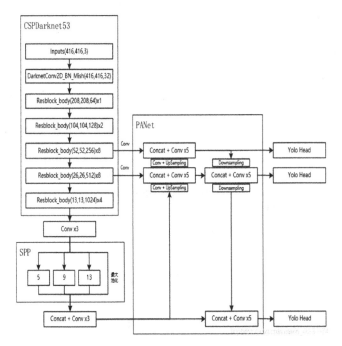

Fig. 4. CSPDarkNet53 network structure diagram

2.3 Control Algorithm

The main application scenario during the conference is the use of PPT. This article takes PPT as an example to implement the control algorithm. The main idea is to use the pyHook package in the Python library to call the global mouse and keyboard events in Windows to provide callbacks. Python applications register event handlers for user input events, such as left and right mouse buttons, and set keyboard and mouse hooks. After the model training, the gesture recognition result is judged, so that the mouse and the keyboard react correspondingly to achieve the purpose of controlling the PPT. The control algorithm is presented in pseudo code as follows:

```
1  list = []
2  while i < strlen(string)
3  do list.append(i)
4  result ← ".join(list[2:8])
5  if result = "dianji":
6  then k.tap_key(k.function_keys [5])
7  elseif result = "xuanzhuan":
8  then k.tap_key(k.control_key)
```

3   Experiment and Result Analysis

3.1   Experimental Platform and Data Set

The experimental environment uses Window10 operating system and PyTroch + YOLO algorithm framework. On the hardware configuration, the CPU uses Intel(R) Core™ i7-8550U CPU @ 1.8 GHz; the GPU is the NVIDIA MX150 2G independent display.

The experiment uses an autonomous data set, which is collected from the real hand of the researcher. The image contains detection targets of different gestures at multiple scales, which is suitable as a data set for gesture detection. Part of the image is shown in Fig. 5. The data set contains 1150 images with a resolution of 320 × 240, labeled with 5 categories: xuanzhuan (rotation), pingyi (translation), zhuaqu (grabbing), suofang (zooming), and dianji (clicking).

Fig. 5. Example of gestures

To achieve the effect, take the dianji (click) action as an example. First, make a click gesture as shown in Fig. 6. After the model predicts a click gesture, the control algorithm makes the corresponding action of playing PPT as shown in Fig. 7.

3.2   Network Training

The data set is divided into training set and test set at a ratio of 7:3. Use the basic YOLOv4 algorithm and PyTorch model to train the data set and get the result.

Fig. 6. An example of the "dianji" gesture

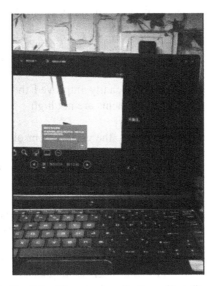

Fig. 7. "dianji" gesture realization effect diagram

3.3 Result Analysis

As shown in Table 1, this experiment uses the accuracy rate P (Precision) as the evaluation standard of the model recognition effect.

Table 1. Different gesture recognition effects

Gesture	Precision/%
PingYi	45.21
XuanZhuan	56.54
DianJi	46.45
SuoFang	42.54
ZhuaQu	59.23

The experimental results show that the method proposed in this paper has preliminary usability. The model can roughly meet the requirements. And can complete the preliminary experimental requirements.

4 Conclusion

The gesture control model using PyTorch + YOLOv4 proposed in this paper has achieved preliminary results. Through the preliminary construction of the PyTorch neural network and the application of the YOLOv4 algorithm, combined with the control algorithm through theoretical analysis and experimental verification, the following conclusions are drawn.

(1) Use PyTorch to quickly build a preliminary neural network model and get preliminary experimental data
(2) The YOLOv4 algorithm has significantly improved the accuracy and speed of YOLOv3, and the hardware requirements are not high

The next research direction can realize the gesture control from simple conference control to the field of smart home, so as to realize a richer and smarter living environment. Or, gesture control can play a role in the field of Internet of Things to realize the interconnection of everything.

Acknowledgment. This work is supported in part by National Key R&D Program Funded Project of China under grant number 2018YFB1700200 and 2019YFE0122600, in part by the Hunan Provincial Key Research and Development Project of China under grant numbers 2019GK2133, in part by the Natural Science Foundation of Hunan Province under grant number 2021JJ50050, 2021JJ50058 and 2020JJ6089, in part by the Scientific Research Project of Hunan Provincial Department of Education under grant number 19B147,in part py the Key Project of the Department of Education in Hunan Province (19A133), in part by the Degree and Postgraduate Education Reform Research Project of Hunan Province Department of Education under grant number 2020JGZD059, in part by the Teaching Reform of Ordinary Colleges and Universities Research project of Hunan Province Department of Education under grant number HNJG-2021–0710,in part by the Open PlatformInnovation Foundation of Hunan Provincial Education Department(grant no. 20K046),and this research was supported by the Special Fund Support Project for the Construction of Innovative Provinces in Hunan (2019GK4009).

References

1. Qi Jing, X., Kun, D.: Research progress of robot visual gesture interaction technology. Robot **39**(04), 565–584 (2017)
2. Bowen, S., Feng, Y.: Monocular camera dynamic gesture recognition and interaction based on deep learning. J. Harbin Univ. Sci. Technol. **26**(01), 30–38 (2021)
3. Fenhua, W., Chao, H., Bo, Z., Qiang, Z.: Gesture recognition based on YOLO algorithm. J. Beijing Inst. Technol. **40**(08), 873–879 (2020)
4. Xuanheng, L., Baosong, D., Yu, P., Bohui, F., Liang, X., Ye, Y., Erwei, Y.: Research on wearable gesture interaction system and recognition algorithm. Small Microcomput. Syst. **41**(11), 2241–2248 (2020)
5. Xiaoyan, X., Huan, Z., Lin, J.: Dynamic gesture recognition based on the characteristics of video data. J. Beijing Univ. Posts Telecommun. **43**(05), 91–97 (2020)
6. Mengli, S., Beiwei, Z., Guanghui, L.: Real-time gesture recognition method based on depth image. Comput. Eng. Des. **41**(07), 2057–2062 (2020)
7. Xiaoping, Y., Xuqi, M., Sai, L.: Improved YOLOv3 pedestrian vehicle target detection algorithm. Sci. Technol. Eng. **21**(08), 3192–3198 (2021)
8. Xiaohu, N., Lei, D.: Overview of typical target detection algorithms for deep learning. Appl. Res. Comput. **37**(S2), 15–21 (2020)
9. Zhijia, L., Xuan, W., Jinbo, Z., Yinhui, X., Xuhui, G.: Improved method of infrared image target detection based on YOLO algorithm. Laser Infrared **50**(12), 1512–1520 (2020)
10. Maurya, H., et al.: Analysis on hand gesture recognition using artificial neural network. Ethics Inf. Technol. **2**(2), 127–133 (2020)
11. Wang, Y., Yang, Y., Zhang, P.: Gesture feature extraction and recognition based on image processing. IIETA **37**(5), 873–880 (2020)
12. Kiselev, I.V., Kiselev, I.V.: Comparative analysis of libraries for computer vision OpenCV and AForge. NET for use in gesture recognition system. J. Phys. Conf. Ser. **1661**(1), 012048 (2020)
13. Liang, C.Y., Yuan, C.H., Feng, T.W.: Hand gesture recognition via image processing techniques and deep CNN. J. Intell. Fuzzy Syst. **39**(3), 4405–4418 (2020)
14. Hoshang, K., et al.: A new framework for sign language alphabet hand posture recognition using geometrical features through artificial neural network (part 1). Neural Comput. Appl. **33**(10), 4945–4963 (2020)
15. Oudah, M., Al-Naji, A., Chahl, J.: Hand gesture recognition based on computer vision: a review of techniques. J. Imaging **6**(8), 73 (2020)
16. Kai, Z., Yi, W., Hailong, H.: Research on recognition and application of hand gesture based on skin color and SVM. J. Comput. Methods Sci. Eng. **20**(1), 269–278 (2020)
17. Mo, T., Sun, P.: Research on key issues of gesture recognition for artificial intelligence. Soft. Comput. **24**(8), 5795–5803 (2020)
18. Shangchun, L., et al.: Multi-object intergroup gesture recognition combined with fusion feature and KNN algorithm. J. Intell. Fuzzy Syst. **38**(3), 2725–2735 (2020)
19. Li, X.: Human–robot interaction based on gesture and movement recognition. Signal Process. Image Commun. **81**, 115686 (2020)
20. Baldissera, F.B., Vargas, F.L.: A light implementation of a 3D convolutional network for online gesture recognition. IEEE Lat. Am. Trans. **18**(2), 319–326 (2020)

A Lightweight FCNN-Driven Approach to Concrete Composition Extraction in a Distributed Environment

Hui Lu[1], Kondwani Michael Kamoto[1], Qi Liu[1(✉)], Yiming Zhang[2], Xiaodong Liu[3], Xiaolong Xu[1], and Lianyong Qi[1]

[1] School of Computer and Software, Engineering Research Center of Digital Forensics, Ministry of Education, Nanjing University of Information Science and Technology, Nanjing 210044, China
{20191221006,qi.liu}@nuist.edu.cn, lianyongqi@qfnu.edu.cn
[2] School of Civil and Transportation Engineering, Hebei University of Technology, Tianjin 300401, China
yiming.zhang@hebut.edu.cn
[3] School of Computing, Edinburgh Napier University, Edinburgh EH14 1DJ, UK
x.liu@napier.ac.uk

Abstract. It is of great significance to study the positive characteristics of concrete bearing cracks, fire and other adverse environment for the safety of human life and property and the protection of environmental resources. However, there are still some challenges in traditional concrete composition evaluation methods. On the one hand, the traditional method needs a lot of experimental work, which is time-consuming and laborious; On the other hand, the cost of new technology is high, and its applicability needs further study. Therefore, this paper proposes an improved lightweight model based on fully connected neural network (FCNN) to discover the relationship between the performance of different concrete mixtures and the visual (image) performance of the final synthesis process, so as to realize the prediction of concrete composition. The model is built in a distributed environment, and it can achieve lightweight and convenient effect through remote call learning model. The experimental results show that the method greatly improves the accuracy of concrete composition prediction.

Keywords: Concrete · Lightweight FCNN · Distributed

1 Introduction

Concrete materials are widely used as building materials. In order to accurately analyze the composition of concrete and obtain the positive characteristics of concrete under adverse environment such as cracks and fire, it is necessary to improve the performance of concrete according to different needs [1]. Therefore, the researchers developed a machine learning model, combined with non-destructive testing method to analyze the composition of concrete. For example, combining Particle Swarm Optimization (PSO)

© ICST Institute for Computer Sciences, Social Informatics and Telecommunications Engineering 2022
Published by Springer Nature Switzerland AG 2022. All Rights Reserved
M. R. Khosravi et al. (Eds.): CloudComp 2021, LNICST 430, pp. 40–46, 2022.
https://doi.org/10.1007/978-3-030-99191-3_4

with Artificial Neural Network (ANN) to analyze the composition and mechanical properties of concrete can effectively solve the problem of multi-variable, multi-output, but the number of research samples for optimal mix design is limited [2, 3]. K-Nearest Neighbor algorithm (KNN) and Finite State Machine (FSM) are also effectively applied to the composition analysis of fresh concrete [4, 5].

For a special type of concrete mix proportion, in the case of small sample size, it is difficult to optimize the parameters of machine learning model to achieve the optimal analysis results. Therefore, the main contribution of this paper is to design three fully connected neural network models, quantify and visually analyze the prediction results, and obtain a best network model for concrete composition prediction. We design a lightweight and efficient Fully Connected Neural Network (FCNN) [6, 7], which is called Three Layer Model with L2 Regularization ($\lambda = 0.001$) (hereinafter referred to as Three Layer Model-L2R ($\lambda = 0.001$)), retaining the characteristics of all data, analyzing the similarity and difference of concrete members, giving accurate prediction results. Finally, the algorithm is deployed on the distributed platform, so that the server hardware does not affect the operation of the algorithm, ensuring the reliability and flexibility of the algorithm [8, 9].

2 Methods

2.1 Three Layer Model-L2R ($\lambda = 0.001$) Overall Network Architecture

The improved fully connected neural network proposed in this paper is a three-layer neural network. The model was designed with two hidden layers (19 units + 38 units), and made use of L2 Regularization (L2R) in the first hidden layer with a λ value of 0.001. The architecture of the model is presented in Fig. 1.

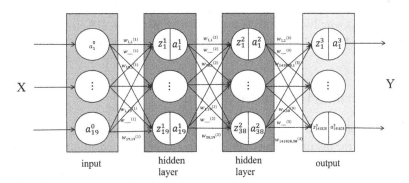

Fig. 1. Three Layer Model with L2 Regularization ($\lambda = 0.001$) model architecture

The network structure is shown in the Fig. 1. The input data is a 19 properties vector of concrete, and the hidden layer has two layers, corresponding to 19 units and 38 units respectively, which means that the 19 dimensional vector is mapped to a 38 dimensional vector through linear mapping, and finally it becomes a 141828 dimensional output. The algorithm idea is that the fully connected neural network is divided into forward propagation and back propagation. Forward propagation gives a predicted value and calculates the error between the predicted value and the real value and the inverse operation optimizes the weights of each link from the gradient direction of error reduction until the training times or the error is within the set range.

2.2 Back Propagation (BP) Algorithm

BP is an optimization process. BP is the most commonly used optimization algorithm in neural networks [10]. This direction is opposite to the forward propagation direction, so it is called back propagation. There are three main equations:

$$W^l = W^l - a\frac{\partial J\left(\alpha^l\right)}{\partial W^l} \tag{1}$$

$$b^l = b^l - a\frac{\partial J\left(\alpha^l\right)}{\partial b^l} \tag{2}$$

$$J\left(a^l\right) = J\left(\sigma\left(Z^l\right)\right) = J(\sigma(W^l a^{l-1} + b^l)) \tag{3}$$

The output value a^l of each neuron was calculated forward; The error term of each neuron is calculated in reverse δ^l; The random gradient descent algorithm iteratively updates the weights w and b, and the loss function J of the output layer l.

2.3 Baseline Model

A baseline model was designed in order to provide a minimum benchmark of performance and allow for meaningful comparison with various model improvements. The baseline model is a multi-layer perceptron with multiple inputs (19 properties), a single hidden layer (19 units), and multiple outputs (141828 scaled pixel values for the mixture image).

3 Deep Learning Distributed System

In this paper, we proposed an improved lightweight fully connected neural network model based on the distributed environment to predict the composition of concrete. The structure of the distributed system is shown in Fig. 2. Users can use any programming language supporting network programming, through the specified IP address or domain name address, according to the interface documentation provided by the system, they can access all kinds of deep learning computing resources provided on the host computer of the system [11–15].

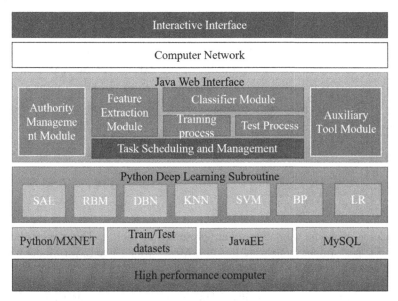

Fig. 2. Architecture of deep learning distributed system

4 Experiment and Analysis

4.1 Datasets

There are three sets of data that are used to build the model, a set of the concrete properties and a set of visual representations of the mixtures. The data sets are comprised of 3523 samples of the concrete properties and their corresponding mixtures.

4.2 Evaluation Metrics

The evaluation criteria used to determine model performance included Mean Squared Error (MSE) that means the expectation of the square of the difference between the estimated value of the parameter and the real value of the parameter. Root Mean Squared Error (RMSE) is the arithmetic square root of the mean square error, and Mean Absolute Error (MAE) is the average of absolute error, which can better reflect the actual situation of predicted value error. Model performance was determined using Structural Similarity Index (SSIM) which is a metric used to measure image quality on a scale of zero (no similarity) to one (perfect similarity).

4.3 Model Performance

To evaluate the effectiveness of improved FCNN Model proposed in this paper, three sets of comparative experiments were carried out on the given dataset.

The experiments so far indicate that we can derive meaningful results using simple model architectures. The MSE, MAE, RMSE, SSIM metrics for the cross-validation and

Table 1. Results of model evaluation on training, testing, and validation sets

Model name	10-fold cross-validation		Validation set			
	MSE	RMSE	MSE	RMSE	MAE	SSIM
Baseline model	0.013 (±0.003)	0.114 (±0.055)	0.987	0.990	0.937	0.968
Baseline model-L2R (λ = 0.001)	0.018 (±0.003)	0.134 (±0.055)	0.987	0.988	0.950	0.984
Three Layer Model-L2R (λ = 0.001)	0.012 (±0.002)	0.110 (±0.043)	0.995	0.992	0.985	0.995

the evaluation using the validation set are presented in Table 1. The metrics show that the next best performing models are Baseline Model with Three Layer Model with L2-Regularization ($\lambda = 0.001$).

Three Layer Model-L2R ($\lambda = 0.001$). This section provides a summary of the modeling process and includes details on the performance of Three Layer Model-L2R ($\lambda = 0.001$). Figure 3 shows the Three Layer Model-L2R ($\lambda = 0.001$) change results of MSE and MAE in each iteration during model training. It is obvious from the Fig. 3 that the training and test curves gradually approach the x-axis with the increase of the number of iterations, that is, they gradually approach the coincidence, that is, the MAE and MSE of the training set and the test set always decrease and approach 0, indicating that the model training effect is good. Besides, the training history shows that there are some minor fluctuations of the testing MSE, with more fluctuation with the MAE. In this paper, in order to show the visual prediction effect, the best and worst outputs generated using the verification set are shown in Fig. 4 and Fig. 5 respectively, in which different colors represent the distribution of different component attributes of concrete. Through the comparison with the original map, it can be seen that the predicted attribute components are basically consistent with the original map, and a good prediction effect

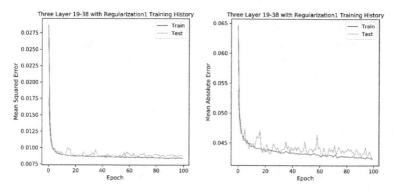

Fig. 3. Three Layer Model-L2R ($\lambda = 0.001$) model training history

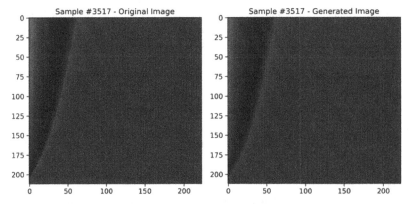

Fig. 4. Best output generated by Three Layer Model-L2R ($\lambda = 0.001$) model for sample

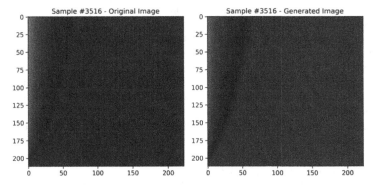

Fig. 5. Worst output generated by Three Layer Model-L2R ($\lambda = 0.001$) model for sample

is achieved. The worst output as shown in Fig. 5 for this model is exceeds the baseline model with which indicates that this model is closer to the best performance.

5 Conclusion

In this paper, we propose a deep learning distributed system, and propose an improved fully connected neural network on this system to discover the correlation between samples of nineteen concrete properties and the resulting mixtures that comprise them. The results of experimentation indicate that a three-layer architecture with 19 units and 38 units in the hidden layers, and L2 regularization ($\lambda = 0.001$) in the first hidden layer has the best performance overall, especially when given challenging unseen data. The recommendation is therefore to make use of this model for future work.

Acknowledgements. This work has received funding from the Key Laboratory Foundation of National Defence Technology under Grant 61424010208, National Natural Science Foundation of China (No. 41911530242 and 41975142), 5150 Spring Specialists (05492018012 and 05762018039), Major Program of the National Social Science Fund of China (Grant No. 17ZDA092), 333 High-Level Talent Cultivation Project of Jiangsu Province (BRA2018332),

Royal Society of Edinburgh, UK and China Natural Science Foundation Council (RSE Reference: 62967_Liu_2018_2) under their Joint International Projects funding scheme and basic Research Programs (Natural Science Foundation) of Jiangsu Province (BK20191398 and BK20180794).

References

1. Zeng, Y., Xiong, N., Park, J.H., Zheng, G.: An emergency-adaptive routing scheme for wireless sensor networks for building fire hazard monitoring. Sensors **10**(6), 6128–6148 (2010)
2. Hsieh, Y., Su, M., Chen, J., Badjie, B.A., Su, Y.: Developing a PSO-based projection algorithm for a porosity detection system using X-ray CT images of permeable concrete. IEEE Access **6**, 64406–64415 (2018)
3. Felix, E.F., Possan, E.: Modeling the carbonation front of concrete structures in the marine environment through ANN. IEEE Lat. Am. Trans. **16**(6), 1772–1779 (2018)
4. Altay, O., Ulas, M., Alyamac, K.E.: Prediction of the fresh performance of steel fiber reinforced self-compacting concrete using quadratic SVM and weighted KNN models. IEEE Access **8**, 92647–92658 (2020)
5. Kumavat, H., Chandak, N.: Experimental study on behavior of normal strength concrete influenced by elevated temperatures. In: 2020 Advances in Science and Engineering Technology International Conferences (ASET), pp. 1–5. IEEE (2020)
6. Wang, Y., Zhang, F., Zhang, X., Zhang, S.: Series AC arc fault detection method based on hybrid time and frequency analysis and fully connected neural network. IEEE Trans. Industr. Inf. **15**(12), 6210–6219 (2019)
7. Mazumdar, M., Sarasvathi, V., Kumar, A.: Object recognition in videos by sequential frame extraction using convolutional neural networks and fully connected neural networks. In: 2017 International conference on energy, communication, data analytics and soft computing (ICECDS), pp. 1485–1488. IEEE (2017)
8. Fang, W., Yao, X., Zhao, X., Yin, J., Xiong, N.: A stochastic control approach to maximize profit on service provisioning for mobile cloudlet platforms. IEEE Trans. Syst. Man Cybern. Syst. **48**(4), 522–534 (2016)
9. Yin, J., Lo, W., Deng, S., Li, Y., Wu, Z., Xiong, N.: Colbar: a collaborative location-based regularization framework for QoS prediction. Inf. Sci. **265**, 68–84 (2014)
10. Ayhan, T., Altun, M.: Approximate fully connected neural network generation. In: 2018 15th International Conference on Synthesis, Modeling, Analysis and Simulation Methods and Applications to Circuit Design (SMACD), pp. 93–96. IEEE (2018)
11. Xiong, Z., Sun, X., Sang, J., Wei, X.: Modify the accuracy of MODIS PWV in China: a performance comparison using random forest, generalized regression neural network and back-propagation neural network. Remote Sens. **13**(11), 2215 (2021)
12. Sun, T., Xiong, J., Wang, Y., Meng, T., Chen, X., Xu, C.: RS-pCloud: a peer-to-peer based edge-cloud system for fast remote sensing image processing. In: 2020 IEEE International Conference on Edge Computing (EDGE), pp. 15–22. IEEE (2020)
13. Zhu, G., Wang, Q., Tang, Q., Gu, R., Yuan, C., Huang, Y.: Efficient and scalable functional dependency discovery on distributed data-parallel platforms. IEEE Trans. Parallel Distrib. Syst. **30**(12), 2663–2676 (2019)
14. Qu, Y., Xiong, N.: RFH: a resilient, fault-tolerant and high-efficient replication algorithm for distributed cloud storage. In: 2012 41st International Conference on Parallel Processing, pp. 520–529 (2012)
15. Li, H., Liu, J., Liu, R.W., Xiong, N., Wu, K., Kim, T.H.: A dimensionality reduction-based multi-step clustering method for robust vessel trajectory analysis. Sensors **17**(8), 1792 (2017)

Triangle Coordinate Diagram Localization for Academic Literature Based on Line Segment Detection in Cloud Computing

Baixuan Tang[1] ⓘ, Jielin Jiang[1] ⓘ, Xiaolong Xu[1]([✉]) ⓘ, Lianyong Qi[2] ⓘ,
Xiaokang Zhou[3] ⓘ, and Yang Chen[4] ⓘ

[1] School of Computer and Software, Nanjing University of Information Science and
Technology, Nanjing 210044, China
njuxlxu@gmail.com
[2] School of Information Science and Engineering, Qufu Normal University, Rizhao 276826,
China
[3] Faculty of Data Science, Shiga University, Japan, and also with the RIKEN Center for
Advanced Intelligence Project, RIKEN, Tokyo, Japan
[4] School of Computer Science, Fudan University, Shanghai, China

Abstract. The localization of triangle coordinate diagram in academic literature is an important step in the process of data mining. However, the detection of triangle coordinate diagram in academic literature mainly depends on manual work, which consumes a lot of time. At present, there is no specific locating method for triangle coordinate diagram. To solve this problem, this paper proposes a method of triangle coordinate diagram localization based on line segment detection, which can be placed on the cloud platform to provide convenience for the functions such as diagram-based retrieval in academic literature database. Technically, this paper uses line segment detection algorithm and line segment merging algorithm to complete triangle coordinate diagram localization. Finally, an experiment is conducted to evaluate the method, which proves the effectiveness of the proposed method.

Keywords: Triangle coordinate diagram · Line segment detection · Academic literature · Diagram localization

1 Introduction

Diagram is an important part of academic literature. As a special non-text data structure in literature, it can reflect the key research methods and conclusions in a great measure. With the explosion of academic literature in recent years, the visual resources in the literature present an explosive growth trend. Database vendors continue to strengthen the disclosure of visual resources in the literature, add diagram-based retrieval, build public knowledge resource pools based on academic visual resources, and carry out related services in the search and open access of resources [1]. At the same time, the academic literature database based on the cloud platform makes it possible to place algorithms

M. R. Khosravi et al. (Eds.): CloudComp 2021, LNICST 430, pp. 47–59, 2022.
https://doi.org/10.1007/978-3-030-99191-3_5

with high requirements on computer performance on the cloud, so that these algorithms can be conveniently applied in more common scenarios. Diagram can also help readers quickly and directly understand the author's intention and the core idea of the literature, which is of great help to readers. Scholars try to help readers by analyzing the diagram in the literature, such as searching and recommending appropriate literature. It can be predicted that the development and construction of visual resources in the paper will further promote the organization and dissemination of academic knowledge and have a broad development space in the field of knowledge service in the future.

Compared with the text content in the literature, there are relatively few studies on the diagrams. One of the main reasons is that in the common academic storage format, PDF, the content is not logically structured, but simply positioned by using localization. In other words, in PDF format, diagrams are stored in a discrete manner, and the elements within the diagrams are structurally independent, so they cannot be located directly from the academic literature.

Nowadays, common research on the localization of diagrams in academic literature is mainly based on the underlying coding of PDF, and the localization of specific types of diagrams according to the prior rules of typesetting and literature writing. To some extent, it has a beneficial effect for the same type of literature in PDF format, which is relatively fixed in typesetting format. However, because it mainly analyses the underlying coding of PDF, it ignores the visual information on the page. Nowadays, there are many kinds of academic literatures, which is difficult to extract information accurately with limited typography rules. At the same time, in reality, a large number of electronic literature data of early literature are stored in the form of image after scanned by paper literature, and diagram localization based on the PDF format is more difficult to apply in this case.

Triangle coordinate diagram usually use three-dimensional percentage coordinates to represent the proportion of an element in a three-component system to the overall structure. As a kind of structural information image, three sides of trigonometry represent three different elements, three vertices represent three origins, and the three-dimensional coordinates of points represent the proportion of each component in an element.

Triangle coordinate diagram can be used as a classification diagram by classifying each element according to its component proportion. Triangle coordinate diagram is widely used in geology, chemistry and statistics, such as the classification of sandstone and greywacke, classification of soil texture, chemical classification of carbonate, representation of population age structure and so on.

Different from the common diagram with rectangle as the border, triangle coordinate diagram is a kind of diagram with a triangle as the border, which makes the locating method of this diagram different from the locating method of common diagram. At present, there is no diagram localization algorithm specifically for triangle coordinate diagram. The method proposed can be combined with diagram retrieval and participate in the work related to triangle coordinate diagram data extraction to save manpower and improve efficiency. Considering the wide application of triangle coordinate diagram in all kinds of literature, it has certain research value to study the localization of triangle coordinate diagram in academic literature.

According to the geometric characteristics of triangle coordinate diagram in literature, a method of triangle coordinate diagram localization based on line segment detection is proposed. At the same time, this method does not require a lot of data annotation, which can save a lot of manpower. Specifically, the contributions of this paper are as follows:

1. A line segment merging method is proposed, which can further process the line segments after line segment detection. This method can merge the segments that are incorrectly segmented and the segments that are repeatedly recognized.
2. A method to locate the triangle coordinate diagram according to the detected line segments is proposed.

The rest of this article is organized as follows: The related work in this article is described in Sect. 2. In Sect. 3, the methods of academic literature triangle coordinate diagram localization are described. Experiment are conducted in Sect. 4. In Sect. 5, we conclude this article and look forward to the future.

2 Related Work

Diagram is an important part of literature, which can express the information that needs complex text description in an intuitive and concise way, so that readers can better understand what the author wants to express [2]. Diagram contains the core content of literature, which has high research value and is an important research object. Lee et al. [3] used machine learning technology to divide 8 million diagrams into five categories according to the content. Through the comparison of their influence with the corresponding literature, it was found that the distribution and types of diagrams remained relatively stable for a long time, but there were differences in different fields. Among them, the higher the influence of literature, it tends to use more schematic diagrams to help readers understand. Apostolova et al. [4] pointed out that the accurate localization and indexing of images in literature has an important impact on the accuracy and efficiency of literature image retrieval.

From the above research, it is not difficult to see that the academic literature diagram has high research value. The research on diagrams in academic literature can be divided into academic diagram retrieval [5], diagram similarity calculation [6], and diagram content analysis and extraction [7]. These researches need to accurately locate the diagrams in the literature before they can be carried out. It can be seen that the accuracy and comprehensiveness of the diagram localization in the literature have a great impact on the follow-up research.

There are two kinds of research objects on the diagram localization of academic literature: Scanned academic literature (including electronic literature in the form of pure pictures, most of which are stored in the form of pictures) and literatures in PDF format (most of the text content is stored in the form of characters). For the method of scanned literature, because the main content of the literature is stored in pictures, the academia treats the problem as a kind of image processing problem to solve. Specifically, this method can be roughly divided into two types, one of which divides the picture from the whole page from top to bottom to get the final diagram area, and then classifies the area to locate the existing diagram in the literature in the picture [8]; Another method starts with pixels, calculates the connectivity between the contents from bottom to top, merges the pixels according to certain rules, and finally merges them into a complete diagram area image [9]. For the PDF format literature method, using the format characteristics of the file, extract specific structure content from it according to certain rules, and locate the diagram by matching keywords and searching for areas without body content near keywords. For example, PDF Figures [10] literature diagram localization tool, published by Allen AI Lab, University of Washington, uses heuristic algorithms to accomplish the task of graph positioning by means of label positioning, area content recognition, and performs well on its own dataset.

In recent years, there have been a large number of methods based on deep learning in academia on the localization of diagram and data fetch in the literature. Ma et al. [11] uses deep neural network to extract the semantics of scatterplots in academic papers, and completes the task of calculating the similarity of two scatterplots. Yu et al. [12] extracted the diagrams from the academic papers on artificial intelligence, classified them and located the diagrams describing the deep learning model, then used these diagrams to generate standard flowcharts and get the corresponding codes. The deep learning method can automatically extract the characteristic information from the dataset, and it performs well in the field of computer vision, such as image classification, target detection, and so on. It surpasses human performance in some tasks [13]. However, at the same time, some studies [14] have shown that the lack of high-quality training data limits the ability of deep learning to solve problems on related tasks. There is a large demand for data to solve problems using deep learning, which also greatly increases the cost of research to solve related problems.

Summarizing previous studies, the following areas need to be improved:

(1) The electronic document encoding based diagram localization method for PDF can only handle documents in PDF format, but cannot handle the problem of diagram localization in a large number of scanned documents (stored as picture format); (2) The method based on deep learning requires manual labeling of a large number of data for the extracted diagram target, which makes it difficult to cope with the lack of related data.

According to the characteristics of triangle coordinate diagram in academic literature, this paper proposes a method of triangle coordinate diagram localization in academic literature based on line segment detection: (1) The literature image is de-noised by Gaussian filter to get low noise image, and the image edge is detected by Sobel operator to obtain the binary image; (2) The original line segment set is obtained by line segment detection of low noise image; (3) Processing the original line segment set: merging the overlapping and wrong segments to get the merged line segment set; (4) According to the relative position between each line segment in the triangle segment set, whether the triangle segment group is a triangle is judged.

3   Triangle Coordinate Diagram Localization

3.1   Gaussian Filter and Sobel Operator

The literature image is de-noised to reduce the redundant noise information in the image, which provides convenience for the next step of line segment detection.

According to the values of red channel R, green channel G and blue channel B of the image, the original image is converted into gray image I by using gray calculation formula.

The gray calculation formula is as follows:

$$I = R \times 0.299 + G \times 0.587 + B \times 0.114 \tag{1}$$

when all the pixels of the image are transformed into gray image by gray operation, Gaussian blur formula is used to convolute the gray image I and Gaussian kernel.

The Gaussian blur formula is as follows:

$$I_\sigma = I * Gaussian_\sigma \tag{2}$$

where * denotes convolution operation, $Gaussian_\sigma$ is a two-dimensional Gaussian kernel with a standard deviation of σ, which is defined as:

$$Gaussian_\sigma = \frac{1}{2\pi\sigma} e^{-(x^2+y^2)/2\sigma^2} \tag{3}$$

where x and y represent the abscissa and ordinate of the pixel respectively; After the whole image is convoluted by Gaussian kernel, the de-noised image is obtained.

In order to better detect the line segments in the image in the next step, Sobel operator filtering is also needed for the image.

Sobel operator contains two convolution kernels, namely transverse convolution kernel and longitudinal convolution kernel. The biggest difference between triangle coordinate diagram and common diagram is that there are segments with an inclination of about 60°. This paper uses these inclined segments as the main basis to judge whether there is a triangle coordinate diagram in the image and locate the triangle coordinate diagram. In practice, there are a large number of transverse straight lines in literature images. Therefore, Sobel transverse convolution kernel is used here to convolute the image. In this way, we can get the image y after filtering out the transverse edge. The formula is as follows:

$$G_x = \begin{bmatrix} -1 & 0 & +1 \\ -2 & 0 & +2 \\ -1 & 0 & +1 \end{bmatrix} * y \tag{4}$$

where $*$ denotes convolution operation, G_x represents the image gradient value of transverse edge detection.

3.2 Line Segment Detector

In this step, line segment detection will be performed on the literature image to obtain the line segment set. Specifically, LSD [15] is used to detect line segment.

The main process is as follows:

(1) Calculate the gradient angle θ and gradient G of each pixel in the image, the formula is:

$$\theta(x, y) = \arctan\left(\frac{g_x(x, y)}{-g_y(x, y)}\right) \tag{5}$$

$$G(x, y) = \sqrt{g_x^2(x, y) + g_y^2(x, y)} \qquad (6)$$

where g_x and g_y represents the horizontal and vertical gradient values of the pixel respectively, the formula is:

$$g_x(x, y) = \frac{i(x+1,y)+i(x+1,y+1)-i(x,y)-i(x,y+1)}{2}$$
$$g_y(x, y) = \frac{i(x,y+1)+i(x+1,y+1)-i(x,y)-i(x+1,y)}{2} \qquad (7)$$

where $i(x, y)$ is the gray value of the pixel at (x, y);

(2) The direction of the pixel is combined into the direction of the line area, and the pixel is filtered by judging the direction of the pixel and the direction of the line area. Select an unselected pixel as the seed point to judge the pixel: The other pixels whose difference between gradient angle and region angle is less than the threshold is added to the line support domain. Every time a new pixel is added to the area, the region angle of the whole line area is update. The angle formula of an area is as follows:

$$\arctan\left(\frac{\sum_j \sin\theta_j}{\sum_j \cos\theta_j}\right) \qquad (8)$$

(3) The diffused region is fitted by rectangle, and an external rectangle containing all pixels in the region is constructed. The main axis angle of the rectangle is calculated, and the main axis angle is set as the angle of the line segment to be extracted;

(4) Verify the line segment and detect the rectangle r. According to the corresponding NFA formula, calculate whether the rectangle r meets the threshold: if not, ignore it; if yes, express the rectangle record as a detected line. The formula is as follows:

$$\text{NFA}(r) = (NM)^{5/2} \cdot B(n, p) \qquad (9)$$

where N and M represent the column width and row width of the image, and the formula of $B(n, p)$ is:

$$B(n, p) = \sum_{j=k}^{n}\binom{n}{j}p^j(1-p)^{n-j} \qquad (10)$$

where n is the total number of pixels in the rectangle and p is the precision;

(5) Go back to step (2), find the next seed point, spread the rest of the image until traversing the whole image, and get the original line segment set of the image.

3.3 Line Segment Merging

LSD has excellent ability to detect line segments. However, a single line segment in the image of literature may be detected as multiple line segments after line segment detection, which will have a negative impact on the locating and type determination of the diagram. Therefore, after line segment detection, it is necessary to merge the line segments according to certain rules: delete the redundant segments and connect the segments that are wrongly segmented.

In this paper, according to the specific situation of the literature, some thresholds are preset. When using this method to identify the diagrams in other literature, the thresholds need to be adjusted according to the situation.

(1) First of all, set the line segment end merging threshold and slope merging threshold. The threshold value can be set according to the page size of literature image, or can be manually specified according to experience;

(2) Then, the redundant segments are merged. Firstly, the redundant line segments with similar length and position are merged. The method is as follows:

Judge whether there are two pairs of endpoints in two line segments, and the distance between the two pairs of endpoints is less than the endpoint merging threshold. If there is a group of line segments that meet the conditions, merge them: According to the formula, the center point of each pair of end points is taken as the end point of the merged line segment, a merged line segment is generated, and two original line segments are deleted. The end coordinates (X, Y) formula of merging line segments is as follows:

$$X = \frac{x_0 + x_1}{2} \tag{11}$$

$$Y = \frac{y_0 + y_1}{2} \tag{12}$$

where (x_0, y_0) and (x_1, y_1) are the two endpoints to be merged;

After that, merge the redundant segments with length difference. The method are as follows: Judge whether the slope difference of two line segments is less than the slope threshold, and whether the maximum distance between the two ends of the shorter line segment and the longer line segment is less than the point line merging threshold.

If the conditions are met, the segments are merged: The shorter segments are deleted, and the longer segments are retained;

(3) Finally, the segments that are wrongly segmented are merged. For the wrong segment, the method is as follows: The distance between two segments is less than the merging threshold, and the slope difference between the two segments is less than the slope threshold.

If the conditions are met, merge segments: Take the two farthest endpoints of two line segments as the two endpoints of the merging line segment, generate a merging line segment, and delete the two original line segments;

(4) Repeat steps (2) and (3) for the line segment set until the set is no longer updated, which means that the line segment merging is completed.

3.4 Diagram Localization

After the above steps, the line segments in the set can represent the frame of the triangle in the literature image to a certain extent. Next, according to certain steps, find the appropriate line segment pair from the set for matching. The steps are as follows:

(1) Classify the line segments in the set according to the slope. Line segments with positive slope form set 1; Line segments with negative slope form set 2.

(2) Select a line segment from set 1. In set 2, select a segment whose absolute value of slope is close to it and whose endpoint is closest to the endpoint of the selected segment in set 1.

(3) Record the selected line segments in set 1 and set 2, and remove the two segments in set 1 and set 2. The two line segments are regarded as the waist of the triangle coordinate diagram in the literature image. Each pair of such line segments locates a triangle coordinate diagram.

(4) Repeat steps (2) to (3) until all line segments in set 1 cannot find qualified line segments in set 2, or one of the sets is empty.

The algorithm from step (2) to step (3) is as follows:

Algorithm 1 matchLine(set1, set2)

1:   for each line1 in set1 do
2:     for each line2 in set2 do
3:       if (|slope of line1 − slope of line2| < threshold)
         and (endpointDistance(line1, line2) < minDistance)
         then
4:         minDistance := endpointDistance(line1, line2)
5:         targetLine := line2
6:       end if
7:     end for
8:     add (line1, targetLine) to targetSet
9:   end for

---

where function endpoint Distance(line1, line2) calculates and returns the minimum distance between two endpoints of line1 and two endpoints of line2.

This paper combines LSD line segment detection [15] and line segment merging to establish a new triangle coordinate diagram localization method. Compared with the common line segment detection methods, we add the line segment merging step after the line segment detection, which is very helpful to judge the diagram type according to the spatial relationship of line segments.

4 Experiment

4.1 Dataset

In order to verify the performance of the proposed method, this paper uses the self-built academic literature triangle coordinate diagram dataset for experiments. We searched the open academic literature dataset for keywords such as "decimal composition", "sand-stones", and "provenance". After manual judgment, 43 literatures containing triangle coordinate diagram were selected and constructed into the self-built dataset of this paper. The dataset contains 43 academic literature pages in the format of pictures, in which each page contains at least one triangle coordinate diagram, and all pages contain 112 triangle coordinate diagrams.

4.2 Experimental Method

An example of a literature image in the dataset (Fig. 1) shows how this method locates triangle coordinate diagrams.

Q
Lm
Biluoco Formation
Biluoco Section
Suorika Section
Sewa Formation
Dongbula Section
Qixiangco Section
Suorika
Gaaco Formation
Demazong
Kelegiongle
F
L Lv
Ls
Figure 6. Ternary diagrams for sandstones of the Sewa, Gaaco, and Biluoco formations. Q, quartz; F, feldspar; L, lithic fragments (Lm, metamorphic; Ls, sedimentary; Lv, volcanic). The black arrows highlight the compositional change consequent to the late Bathonian tectonic event.
Sandstone compositions are different in the north Biluoco and Suorika sections of the Abushan Formation. In the north Biluoco section, sandstones of the Abushan Formation are litho-quartzose and quartzo-lithic volcaniclastic (average composition QFL = 46:9:45, LmLsLv = 3:24:73) (Table S2). Intermediate to felsic volcanic rock fragments prevail over limestone and minor sandstone clasts. In the Suorika area, sandstone samples are litho-quartzose and quartzo-lithic sedimentaclastic (average composition QFL = 51:47:2, LmLsLv = 8:89:2) (Table S2), with dominant limestone and only minor sandstone and volcanic rock fragments.

Fig. 1. An image in the dataset

(1) Firstly, Sobel operator and Gaussian filter are performed on the literature image to get Fig. 2.

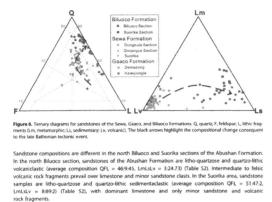

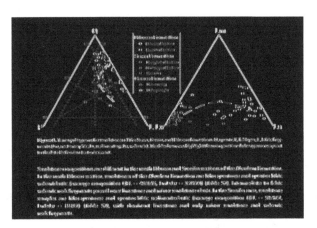

Fig. 2. The image after performed

(2) Line segment detection is performed on the image from the previous step to get the set of line segments. Draw all line segments in the set on literature image, as shown in Fig. 3. (Where each line segment is drawn in a random color, the same below).

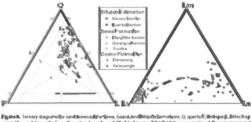

Fig. 3. The image drawn with line segments in the set

(3) Filter out the line segments whose length and angle do not meet the rules in the line segment set of the previous step. Draw the filtered line segment set on the literature image, as shown in Fig. 4. (End points of line segments are marked with red dots).

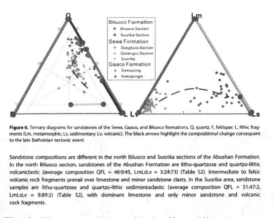

Q
Lm
L
Lv
Ls
Biluoco Formation
Biluoco Section
Suorika Section
Sewa Formation
Dongbula Section
Qixiangco Section
Suorika
Gaaco Formation
Demazong
Kelegiongle
Figure 6. Ternary diagrams for sandstones of the Sewa, Gaaco, and Biluoco formations. Q, quartz; F, feldspar; L, lithic fragments (Lm, metamorphic; Ls, sedimentary; Lv, volcanic). The black arrows highlight the compositional change consequent to the late Bathonian tectonic event.
Sandstone compositions are different in the north Biluoco and Suorika sections of the Abushan Formation. In the north Biluoco section, sandstones of the Abushan Formation are litho-quartzose and quartzo-lithic volcaniclastic (average composition QFL = 46:9:45, LmLsLv = 3:24:73) (Table S2). Intermediate to felsic volcanic rock fragments prevail over limestone and minor sandstone clasts. In the Suorika area, sandstone samples are litho-quartzose and quartzo-lithic sedimentaclastic (average composition QFL = 51:47:2, LmLsLv = 8:89:2) (Table S2), with dominant limestone and only minor sandstone and volcanic rock fragments.

Fig. 4. The image drawn with the filtered line segments

(4) For the line segment set in the previous step, the line segments are merged according to the method proposed in this paper. After that, the line segment set is drawn on the literature image, as shown in Fig. 5.

(5) Search and match the most appropriate line segment from the set in the previous step, and set them as a triangle segment group. Each triangle segment group represents a triangle coordinate diagram, as shown in Fig. 6. (Different triangle coordinate diagrams are represented by triangle boxes of different colors.)

The experiment uses the method in this paper to locate the triangle coordinate diagram in the dataset. The results are given as a triangle box on the rendered page. If no triangle coordinate diagram is found, no box is given in the corresponding area. The result of the

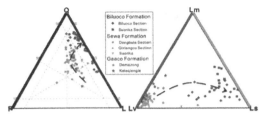

Figure 6. Ternary diagrams for sandstones of the Sewa, Gaaco, and Biluoco formations. Q, quartz; F, feldspar; L, lithic fragments (Lm, metamorphic; Ls, sedimentary; Lv, volcanic). The black arrows highlight the compositional change consequent to the late Bathonian tectonic event.

Sandstone compositions are different in the north Biluoco and Suorika sections of the Abushan Formation. In the north Biluoco section, sandstones of the Abushan Formation are litho-quartzose and quartzo-lithic volcaniclastic (average composition QFL = 46:9:45, LmLsLv = 3:24:73) (Table S2). Intermediate to felsic volcanic rock fragments prevail over limestone and minor sandstone clasts. In the Suorika area, sandstone samples are litho-quartzose and quartzo-lithic sedimentaclastic (average composition QFL = 51:47:2, LmLsLv = 8:89:2) (Table S2), with dominant limestone and only minor sandstone and volcanic rock fragments.

Fig. 5. The image drawn with the merged line segments

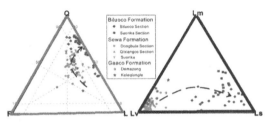

Figure 6. Ternary diagrams for sandstones of the Sewa, Gaaco, and Biluoco formations. Q, quartz; F, feldspar; L, lithic fragments (Lm, metamorphic; Ls, sedimentary; Lv, volcanic). The black arrows highlight the compositional change consequent to the late Bathonian tectonic event.

Sandstone compositions are different in the north Biluoco and Suorika sections of the Abushan Formation. In the north Biluoco section, sandstones of the Abushan Formation are litho-quartzose and quartzo-lithic volcaniclastic (average composition QFL = 46:9:45, LmLsLv = 3:24:73) (Table S2). Intermediate to felsic volcanic rock fragments prevail over limestone and minor sandstone clasts. In the Suorika area, sandstone samples are litho-quartzose and quartzo-lithic sedimentaclastic (average composition QFL = 51:47:2, LmLsLv = 8:89:2) (Table S2), with dominant limestone and only minor sandstone and volcanic rock fragments.

Fig. 6. The image drawn with the triangle boxes

experiment is checked manually. For the results of a triangle coordinate diagram, there are four possible kinds of results: correct, wrong, missing, and extra.

"Correct" means that the box given by the method can be positioned to the frame of the triangle coordinate diagram, and does not include other area that do not belong to the diagram; "Wrong" means that the number of triangle boxes given by the method is the same as the actual number of triangle coordinate diagram, but the given triangle boxes are where there is no triangle coordinate diagram or the given triangle box does not overlap with the triangle coordinate diagram; "Missing" means that the number of triangle boxes given by the method is less than the actual number of triangle coordinate diagrams, that is, some triangle coordinate diagrams fail to be given the corresponding triangle boxes on the result page; "Extra" means that the number of triangle boxes given by the method exceeds the number of actually existing triangle coordinate diagrams on the page.

4.3 Experimental Results and Numerical Analysis

Through experiments and manual verification, there are 112 triangle coordinate diagrams in 43 pages. The method in this paper gives 76 diagrams position results, of which 75 are "correct", 37 are "missing", 1 is "extra", and no "wrong"; The precision rate of the method is 98.68%, and the recall rate is 66.96%.

Experimental results show that this method has high precision, but low recall. The higher precision is attributed to the strict decision rules of the method. However, because of this, the strict decision rules have a certain impact on the recall rate. For example, when the data points are close to the frame of triangle coordinate diagram, when detecting the line segment of the frame, because of the existence of the data points on the frame, the frame line segment may be recognized as a multi-segment line segment or not a line segment (in order to avoid this problem, we introduce the step of line segment merging. However, this cannot completely avoid the problem), which will have an impact on the recall rate.

5 Conclusion

This paper solves the problem of academic literature triangle coordinate diagram localization. A new triangle coordinate diagram localization method is established by line segment detection and line segment merging. The purpose of locating triangle coordinate diagram in academic literature is realized. This method regards the problem of diagram localization as an image processing problem: Compared with the method based on the coding information in PDF format literature, this method can solve the problem of literature diagram localization in the scanning format of image; Compared with the method based on deep learning, this method does not need a lot of manpower to label data and can save manpower cost.

In this method, after detecting the position of line segment by line segment detection, the line segments are merged. Due to the merging of line segments, the wrong detection of line segment group can be avoided.

Nevertheless, there are still some improvements needed for this method.

(1) In the line segment merging step, it is necessary to manually set an appropriate threshold as the basis for line segment merging or not. Clustering the length of line segments and setting the threshold based on it may be a better way to make the generalization ability of the method stronger.

(2) When judging the triangle coordinate diagram, the model adopts the rules set manually to filter the line segments. This means that when dealing with other types of triangle coordinate diagram, it needs to be set according to the specific conditions of those diagrams. For example, this method can not effectively identify asymmetric triangle coordinate diagrams, triangle coordinate diagrams with inclined bottom edges or inverted triangle coordinate diagrams, which is one of the problems to be solved in the follow-up.

Acknowledgement. This research is supported by the National Natural Science Foundation of China under grant no. 42050102.

References

1. Rong, H., et al.: Integrated framework and visual knowledgometrics exploration for analyzing visual resources in academic literature. J. China Soc. Sci. Techn. Inf. **36**(2), 141–151 (2017)
2. Hao, F., et al.: Research on reading effect of the information diagram in the data news: evidence from the eye movement. Librar. Inf. Serv. **63**(8), 74–86 (2019)
3. Lee, P.S., West, J.D., Howe, B.: Viziometrics: analyzing visual information in the scientific literature. IEEE Trans. Big Data **4**(1), 117–129 (2016)
4. Apostolova, E., You, D., Xue, Z., et al.: Image retrieval from scientific publications: text and image content processing to separate multipanel figures. J. Am. Soc. Inform. Sci. Technol. **64**(5), 893–908 (2013)
5. Leibe, B., Matas, J., Sebe, N., Welling, M. (eds.): ECCV 2016. LNCS, vol. 9909. Springer, Cham (2016). https://doi.org/10.1007/978-3-319-46454-1
6. Ma, Y., Tung, A.K.H., Wang, W., Gao, X., Pan, Z., Chen, W.: ScatterNet: a deep subjective similarity model for visual analysis of scatterplots. IEEE Trans. Visual Comput. Graph. **26**(3), 1562–1576 (2020)
7. Yu, C., Levy, C.C., Saniee, I.: Convolutional neural networks for figure extraction in historical technical documents. In: 2017 14th IAPR International Conference on Document Analysis and Recognition (ICDAR), pp. 789–795 (2017)
8. Chen, K., Seuret, M., Liwicki, M., Hennebert, J., Ingold, R.: Page segmentation of historical document images with convolutional autoencoders. In: 2015 13th International Conference on Document Analysis and Recognition (ICDAR), pp. 1011–1015. Tunis, Tunisia (2015)
9. Simon, A., Pret, J.-C., Johnson, A.P.: A fast algorithm for bottom-up document layout analysis. IEEE Trans. Pattern Anal. Mach. Intell. **19**(3), 273–277 (1997)
10. Clark, C., Divvala, S.: PDFFigures 2.0: Mining figures from research papers, 2016 IEEE/ACM Joint Conference on Digital Libraries (JCDL), pp. 143–152. Newark, NJ, USA (2016)
11. Ma, Y.X., et al.: ScatterNet: a deep subjective similarity model for visual analysis of scatterplots. IEEE Trans. Visual Comput. Graph. **26**(3), 1562–1576 (2020)
12. Yu, C., Levy, C.C., Saniee, I.: Convolutional neural networks for figure extraction in historical technical documents. In: 2017 14th IAPR International Conference on Document Analysis and Recognition (ICDAR), pp. 789–795. Kyoto, Japan (2017)
13. He, K., Zhang, X., Ren, S., Sun, J.: Deep residual learning for image recognition. In: 2016 IEEE Conference on Computer Vision and Pattern Recognition (CVPR), pp. 770–778. Las Vegas, NV, USA (2016)
14. Li, P., Jiang, X., Shatkay, H.: Extracting figures and captions from scientific publications. In: Proceedings of the 27th ACM International Conference on Information and Knowledge Management, pp. 1595–1598. Torino, Italy (2018)
15. Gioi, R.G., et al.: LSD: a fast line segment detector with a false detection control. IEEE Trans. Pattern. Anal. Mach. Intell. **32**(4), 722–732 (2010)

Optimizing Fund Allocation for Game-Based Verifiable Computation Outsourcing

Pinglan Liu, Xiaojuan Ma, and Wensheng Zhang[(✉)]

Computer Science Department, Iowa State University, Ames, IA 50011, USA
{pinglan,xiaojuan,wzhang}@iastate.edu

Abstract. This paper considers the setting where a cloud server executes tasks submitted by multiple clients. Every client wishes to assure honest execution of the tasks by employing a trusted third party (TTP) to verify with a probability. The cloud server makes a deposit for each task it takes, each client allocates a budget for each task submitted, and every party has its limited fund. We study how to allocate the funds optimally such that: a economically-rational cloud server honestly computes each task; the server's wage is maximized; the delay for task verification is minimized. Game theory is applied to formulate these problems, and optimal solutions are developed. Each solution is evaluated through rigorous proofs. To the best of our knowledge, this is the first work on optimizing fund allocation for verifiable outsourcing of computation in the setting of one server and multiple clients, based on game theory.

Keywords: Outsourcing · Computation verification · Game theory · Optimization

1 Introduction

The popularity of cloud services promotes computation outsourcing. Clients outsource heavy computational tasks (e.g., data mining, machine learning) to a cloud server with rich resources to handle them. The server aims to efficiently utilize its resources and maximizes its profit from the computation. Each client desires to pay no more than a certain predefined budget and gets correct computation results with short latency.

To assure that the server returns correct results, verifiable outsourced computation mechanisms should be in place. A large variety of verification schemes have been proposed in the literature. They can rely on cryptography [1–12], trusted hardware [13–16], redundant system (with at least one trusted server) [17,18], game theory [19–26], or combinations of the above. The approaches purely relying on cryptography or trusted hardware usually have high costs and/or low performance/scalability, while the game-based approaches have been more appealing for their lower costs due to the practical assumption of economically-rational participants. Hence, we also apply game theory in our study.

M. R. Khosravi et al. (Eds.): CloudComp 2021, LNICST 430, pp. 60–71, 2022.
https://doi.org/10.1007/978-3-030-99191-3_6

We adopt the basic model that each client outsources her tasks to only one server (without redundancy) but with probabilistic auditing. Additionally, for each task, the server is required to make a deposit, which can be taken by the client when the server is found misbehaving; each client should prepare a *budget* that includes the wage paid to the server (if the server is not found dishonest) and the cost for hiring a trusted third party (TTP) to check the result returned by the server (i.e., auditing). A relation among the deposit, wage and the auditing probability can be found such that, the server's most beneficial strategy is to act honestly as long as the condition is satisfied.

It is natural to assume the cloud has a certain fund to spend as deposits for the tasks it take. However, the fund is limited at a time and should be spent smartly so that the server can maximize its benefit, which we measure as the wage it can earn. A client is also assumed to have certain fund for the tasks she outsources. The client's fund is limited too, and thus should be smartly spent as well to maximize her benefit, which we measure as the delay that she has to experience when waiting for her tasks to complete. Here, the client's spending strategy includes: first, how to distribute a given amount of fund to the tasks that are submitted simultaneously or within the same time window; second, for each of the tasks, how to further divide the assigned budget for paying the server's wage and for hiring a TTP respectively. *How can we smartly allocate the server and the clients' funds to maximize their profits?* To the best of our knowledge, this is a question that has not been raised or answered in the literature. The focus of this paper is to formulate and solve this problem.

We formulate the problem as follows. First, we formulate a per-task game-based outsourcing model. The model enforces a secure relation among three components, the server's deposit, the server's wage and the client's auditing probability, where the latter two determine the client's budget, to ensure the server's best choice to be compute honestly. In addition, the model has the attractive property that, the wage and the auditing probability are not fixed but functions of the server's deposit and the client's budget; the larger is the deposit and/or the budget, the larger is the wage and the smaller is the auditing probability. Note that, larger wage and smaller auditing probability (and thus shorter delay) are desired by the server and the client, respectively. Second, we formulate the interactions between the server and clients into an infinite extensive game with perfect information. Within this game, the server and the clients are the parties; the different ways to dividing the server's fund into the tasks' deposits and to dividing the clients' funds into the tasks' budgets are the parties' actions; and the parties' utilities are defined as functions of the actions.

To solve the formulated problem, we develop algorithms that find the Nash Equilibria of the games, which are also the optimal solutions that maximize the server's wage and minimize the clients' delays in two settings: there is one client or multiple clients in the system.

In the following, Sect. 2 introduces the system model and the per-task game-based outsourcing model. Section 3 defines the game between the server and the clients. Sections 4 and 5 develop the solutions. Finally, Sect. 6 concludes the paper.

2   System Architecture

System Model. We consider a system consisting of a cloud service provider (called cloud server or *server* hereafter), m *clients* that need to outsource computation tasks to the server, and some trusted third parties (called *TTPs* hereafter) which the clients can resort to for verifying outsourced computation.

The server, denoted as S, is not completely trusted and its execution of the tasks outsourced by the clients may not always be correct. However, we assume the server is economically rational; that is, it always aims to maximize its profit and will not misbehave if that would cause penalty. As to be elaborated in Sect. 2, we introduce a game-based approach to guarantee that the server honestly executes the outsourced tasks. We assume that the server is willing to use a certain amount of fund as deposit to assure its client of its honest behavior.

We denote the m clients as $C_1, \cdots, C_m$. The tasks outsourced by each client C_i are denoted as $t_{i,j}$ for $j = 1, \cdots, n_i$, where n_i is the number of such tasks. Each task $t_{i,j}$ is associated with two costs denoted as $c_{i,j}$ and $\hat{c}_{i,j}$, where $c_{i,j}$ is the server's cost to execute the task and $\hat{c}_{i,j}$ is each TTP's cost to execute the task. To simplify the presentation, we assume the execution time is proportional to the costs; that is, assuming k is a certain constant, the server's execution time of the task is $k \cdot c_{i,j}$ and each TTP's execution time of the task is $k \cdot \hat{c}_{i,j}$. Each client C_i allocates a budget $b_{i,j}$ for each task $t_{i,j}$, where $b_{i,j} \geq c_{i,j}$ so that the server is willing to take the task.

Each TTP can be hired at the price of $\hat{c}_{i,j}$ by a client to check if the server's execution is correct via re-execution. A TTP can also be a cloud server that has a trusted execution environment (TEE) such as Intel SGX enclave.

Finally, we assume that the server, the clients and the TTPs can access a blockchain system so that no any centralized trusted authority is required.

Per-task Game-Based Outsourcing Model. To ensure that the server honestly executes tasks, we adopt a game theoretic approach as follows. For each task $t_{i,j}$, the server should make a deposit of $d_{i,j}$ and client C_i should promise a budget with a certain expected value of $b_{i,j}$.

After the client outsources $t_{i,j}$ to the server, with a probability denoted as $p_{i,j}$ it also hires a TTP to execute the task. After the client has received a result of computation task from the server and/or the TTP, funds are distributed between the client and the server as follows: If no TTP is hired, or the results returned by the server and the hired TTP are the same, the client should pay a wage denoted as $w_{i,j}$, where $w_{i,j} \geq c_{i,j}$, to the server, and the server should also be returned with its deposit $d_{i,j}$. If the results returned by the server and the TTP are different, deposit $d_{i,j}$ should be given to the client. Hence,

$$b_{i,j} = w_{i,j} + p_{i,j} \cdot \hat{c}_{i,j}. \tag{1}$$

Also, as stated in the following theorem (proved in [27]), is the sufficient condition to deter the server from misbehaving and ensure it honestly executes task $t_{i,j}$.

Theorem 1. *If $w_{i,j} \geq c_{i,j}$ and $p_{i,j} \geq \frac{c_{i,j}}{w_{i,j}+d_{i,j}}$, an economically rational server must execute task $t_{i,j}$ honestly and submit a correct result to the client.*

3   Optimization Problem

Game between The Server and The Clients. We model the interactions between the server and the clients as an infinite extensive game with perfect information, denoted as $G = (P, A, U)$. Here, $P = \{S, C_1, \cdots, C_m\}$ is the set of players. A is the set of actions taken by the players, including (i) all possibilities that each C_i can split its budget b_i to n_i tasks and (ii) all possibilities that S can split its deposit fund d to the $n = \sum_{i=1}^{m} n_i$ tasks. Hence, the action set each C_i can take is denoted as $A_{c,i} = \{(b_{i,1}, \cdots, b_{i,n_i}) \mid \sum_{j=1}^{n_i} b_{i,j} = b_i\}$, where b_i is C_i's total budget for its tasks, and each action $(b_{i,1}, \cdots, b_{i,n_i})$ is one possible division of b_i to n_i tasks; the action set S can take is denoted as $A_s = \{(d_{1,1}, \cdots, d_{m,n_m}) \mid \sum_{i=1}^{m} \sum_{j=1}^{n_i} d_{i,j} = d\}$, where d is the server's fund for deposits, and each action $(d_{1,1}, \cdots, d_{m,n_m})$ is one possible division of d to n tasks. $U = \{U_s, U_{c,1}, \cdots, U_{c,m}\}$ are the players' utility functions.

Constraints on Budgets and Deposit. According to the above definitions of the clients' and the server's actions, the following constraints are obvious:

$$\sum_{j=1}^{n_i} b_{i,j} = b_i, \ \forall\, i \in \{1, \cdots, m\}, \ and \ \sum_{i=1}^{m} \sum_{j=1}^{n_i} d_{i,j} = d. \tag{2}$$

For each task $t_{i,j}$, the server's deposit for it should be at least $\hat{c}_{i,j}$, to compensate client C_i's cost for hiring a TTP if the server is found dishonest. Hence, we have the following constraint:

$$d_{i,j} \geq \hat{c}_{i,j}. \tag{3}$$

Regarding budget $b_{i,j}$ for $t_{i,j}$, according to Eq. (1), it includes wage $w_{i,j}$ paid to the server for honest computation and the expected cost to hire TTP. First, based on Theorem 1 and that TTP should be hired as infrequently as possible, we set

$$p_{i,j} = \frac{c_{i,j}}{w_{i,j} + d_{i,j}}. \tag{4}$$

Second, $w_{i,j} \geq c_{i,j}$ must hold to incentive the server. Because $b_{i,j} = w_{i,j} + \frac{c_{i,j}\hat{c}_{i,j}}{w_{i,j}+d_{i,j}}$, which is from Equations (1) and (4), is an increasing function of $w_{i,j}$, it holds that $w_{i,j} \geq c_{i,j}$ is equivalent to $b_{i,j} \geq c_{i,j} + \frac{c_{i,j}\hat{c}_{i,j}}{c_{i,j}+d_{i,j}}$. Further due to $d_{i,j} \geq \hat{c}_{i,j}$, we set

$$b_{i,j} \geq c_{i,j} + \frac{c_{i,j}\hat{c}_{i,j}}{c_{i,j} + \hat{c}_{i,j}}, \tag{5}$$

which implies $b_{i,j} \geq c_{i,j} + \frac{c_{i,j}\hat{c}_{i,j}}{c_{i,j}+d_{i,j}}$ and $w_{i,j} \geq c_{i,j}$.

Utility Functions. Server S aims to maximize its total wage $\sum_{i=1}^{m} \sum_{j=1}^{n_i} w_{i,j}$ under the constraints of (1), (4), (2), (3) and (5). From (1) and (4), it holds that $b_{i,j} = w_{i,j} + \frac{c_{j,j}\hat{c}_{i,j}}{w_{i,j}+d_{i,j}}$ which can be written as a quadratic equation for variable $w_{i,j}$ as $w_{i,j}^2 + w_{i,j}(d_{i,j} - b_{i,j}) + c_{j,j}\hat{c}_{i,j} - b_{i,j}d_{i,j} = 0$. Then, we have

$$w(b_{i,j}, d_{i,j}) = \frac{b_{i,j} - d_{i,j} + \sqrt{(b_{i,j} + d_{i,j})^2 - 4c_{i,j}\hat{c}_{i,j}}}{2}. \tag{6}$$

Therefore, the utility of server S is $U_s(A_s, A_{c,1}, \cdots, A_{c,m}) = \sum_{i=1}^{m} \sum_{j=1}^{n_i} w(b_{i,j}, d_{i,j})$. Each C_i aims to minimize the expected time for verifying its n_i tasks. For each task $t_{i,j}$, the expected verification time, denoted as $T_{i,j}$, is

$$T_{i,j}(b_{i,j}, d_{i,j}) = k \cdot (b_{i,j} - w(b_{i,j}, d_{i,j})) = k \cdot \frac{b_{i,j} + d_{i,j} - \sqrt{(b_{i,j} + d_{i,j})^2 - 4c_{i,j}\hat{c}_{i,j}}}{2}.$$

Then, the utility of client C_i is defined as $U_{c,i}(A_s, A_{c,i}) = \sum_{j=1}^{n_i} [T_{i,j}(b_{i,j}, d_{i,j})]$.

Nash Equilibrium of the Game. A Nash equilibrium of the game is a combination of action, denoted as $(A*_s, A*_{c,1}, \cdots, A*_{c,m})$, taken by the server and the clients respectively, such that: for the server and any $A_s \neq A*_s$, $U_s(A_s, A*_{c,1}, \cdots, A*_{c,m}) \leq U_s(A*_s, A*_{c,1}, \cdots, A*_{c,m})$; for each client $i \in \{1, \cdots, m\}$ and any $A_{c,i} \neq A*_{c,i}$, $U_{c,i}(A*_s, A_{c,i}) \leq U_{c,i}(A*_s, A*_{c,i})$.

4 Setting I: Server S vs Single Client C_i

4.1 Client's Optimization Problem

The client's purpose is to minimize her utility, i.e., the expected time for verifying her tasks. Hence, the client's optimization problem is as follows. (Note: parameter k is ignored for the simplicity of exposition.)

$$\min \sum_{j=1}^{n_i} \frac{b_{i,j} + d_{i,j} - \sqrt{(b_{i,j} + d_{i,j})^2 - 4c_{i,j}\hat{c}_{i,j}}}{2} \qquad (7)$$

$$s.t., \sum_{j=1}^{n_i} d_{i,j} = d; \ \sum_{j=1}^{n_i} b_{i,j} = b_i; d_{i,j} \geq \hat{c}_{i,j}; \ b_{i,j} \geq c_{i,j} + \frac{c_{i,j}\hat{c}_{i,j}}{c_{i,j} + \hat{c}_{i,j}}. \qquad (8)$$

4.2 Server's Optimization Problem

The server's purpose is also to maximize its utility, i.e., the total wage earned from the client. Hence, its optimization problem is as follows.

$$\max \sum_{j=1}^{n_i} \frac{b_{i,j} - d_{i,j} + \sqrt{(b_{i,j} + d_{i,j})^2 - 4c_{i,j}\hat{c}_{i,j}}}{2}, \ s.t., \ constraints \ (8). \qquad (9)$$

Note that, the sum of the above two objective functions is

$$(7) + (9) = \sum_{j=1}^{n_i} b_{i,j} = b_i.$$

Hence, the objective of the server's optimization problem can be re-written to

$$\max \ b_i - \sum_{j=1}^{n_i} \frac{b_{i,j} + d_{i,j} - \sqrt{(b_{i,j} + d_{i,j})^2 - 4c_{i,j}\hat{c}_{i,j}}}{2},$$

which is further equivalent to min $\sum_{j=1}^{n_i} \frac{b_{i,j}+d_{i,j}-\sqrt{(b_{i,j}+d_{i,j})^2-4c_{i,j}\hat{c}_{i,j}}}{2}$. Therefore, the above two optimization problems are equivalent: a solution to the
client's optimization problem is also a solution to the server's optimization problem; thus it is also the Nash equilibrium of the game.

4.3   Proposed Algorithm

Due to the equivalence of the above two optimization problems, we only need
to solve one of them. Next, we develop the algorithm, formally presented in
Algorithm 1, to find the solution to the client's optimization problem. The core
of the algorithm is to solve the following optimization problem, which is re-
written from the afore-presented client's optimization problem.

$$\min \sum_{j=1}^{n_i} f(s_{i,j}, i, j)$$

$$where \ f(x, i, j) = \frac{x - \sqrt{x^2 - 4c_{i,j}\hat{c}_{i,j}}}{2}$$

$$s.t. s_{i,j} = b_{i,j} + d_{i,j} \ and \ constraints \ (8) \tag{10}$$

Note that, $f(x, i, j)$ is the client's utility associated with each task $t_{i,j}$, when the
task is assigned with x as the sum of $b_{i,j}$ and $d_{i,j}$. In the algorithm, we also use
a partial derivative function of $f(x, i, j)$, which is defined as

$$f'(x, i, j) = \frac{\partial f(x, i, j)}{\partial x}. \tag{11}$$

After the client and server exchange with each other their budget and deposit
(i.e., b_i and d), they each run Algorithm 1 to optimally allocate $b_i + d$ to the
n_i tasks, i.e., each task $t_{i,j}$ is assigned with budget $b_{i,j}$ and deposit $d_{i,j}$ where
$\sum_{j=1}^{n_i} b_{i,j} = b_i$ and $\sum_{j=1}^{n_i} d_{i,j} = d$, with the goal of maximizing the client's utility.
Intuitively, the algorithm runs in the following three phases:

In the first phase, each task $t_{i,j}$ is assigned an initial value for $s_{i,j}$, which
denotes the sum of $b_{i,j}$ and $d_{i,j}$. Here, the initial value is set to $\hat{c}_{i,j}+c_{i,j}+\frac{c_{i,j}\hat{c}_{i,j}}{c_{i,j}+\hat{c}_{i,j}}$
in order to satisfy constraints (8). After this phase completes, $s = b_i + d -$
$\sum_{j=1}^{n_i}(\hat{c}_{i,j} + c_{i,j} + \frac{c_{i,j}\hat{c}_{i,j}}{c_{i,j}+\hat{c}_{i,j}})$ remains to be allocated in the second phase.

In the second phase, s is split into units each of size δ and the units are further
assigned to the tasks step by step. Specifically, with each step, one remaining
unit is assigned to task $t_{i,j}$ whose $f'(s_{i,j}, i, j)$ is the minimal among all the tasks;
this way, the units are assigned in a greedy manner to maximize the total utility
of all the n_i tasks.

After the b_i+d have been greedily assigned to all the tasks, in the third phase,
$s_{i,j}$ is further split into $b_{i,j}$ and $d_{i,j}$ such that, the shorter verification time a
task has, the larger deposit is assigned to it. This way, the server's deposit can
be reclaimed as soon as possible from the tasks.

Algorithm 1. Optimizing Resource Allocation (Server S v.s. Client C_i with Static Task Set)

Input: b_i - total budget of client C_i; d - total deposit of server S; n_i - total number of tasks; task set $\{t_{i,1}, \cdots, t_{i,n_i}\}$ and associated costs $\{c_{i,1}, \cdots, c_{i,n_i}\}$ and $\{\hat{c}_{i,1}, \cdots, \hat{c}_{i,n_i}\}$.
Output: $\{b_{i,1}, \cdots, b_{i,n_i}\}$ and $\{d_{i,1}, \cdots, d_{i,n_i}\}$.
Phase I: Initialization.

1: **for** $j \in \{1, \cdots, n_i\}$ **do**
2:     $s_{i,j} \leftarrow (\hat{c}_{i,j} + c_{i,j} + \frac{c_{i,j}\hat{c}_{i,j}}{c_{i,j}+\hat{c}_{i,j}})$ ▷ meet constraints (8)

Phase II: Greedy Allocation of the Remaining Fund.

1: $s \leftarrow [b_i + d - \sum_{j=1}^{n_i}(\hat{c}_{i,j} + c_{i,j} + \frac{c_{i,j}\hat{c}_{i,j}}{c_{i,j}+\hat{c}_{i,j}})]$ ▷ remaining fund to distribute
2: **while** $s \geq \delta$ **do**   ▷ distribute remaining fund in unit δ
3:     $j* \leftarrow \arg\min_{j\in\{1,\cdots,n_i\}} f'(s_{i,j}, i, j)$
4:     $s_{i,j*} \leftarrow (s_{i,j*} + \delta)$; $s \leftarrow (s - \delta)$

Phase III: Splitting Sum to Budget/Deposit.

1: $d' \leftarrow d - \sum_{j=1}^{n_i} \hat{c}_{i,j}$
2: $tempSet = \{1, \cdots, n_i\}$
3: **while** $tempSet \neq \emptyset$ **do**
4:     $j* = \arg\min_{j\in\{1,\cdots,n_i\}} f(s_{i,j}, i, j)$ ▷ find the task with the shortest verification time
5:     $x \leftarrow \min\{d', s_{i,j*} - \hat{c}_{i,j*} - (c_{i,j} + \frac{c_{i,j}\hat{c}_{i,j}}{c_{i,j}+\hat{c}_{i,j}})\}$
6:     $d_{i,j*} \leftarrow (\hat{c}_{i,j*} + x)$ ▷ assign as much deposit to task with the shortest verification time
7:     $b_{i,j*} \leftarrow (s_{i,j*} - d_{i,j*})$
8:     $d' \leftarrow (d' - x)$
9:     $tempSet \leftarrow (tempSet - \{j*\})$

4.4   Analysis

It can be proved that Algorithm 1 finds an optimal solution for the client's optimization problem (which is also a solution for the server's optimization problem), and the solution is a Nash equilibrium of the game between the client and the server. We develop the proof in the following steps. First, we introduce an optimization problem, as follows, which is relaxed from (10):

$$\min \sum_{j=1}^{n_i} f(s_{i,j}, i, j) = \sum_{j=1}^{n_i} \frac{s_{i,j} - \sqrt{s_{i,j}^2 - 4c_{i,j}\hat{c}_{i,j}}}{2} \tag{12}$$

$$s.t. -s_{i,j} + c_{i,j} + \frac{c_{i,j}\hat{c}_{i,j}}{c_{i,j}+\hat{c}_{i,j}} + \hat{c}_{i,j} \leq 0. \tag{13}$$

Second, we derive the following Lemmas.

Lemma 1. *The optimization problem defined in* (12) *has a unique solution.*

Lemma 2. *Phases I and II of Algorithm 1 find the unique solution to the optimization problem defined in* (12).

Lemma 3. *Phase III of Algorithm 1 converts a solution of the problem defined in (12) to a solution of the problem defined in (10).*

Based on the above lemmas, we therefore have the following theorem:

Theorem 2. *Algorithm 1 finds a solution of the problem defined in (10).*

Finally, it can also be proved the following theorem:

Theorem 3. *Algorithm 1 finds a Nash equilibrium of the game between server S and client C_i.*

The proofs for the above lemmas and theorems can be found in [27].

5 Setting II: Server S vs Clients $C_1, \cdots, C_m$

Different from the previous context of single client, optimizing for the server's utility and for each client's utility are not equivalent. So we cannot solve it in one step. Instead, we tackle the problem in two steps: we first optimize for the server's utility, which produces an allocation of the server's deposits to the clients; then, we optimize for each client's utility based on the client's budget and the deposit allocated by the server.

5.1 Algorithm

We propose an algorithm, formally presented in Algorithm 3, which runs in the following two steps.

First, we solve the server's optimization problem, which produces the optimal allocation of the server's deposits to the clients that maximizes the server's wages. Thus, the optimization problem can be defined as follows:

$$\max \sum_{i=1}^{m} \sum_{j=1}^{n_i} w(b_{i,j}, d_{i,j}), where \ w(x, y) \ is \ defined \ as \ in \ (6)$$

$$s.t. \text{ constraints } (8). \tag{14}$$

Because

$$\sum_{i=1}^{m} b_i - \sum_{i=1}^{m} \sum_{j=1}^{n_i} w(b_{i,j}, d_{i,j}) = \sum_{i=1}^{m} \sum_{j=1}^{n_i} [b_{i,j} - w(b_{i,j}, d_{i,j})]$$

$$= \sum_{i=1}^{m} \sum_{j=1}^{n_i} \frac{b_{i,j} + d_{i,j} - \sqrt{(b_{i,j} + d_{i,j})^2 - 4c_{i,j}\hat{c}_{i,j}}}{2} = \sum_{i=1}^{m} \sum_{j=1}^{n_i} f(b_{i,j} + d_{i,j}, i, j),$$

the objective function of the above optimization problem, i.e., (14), is equivalent to min $\sum_{i=1}^{m} \sum_{j=1}^{n_i} f(b_{i,j} + d_{i,j}, i, j)$. Furthermore, let $s_{i,j} = b_{i,j} + d_{i,j}$, and then the above optimization problem can be converted to:

$$\min \sum_{i=1}^{m} \sum_{j=1}^{n_i} f(s_{i,j}, i, j), \, where \, f(x,i,j) \text{ is defined as in (10)},$$

s.t.

$$s_{i,j} \geq c_{i,j} + \frac{c_{i,j}\hat{c}_{i,j}}{c_{i,j} + \hat{c}_{i,j}} + \hat{c}_{i,j}, \sum_{j=1}^{n_i} s_{i,j} \geq b_i + \sum_{j=1}^{n_i} \hat{c}_{i,j}, \sum_{i=1}^{m}\sum_{j=1}^{n_i} s_{i,j} = \sum_{i=1}^{m} b_i +(15)$$

Here, the constraints are derived from constraints (8). This optimization problem can be solved in three phases, as formally presented in Algorithm 2.

Algorithm 2. Optimal Splitting of Deposit (Server S v.s. Client C_i, $i = 1, \cdots, m$, with Static Task Set)

Input: b_i - total budget of each client C_i; d: total deposit of server S; n_i - total number of tasks from each C_i; task set $\{t_{1,1}, \cdots, t_{1,n_1}, \cdots, t_{m,1}, \cdots, t_{m,n_m}\}$ and associated costs $\{c_{1,1}, \cdots, c_{1,n_1}, \cdots, c_{m,1}, \cdots, c_{m,n_m}\}$ and $\{\hat{c}_{1,1}, \cdots, \hat{c}_{1,n_1}, \cdots, \hat{c}_{m,1}, \cdots, \hat{c}_{m,n_m}\}$.
Output: deposit d_i allocated to each client C_i.
Phase I: Initialization.

1: **for** $i \in \{1, \cdots, m\}$ **do**
2:     **for** $j \in \{1, \cdots, n_i\}$ **do**
3:         $s_{i,j} \leftarrow (\hat{c}_{i,j} + c_{i,j} + \frac{c_{i,j}\hat{c}_{i,j}}{c_{i,j}+\hat{c}_{i,j}})$

Phase II: Greedy Allocation of Clients' Remaining Budgets.

1: **for** $i \in \{1, \cdots, m\}$ **do**
2:     $b_i' \leftarrow b_i - \sum_{j=1}^{n_i}(c_{i,j} + \frac{c_{i,j}\hat{c}_{i,j}}{c_{i,j}+\hat{c}_{i,j}})$
3:     **while** $b_i' \geq \delta$ **do**
4:         $j* = \arg\min_{j\in\{1,\cdots,n_i\}} f'(s_{i,j}, i, j)$.
5:         $s_{i,j*} \leftarrow (s_{i,j*} + \delta); b_i' \leftarrow (b_i' - \delta)$

Phase III: Greedy Allocation of Remaining Deposit to tasks.

1: $d' \leftarrow d - \sum_{i=1}^{m} \sum_{j=1}^{n_i} \hat{c}_{i,j}$
2: $TS = \{(1,1), \cdots, (1, n_1), \cdots, (m, 1), \cdots, (m, n_m)\}$
3: **while** $d' \geq \delta$ **do**
4:     $(i*, j*) = \arg\min_{(i,j)\in TS} f'(s_{i,j}, i, j)$
5:     $s_{i*,j*} \leftarrow (s_{i*,j*} + \delta); d' \leftarrow (d' - \delta)$

Phase IV: Preparing the Output.

1: **for** $i \in \{1, \cdots, m\}$ **do**
2:     $d_i \leftarrow \sum_{j=1}^{n_i} s_{i*,j*} - b_i$

In the second step, it is already known the server's deposits allocated to the clients. Because the budget of each client is also known, each server-client pair can run Algorithm 1, presented in the previous section, to find out the optimal allocation of budget/deposit to the client's tasks to minimize the client's utility.

Algorithm 3. Optimal Resource Allocation (Server S v.s. Client C_i, $i = 1, \cdots, m$, with Static Task Set)

Input: b_i - total budget of each client C_i; d - total deposit of server S; $\{n_i\}$ - total number of tasks from each C_i for $i = 1, \cdots, m$; task set $\{t_{1,1}, \cdots, t_{1,n_1}, \cdots, t_{m,1}, \cdots, t_{m,n_m}\}$ and associated costs $\{c_{1,1}, \cdots, c_{1,n_1}, \cdots, c_{m,1}, \cdots, c_{m,n_m}\}$ and $\{\hat{c}_{1,1}, \cdots, \hat{c}_{1,n_1}, \cdots, \hat{c}_{m,1}, \cdots, \hat{c}_{m,n_m}\}$.

Output: $\{b_{1,1}, \cdots, b_{1,n_1}, \cdots, b_{m,1}, \cdots, b_{m,n_m}\}$ and $\{d_{1,1}, \cdots, d_{1,n_1}, \cdots, d_{m,1}, \cdots, d_{m,n_m}\}$.

1: $\{d_1, \cdots, d_m\} \leftarrow$ Algorithm 2
2: **for** $i \in \{1, \cdots, m\}$ **do**   ▷ for each client
3:     $(\{b_{i,1}, \cdots, b_{i,n_i}\}, \{d_{i,1}, \cdots, d_{i,n_i}\}) \leftarrow$ Algorithm 1.

5.2   Analysis

To analyze the solution, the following can be proved: First, the optimization problem defined in (15) has only one unique solution. Second, Algorithm 2 solves the optimization problem defined in (15). Third, the optimization problem defined in (15) is equivalent to the one defined in (14). Finally, the budget and deposit allocation strategy produced by Algorithm 3 is a Nash equilibrium.

Lemma 4. *The optimization problem defined in* (15) *has one unique solution.*

Theorem 4. *Phases I-III of Algorithm* 2 *solves optimization problem* (15).

Lemma 5. *Optimization problem* (14) *is equivalent to that defined in* (15).

Theorem 5. *Algorithm* 3 *finds a Nash Equilibrium for the game between server* S *and* m *clients* $C_1, \cdots, C_m$.

The proofs for the above lemmas and theorems can be found in [27].

6   Conclusions and Future Works

In this paper, we study the verifiable computation outsourcing problem in the setting where a cloud server services a set of tasks submitted by multiple clients. We adopt a game-based model, where the cloud server should make a deposit for each task it takes, each client should allocate a budget that includes the wage paid to the server and the possible cost for hiring TTP for each task it submits, and every party (i.e., each of the server and the clients) has its limited fund that can be used for either deposits or task budgets. We study how the funds should be optimally allocated to achieve the three-fold goals: a rational cloud server should honestly compute each task it takes; the server's wages earned from computing the tasks are maximized; and the overall delay experienced by each task for verifying her tasks is minimized. Specifically, we apply game theory to formulate the optimization problems, and develop the optimal or heuristic solutions for two application scenarios: one client outsources a set of tasks to the server; multiple clients outsource a set of tasks to the server. For each of the solutions, we analyze the solutions through rigorous proofs.

In the future, we will study in more depth the setting where there are multiple clients submitting dynamic sequences of tasks to the server. As it is challenging to develop optimal solution for the currently-defined general setting, we will explore to refine the problem with reasonable constraints and then develop an optimal solution for it.

Acknowledgement. The work is partly supported by NSF under grant CNS-1844591.

References

1. Gennaro, R., Gentry, C., Parno, B.: Non-interactive verifiable computing: outsourcing computation to untrusted workers. In: Rabin, T. (ed.) CRYPTO 2010. LNCS, vol. 6223, pp. 465–482. Springer, Heidelberg (2010). https://doi.org/10.1007/978-3-642-14623-7_25
2. Parno, B., Raykova, M., Vaikuntanathan, V.: How to delegate and verify in public: verifiable computation from attribute-based encryption. In: Cramer, R. (ed.) TCC 2012. LNCS, vol. 7194, pp. 422–439. Springer, Heidelberg (2012). https://doi.org/10.1007/978-3-642-28914-9_24
3. Catalano, D., Fiore, D.: Practical homomorphic MACs for arithmetic circuits. In: Johansson, T., Nguyen, P.Q. (eds.) EUROCRYPT 2013. LNCS, vol. 7881, pp. 336–352. Springer, Heidelberg (2013). https://doi.org/10.1007/978-3-642-38348-9_21
4. Parno, B., Howell, J., Gentry, C., Raykova, M.: Pinocchio: nearly practical verifiable computation. In: IEEE Symposium on Security and Privacy, pp. 238–252. IEEE (2013)
5. Abadi, A., Terzis, S., Dong, C.: VD-PSI: verifiable delegated private set intersection on outsourced private datasets. In: Gros21klags, J., Preneel, B. (eds.) FC 2016. LNCS, vol. 9603, pp. 149–168. Springer, Heidelberg (2017). https://doi.org/10.1007/978-3-662-54970-4_9
6. Costello, C., et al.: Geppetto: versatile verifiable computation. In: IEEE Symposium on Security and Privacy, pp. 253–270. IEEE (2015)
7. Fiore, D., Fournet, C., Ghosh, E., Kohlweiss, M., Ohrimenko, O., Parno, B.: Hash first, argue later: adaptive verifiable computations on outsourced data. In: Proceedings of the 2016 ACM SIGSAC Conference on Computer and Communications Security, pp. 1304–1316 (2016)
8. Setty, S.T., McPherson, R., Blumberg, A.J., Walfish, M.: Making argument systems for outsourced computation practical (sometimes). NDSS 1(9), 17 (2012)
9. Setty, S., Vu, V., Panpalia, N., Braun, B., Blumberg, A.J., Walfish, M.: Taking proof-based verified computation a few steps closer to practicality. In: 21st USENIX Security Symposium (USENIX Security 2012), pp. 253–268 (2012)
10. Goldwasser, S., Kalai, Y.T., Rothblum, G.N.: Delegating computation: interactive proofs for muggles. J. ACM (JACM) **62**(4), 1–64 (2015)
11. Ben-Sasson, E., Chiesa, A., Spooner, N.: Interactive oracle proofs. In: Hirt, M., Smith, A. (eds.) TCC 2016. LNCS, vol. 9986, pp. 31–60. Springer, Heidelberg (2016). https://doi.org/10.1007/978-3-662-53644-5_2
12. Wahby, R.S., et al.: Full accounting for verifiable outsourcing. In: Proceedings of the 2017 ACM SIGSAC Conference on Computer and Communications Security, pp. 2071–2086 (2017)

13. Brandenburger, M., Cachin, C., Kapitza, R., Sorniotti, A.: Blockchain and trusted computing: problems, pitfalls, and a solution for hyperledger fabric (2018). arXiv preprint: arXiv:1805.08541
14. Xiao, Y., Zhang, N., Lou, W., Hou, Y.T.: Enforcing private data usage control with blockchain and attested off-chain contract execution (2019). arXiv preprint: arXiv:1904.07275
15. Cheng, R., et al.: Ekiden: a platform for confidentiality-preserving, trustworthy, and performant smart contracts. In: IEEE European Symposium on Security and Privacy (EuroS&P). IEEE, pp. 185–200 (2019)
16. Tramer, F., Boneh, D.: Slalom: Fast, verifiable and private execution of neural networks in trusted hardware (2018). arXiv preprint: arXiv:1806.03287
17. Canetti, R., Riva, B., Rothblum, G.N.: Practical delegation of computation using multiple servers. In: Proceedings of the 18th ACM Conference on Computer and Communications Security, pp. 445–454 (2011)
18. Avizheh, S., Nabi, M., Safavi-Naini, R., Venkateswarlu, M.K.: Verifiable computation using smart contracts. In: Proceedings of the 2019 ACM SIGSAC Conference on Cloud Computing Security Workshop, pp. 17–28 (2019)
19. Nix, R., Kantarcioglu, M.: Contractual agreement design for enforcing honesty in cloud outsourcing. In: Grossklags, J., Walrand, J. (eds.) GameSec 2012. LNCS, vol. 7638, pp. 296–308. Springer, Heidelberg (2012). https://doi.org/10.1007/978-3-642-34266-0_18
20. Pham, V., Khouzani, M.H.R., Cid, C.: Optimal contracts for outsourced computation. In: Poovendran, R., Saad, W. (eds.) GameSec 2014. LNCS, vol. 8840, pp. 79–98. Springer, Cham (2014). https://doi.org/10.1007/978-3-319-12601-2_5
21. Belenkiy, M., Chase, M., Erway, C.C., Jannotti, J., Küpçü, A., Lysyanskaya, A.: Incentivizing outsourced computation. In: Proceedings of the 3rd International Workshop on Economics of Networked Systems, pp. 85–90 (2008)
22. M. Khouzani, V. Pham, and C. Cid, "Incentive engineering for outsourced computation in the face of collusion. In: Proceedings of WEIS (2014)
23. Küpçü, A.: Incentivized outsourced computation resistant to malicious contractors. IEEE Trans. Depend. Secure Comput. **14**(6), 633–649 (2015)
24. Dong, C., Wang, Y., Aldweesh, A., McCorry, P., van Moorsel, A.: Betrayal, distrust, and rationality: smart counter-collusion contracts for verifiable cloud computing. In: Proceedings of the 2017 ACM SIGSAC Conference on Computer and Communications Security, pp. 211–227 (2017)
25. Liu, P., Zhang, W.: A new game theoretic scheme for verifiable cloud computing. In: IEEE 37th International Performance Computing and Communications Conference (IPCCC), pp. 1–8. IEEE (2018)
26. Liu, P., Zhang, W.: Game theoretic approach for secure and efficient heavy-duty smart contracts. In: 2020 IEEE Conference on Communications and Network Security (CNS), pp. 1–9. IEEE (2020)
27. Liu, P., Ma, X., Zhang, W.: Optimizing fund allocation for game-based verifiable computation outsourcing. CoRR, vol. abs/2103.06440 (2021). https://arxiv.org/abs/2103.06440

A Survey of Face Image Inpainting Based on Deep Learning

Shiqi Su[1]🆔, Miao Yang[2]🆔, Libo He[3]🆔, Xiaofeng Shao[1]🆔, Yuxuan Zuo[1]🆔, and Zhenping Qiang[1](✉)🆔

[1] College of Big Data and Intelligent Engineering, Southwest Forestry University,
Kunming 650224, China
qzp@swfu.edu.cn
[2] Yunnan Institute of Product Quality Supervision and Inspection,
Kunming 650214, China
[3] Information Security College, Yunnan Police College, Kunming 650223, China

Abstract. In recent years, deep learning has become the mainstream method of image inpainting. It can not only repair the texture of the image, obtain high-level abstract features of the image, but also recover semantic images such as human faces. Among these methods, attention mechanisms, semantic methods, and progressive networks have become very promising image inpainting models. These models implement end-to-end image inpainting and generate visually reasonable and clear image structure and texture. This paper briefly describes the face inpainting technology and summarizes the existing face image inpainting methods. We try to collect most of the face inpainting methods based on deep learning, divide them into attentional, semantic-based, and progressive inpainting networks, and prorate the methods proposed by researchers in each category in recent years. Then we summarize the dataset proposed by the predecessors and the evaluation index of the algorithm performance. Finally, we summarize the current situation and future development trends of face inpainting.

Keywords: Face inpainting · Deep learning · Attention inpainting · Semantic inpainting

1 Introduction

Image is one of the common information carriers in all walks of life. Because a large amount of image information is destroyed, editing software that can edit images without leaving traces is not feasible. Therefore, an algorithm or system is needed that can edit images without leaving any trace. Image inpainting is a technical process to infer and restore the damaged or missing area content based on the known content of the image so that the image inpainting meets the needs of human visual perception as closely as possible. It can be extended to face inpainting. With the improvement of image processing tools and the flexibility

M. R. Khosravi et al. (Eds.): CloudComp 2021, LNICST 430, pp. 72–87, 2022.
https://doi.org/10.1007/978-3-030-99191-3_7

of digital image editing, automatic image inpainting has become an important application in computer vision and an important stimulating research topic in the field of image processing.

Nowadays, image inpainting has become an active research direction in the field of computer technology, and face inpainting, as one of its branches, is of great significance. Face inpainting is to restore damaged or occluded incomplete face images, but it is difficult to grasp the semantic structure. With the rapid development of image inpainting technology, the problems to be solved are becoming more and more complex. In real life, the lack of face image has caused major work-related problems in all walks of life, and face image inpainting technology can solve this problem intelligently and effectively. It can be applied to many practical applications related to face and has important research value. Due to different postures, expressions and occlusion, face inpainting is a difficult task. Therefore, a good inpainting algorithm should ensure the authenticity of the output, including the topology between eyes, nose, and mouth, as well as the consistency of posture, gender, race, and expression.

We summarize the face image inpainting method based on deep learning. The rest of the paper is organized as follows: Sect. 2 presents the review of the literature, including attention-based, semantic-based, and progressive inpainting methods. Section 3 presents datasets and scoring metrics commonly used in face image inpainting. Section 4 summarizes the current status and future development trends of face image inpainting.

2   Face Inpainting Method Based on Deep Learning

With the development of technology, the emergence of deep learning technologies, such as generative adversarial networks (GAN) [1]and convolutional neural networks (CNN) [2], has accelerated the development of the technology face inpainting. These deep learning-based image inpainting methods can already learn rich face semantic information from huge datasets, then fill in the missing information in the image end-to-end, and can achieve better effects. The key to facial inpainting is to maintain the correctness of the facial structure and the rationality of the detailed texture after the inpainting. The traditional image inpainting methods [3–5] did not have the ability to capture high-level semantics and consider the face as a whole, even more, are not suitable for the completion of large-area face images, so they cannot restore the facial image.

Although CNN can capture the abstract information of the image, and GAN can use supervised learning to strengthen the effect of generating the network, the results of these methods for face inpainting alone are not very satisfactory, most researchers now combine the two to inpainting images. In addition, there is also Shift-Net [6] proposed based on texture and CNN; since U-net [7] can use a few images for end-to-end training, some researchers have also proposed many inpainting methods based on this. As demand continues to increase, some researchers have proposed semantic inpainting methods. Pathak et al. [8] proposed the Encoder-Decoder network structure, although the context encoder can capture the semantics of appearance and visual structure, the context encoder is used for semantic inpainting, the result is not ideal; the literature [9] had added the global context discriminator and the local context discriminator to the literature [8] to discriminate the consistency of the generation effect from both the global and local point of view, and can improve clarity and the contrast of the local area, and proposed a full convolution for image inpainting. And there are kinds of literature [10,11] that use this type of method. Although it can use full convolution to restore free template images of any resolution, the inpainting effect is not ideal when inpainting images with very complex semantic information.

To make full use of the mask information, different researchers have proposed different convolution methods [12–16]. Jo et al. [12] proposed an encoder-decoder architecture similar to U-net. All convolution layers are gated convolution networks, which enable an image editing system. It is a system with a free-form mask, sketches, and color as inputs. Liu et al. [16] used partial convolution, where convolution was limited to valid pixels to reduce artifacts caused by differences in the distribution between masked and uncovered areas, but this method can create damaged structures when the missing areas became continuous and relatively large.

In addition, image inpainting in the practical application includes free-form or irregular holes. Compared with regular holes, these holes needed different optimization processes or attention mechanisms [17], so an attention-based face image inpainting method was introduced; there are also methods based on semantic; furthermore, some also proposed to divide the task of image inpainting into several subproblems for progressive inpainting. The multi-stage network model generally has higher efficiency. These methods are introduced in turn below.

2.1 Attention-Based Image Inpainting

In the field of computer vision, an attention mechanism is introduced to process visual information. It looks for the most important part of result generation and improves the performance of segmentation, re-recognition, and tracking algorithms. Attention mechanism is a technology that enables the model to focus on important information and make full use of it. Most of the research work on the combination of deep learning and visual attention mechanism focuses on using a mask to form the attention mechanism. The principle of the mask is to identify the key features in the picture data through another layer of new weight. Through learning and training, the deep neural network can learn the areas that need attention in the picture, which forms attention.

In recent years, attention based on the relationship between context and mask is often used in image inpainting tasks [18–32]. Yu et al. [20] innovatively added a context-aware module to their coarse-to-fine architecture, which focused on relevant feature patches at any location to improve the inpainting results. Literature [21] used partial convolution instead of vanilla convolution on the basis of [20]. Xie et al. [19] designed a two-way attention map estimation module for feature renormalization and mask update in the feature generation process. He et al. [22] proposed an image inpainting model based on the inside-outside attention layer (IOA). IOA can generate images with free-form masks while maintaining high contextual semantic consistency and visual reality. Liu et al. [30] used a coherent layer of semantic attention in a refined network to ensure semantic correlation between exchange features. Wang et al. [33] developed a multi-scale attention module in the architecture to make flexible use of background content. The Pluralistic image completion (PIC) method [34] employed a self-attention layer that uses short-term and long-term context information to ensure a consistent appearance. Zeng et al. [35] applied an attention mechanism to build an attention delivery network that used advanced semantic information to inpainting low-level image features. These image inpainting algorithms demonstrate the effectiveness of the attention mechanism.

The attention of each round of the traditional attention mechanism is calculated independently of each other and will interfere with each other during fusion. The convolutional neural network can not explicitly borrow or copy information from distant spatial positions, which is the reason for image structure distortion and texture blur. Although the context attention layer can improve the performance compared with the traditional convolution, and the facial image inpainting model uses the attention mechanism to borrow features from the background, the inpainting results still lack fine texture details, and the pixels are inconsistent with the background.

2.2   Semantic-Based Image Inpainting

The attention-based image inpainting method obtains information from the background area far away from the mask to propagate to the mask area, but in the process of propagation, it will produce fuzzy results because of the misleading part of the information of the newly recovered mask. Facial images usually contain unique patterns, a few repetitive structures, and the semantic content is specific. When the face image is lost, it is more difficult to complete and restore, which makes face inpainting a challenging problem. Because the face image is highly structured and has several key semantic components, such as eyes and mouth, the semantic information of the face can be used to inpainting it better.

Semantic inpainting needs to fill a large number of missing areas according to known data. Such as [30,33,36–43], it infered the content of any large missing area in the image according to the semantic information of the image. Face inpainting is the most representative type of semantic inpainting. The general context will produce fewer ideal results. For example, the context encoder (CE) proposed by Pathak et al. [8] first used the deep neural network to generate missing regions, and the context encoder fills the loophole by extracting features from the original image. However, the disadvantage of this method is that the generated image contains too many visual artifacts. Semantic inpainting is not an attempt to reconstruct real images, but to fill this loophole with realistic content. Raymond et al. [37] proposed a new semantic image inpainting method. This method combined weighted semantic loss in the trained generative model to determine the most similar coding information between the implicit space and the missing image and then predicts the missing content through the generative model. This method is superior to the common semantic-based algorithm CE and can generate reasonable and clear edge information, but there are examples of inpainting failures. Many methods use the prior knowledge or strategies in specific fields to solve the corresponding problems, such as the face super-resolution (SR) method, which uses the prior knowledge of the face to better SR inpainting the face. Shen et al. [44] used face semantic tags as global a priori and local constraints to eliminate ambiguity. They used the face analysis network to generate the semantic tags of the fuzzy input image, and then took the fuzzy image and semantic tags as the input to inpainting the image from coarse to fine network. Zhang et al. [39] proposed a new semantic image inpainting method-the squeeze excitation network deep revolution general adaptive network (SE-DCGAN). Zhang et al. [40] proposed a progressive generative network (PGN), which regarded semantic image inpainting as a step-by-step learning process, but its model did not have good inpainting results for free-form or complex images (e.g., face images).

In the above two methods, if semantic and attention are combined, better processing results will be achieved. Liu et al. [30] used a coherent semantic attention layer to ensure the semantic correlation between exchange features, proposed a coarse-fine network, and added the fine inpainting network of coherent semantic attention (CSA) layer. By modeling the semantic correlation between hole features, it can not only maintain the structure of context but also predict the missing parts more effectively. Wang et al. [41] improved the original image inpainting algorithm model [30] based on U-net and Visual Geometry Group Network (VGG) and designed a semantic focus layer to learn the relationship between missing region features in the image inpainting task. Qiu et al. [38] proposed a two-step confrontation model semantic structure reconstructor and texture generator, which used the semantic structure graph based on unsupervised segmentation to train the semantic structure reconstructor and maintain the consistency between the missing part and the whole picture, spatial channel attention module (SCA) was introduced to obtain fine-grained texture.

2.3   Progressive-Based Image Inpainting

Although some of the above methods have good results, these methods are still challenging for the task of face image inpainting because the generated image should have a good visual effect and fast processing speed. Optimization-based methods such as [45] can produce inpainting results that were visually considered natural, but its calculation speed was very slow, and it was slower to process images with high resolution; the CE [8] is very fast, but sometimes it cannot restore a satisfactory structure. Therefore, researchers have developed a new method, the progressive-based method [11,13,15,18,20,22,30,40,41,46–54], so as to reduce the difficulty of training depth in the inpainting network.

For example, [13,20,22,30,48,52], these methods are two-stage network structures composed of a coarse-fine network. In the first stage, the image need to be processed is roughly inpainting, and then the roughly processed image is used as the input of the fine stage, so as to further strengthen the structure and texture details of the face image. Xiong et al. [47] proposed a foreground aware inpainting method, which involved three stages: contour detection, contour completion, and image completion, so as to eliminate structure inference and content illusion. Song et al. [11] introduced additional manual labels in segmentation prediction and guidance Network (SPG-net), but it was often unavailable in practical application, so this method was difficult to be directly used for image restoration. Huang et al. [52] proposed a new semantic aware context aggregation module (SACA) to solve the problem of generating fuzzy content. By using the internal semantic similarity of the input feature graph, the remote context information is aggregated from the semantic point of view. SACA suppresses the influence of misleading hole features in context aggregation by learning the relationship between pixels and semantics and significantly reduces the computational burden. The multi-stage method can alleviate the difficulty of deep maintenance network training.

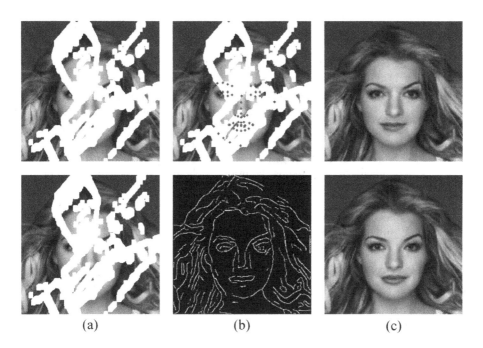

(a)   (b)   (c)

Fig. 1. Results of Lafin (upper) and edge connect (lower) algorithms. (a) input image, (b) presents the version of the landmark on the masked image (top), generated edges (bottom), (c) generated result.

Nazeri et al. [15] proposed a two-stage confrontation model called edgeconnect, which first predicted the edge of the missing area, and then generated the
edge-guided inpainting results. However, the edge is not an ideal semantic structure because it loses a lot of region information and color information. Yang
et al. [55] introduced a generator called landmark guided face painter (Latin),
which was composed of face landmark prediction subnet and image inpainting
subnet to solve the problem of face inpainting. The face landmark prediction
subnet module reflects the topology, pose, and expression of the target face to
be restored. The image inpainting subnet uses the predicted landmark as a guide,
and uses the spatial context to connect the temporal feature mapping to ensure
the consistency of attributes. Table 1 is a brief comparison of edgeconnect, lafin
method in terms of network structure, generator, and input images required for
image processing. Figure 1 shows the results of edgeconnect and Lafin algorithms.

Table 1. Table comparison between Edgeconnect [15] and Lafin [55] methods.

	Edgeconnect	Lafin
Networks	Edge generator, image completion network	Landmark prediction module, image inpainting module
Input	Mask, Edge map, Grayscale	Corrupted image, landmarks
Convolution	Dilated conv	Dilated conv, gated conv
Defect	The edge generator model cannot accurately depict edges in highly textured areas	The inpainting results after missing many central areas are not so ideal, so are landmarks
Advantage	The prior information with high correlation and low generation difficulty is selected as the prior information of the next stage. The edge information restored by the algorithm is accurate and will not appear as false content	Face key points are neat, sufficient, and robust, which can be used as the supervision of face inpainting. It is a simple and a reliable way of data expansion

3   Datasets and Evaluation Indicators

3.1   Dataset

For face image inpainting, researchers have proposed many public datasets and
large datasets to evaluate the applicability of their algorithms. Face image
inpainting also belongs to a part of image inpainting. Adding images such as
the natural and street view in the training process will improve the inpainting
result. Table 2 introduces some datasets used by predecessors, and Fig. 2 shows
sample images of common datasets.

Table 2. Datasets introduction.

Dataset	Year	Number	Attribute	Affiliated
CAS-PEAL [56]	2008	99,594	Different postures in a specific environment	Institute of computing technology, Chinese Academy of Sciences
ImageNet [57]	2009	14,197,122	21841 categories	Stanford University Vision Research Laboratory
Helen Face [58]	2012	2330	All images are marked with 68 feature points	University of Illinois, Urbana-Champaign and Adobe Systems Inc
CASIA-WebFace [59]	2014	494,414	10575 people	National Laboratory of Pattern Recognition; institute of Automation, Chinese Academy of Sciences
Places2 [60]	2017	10 million+	Including more than 400 unique scene categories	Massachusetts Institute of Technology
CelebA [61]	2018	202,599	Each image is marked with features	Chinese University of Hong Kong

3.2 Evaluating Indicator

Generally, in face inpainting, the evaluation index is usually used to objectively evaluate the advantages and disadvantages of image processing algorithms, and highlight the advantages of the algorithms propose by researchers in comparative experiments. Generally speaking, each subdivided field has corresponding indicators. In image inpainting, the evaluation indicators are basically universal and can be evaluated by comparing the image inpainting with the real image, that is, there are reference image evaluation indicators. Accordingly, a series of indicators are proposed: mean square error (MSE), structural similarity index (SSIM), peak signal to noise ratio (PSNR), etc. these indicators are common. PSNR and SSIM are mostly used in image inpainting, so the results are more convincing.

Structural Similarity Index (SSIM). SSIM [62] is a comprehensive reference image quality assessment index proposed by the University of Texas at Austin, it is used to estimate the similarity between image inpainting and original image. When the two pictures are exactly the same, the value of SSIM is 1. Structural similarity theory holds that natural images are highly structured, that is, there is a strong correlation between pixels, which contains important information of object structure in the visual scenes. The mean is used as the estimate of brightness, the standard deviation as the estimate of contrast, and the covariance as the measure of structural similarity. Given two images x and y, the structural similarity of the two images is expressed as:

$$SSIM(x,y) = \frac{(2\mu_x\mu_y + c_1)(2\sigma_{xy} + c_2)}{(\mu_x^2 + \mu_y^2 + c_1)(\sigma_x^2 + \sigma_y^2 + c_2)} \qquad (1)$$

Fig. 2. Common dataset samples. From top to bottom are CASCIA dataset (a), CelebA dataset (b), Helen Face dataset (c), CAS-PEAL dataset (d), Place2 dataset (e).

here μ_x, and μ_y are the mean values of x and y respectively, σ_x^2 and σ_y^2 are the variances of x and y respectively, σ_{xy} is the covariance of x and y; $c_1 = (k_1 L)^2, c_2 = (k_2 L)^2$ are two constants, in case the fraction is zero, L is the range of pixel values, $k_1 = 0.01, k_2 = 0.03$ are the default values. The value range of SSIM is 0–1.

Peak Signal to Noise Ratio (PSNR)). PSNR [62] is the most widely used objective standard for evaluating images. It is generally used to evaluate the quality of the repaired face image compared with the real face image. The higher the PSNR, the smaller the distortion after compression. PSNR is widely used, but its value cannot well reflect the subjective feeling of human eyes. General value range: 20–40. The larger the value, the better the video quality. Usually, after image compression, the output image will be different from the original image to some extent. PSNR performs statistical analysis based on the gray value of image pixels. Due to the differences in human visual characteristics, the evaluation results are usually inconsistent with people's main feelings, but it is still a valuable evaluation index. In order to measure the quality of the processed face image, we usually refer to the PSNR value to measure whether a processing program is satisfactory. PSNR can be simply defined by mean square error MSE. Given an original image I with a size of $m \times n$ and a processed face image K, the mean square error is defined as:

$$MSE = \frac{1}{mn}\Sigma_{j=0}^{m-1}\Sigma_{j=0}^{n-1}[I(i,j) - K(i,j)]^2 \tag{2}$$

among them: $I(i,j), K(i,j)$ respectively represent the pixel value at the corresponding coordinate, and m and n are the height and width of the image respectively. The formula of PSNR is as follows:

$$PSNR = 10lg(\frac{MAX_I^2}{MSE}) \tag{3}$$

among them: MAX_I^2 is the maximum value of the picture color.

The evaluation results of some inpainting methods on common datasets are shown in Table 3. It can be seen from Table 3 that the values of PSNR and SSIM based on the progressive face inpainting method are relatively stable, and there is no low score, and SSIM almost exceeds 90%.

Table 3. Table lists the quantitative evaluation results of the above-mentioned various image inpainting algorithms based on deep learning, the values of which are from various original documents. "+" means that the larger the value of this index, the better.

Category	Method	Dataset	Mask	PSNR$^+$	SSIM$^+$
Attention-based	[18]	Place2	Center mask	26.17	0.91
	[19]	Place2	Mask ratio = (0.2, 0.3]	25.59	0.785
	[20]	Place2	Rule mask	18.91	–
	[21]	CelebA	–	**40.86**	–
	[22]	CelebA	Center mask	26.84	0.921
	[23]	CelebA	Center mask	32.23	**0.933**
	[27]	CelebA	Mask ratio = (0.3, 0.4]	26.67	0.874
	[30]	CelebA	Center mask	26.54	0.931
	[34]	ImageNet	Center mask	20.10	–
	[25]	Place2	Random mask	–	0.781
Semantic-based	[36]	CelebA	Center mask	19.18	0.920
	[37]	CelebA	Random mask	22.8	–
	[38]	CelebA	Center mask	**32.23**	**0.933**
	[40]	CelebA	50% mask	19.10	0.802
	[44]	Helen Face	Center mask	21.45	0.851
	[52]	CelebA	Mask ratio = (0.3, 0.4]	27.21	0.895
Progressive-based	[15]	CelebA	Mask ratio = (0.4, 0.5]	25.28	0.846
	[22]	CelebA	Center mask	26.84	0.921
	[41]	ImageNet	–	25.74	0.934
	[46]	CelebA	–	26.60	0.920
	[47]	Place2	–	**29.86**	0.938
	[51]	CelebA	Mask ratio = (0.2, 0.3]	29.01	**0.955**
	[53]	Place2	Mask ratio = (0.2, 0.3]	25.66	0.914

4   Conclusion

With the continuous development of deep learning technology and urgent application needs, the task of face image inpainting has attracted the attention of researchers from all walks of life and become an important and challenging research topic in the field of computer vision. In this paper, different types of methods are introduced, including attention-based methods, semantic-based methods, and progressive inpainting methods; secondly, the commonly used datasets and performance evaluation indexes of face image inpainting in the existing literature are summarized. Through quantitative evaluation and comparison of inpainting effects, it is proved that the current face disocclusion technology based on deep learning has a good experimental effect.

Based on the classification and summary of the existing image inpainting methods, aiming at the problems still existing in the current research task, this paper makes the following prospects for its future research direction and development trend:

1) The essence of image inpainting is a computer vision task to guess and complete the missing area by mining known information. It is an inevitable demand to improve the inpainting quality to effectively extract the known information and establish the information associated with the unknown content. Improving the learning ability of image feature expression of inpainting model is still one of the problems worthy of in-depth exploration.

2) At present, most of the datasets used in the literature are European and American face datasets, so the test results of Asian faces are not ideal. Therefore, it is necessary to establish a dataset belonging to Asian face features to make the algorithm more consistent with Asian face attributes.

3) Generative adversarial network plays a key role in image generation and is also adopted by most image inpainting methods. However, at present, generative adversarial network still has its own defects, such as mode collapse and unstable training. How to solve these problems will also become a challenge in image inpainting research.

Acknowledgements. This work was funded by the National Natural Science Foundation of China (12163004), the basic applied research program of Yunnan Province (202001AT070135, 202101AS070007, 202002AD080002, 2018FB105).

References

1. Goodfellow, I., et al.: Generative adversarial nets. In: Advances in Neural Information Processing Systems, vol. 27 (2014)
2. Krizhevsky, A., Sutskever, I., Hinton, G.E.: ImageNet classification with deep convolutional neural networks. Adv. Neural. Inf. Process. Syst. **25**, 1097–1105 (2012)
3. Bertalmio, M., Sapiro, G., Caselles, V., Ballester, C.: Image inpainting. In: Proceedings of the 27th Annual Conference on Computer Graphics and Interactive Techniques, pp. 417–424 (2000)
4. Barnes, C., Shechtman, E., Finkelstein, A., Goldman, D.B.: PatchMatch: a randomized correspondence algorithm for structural image editing. ACM Trans. Graph. **28**(3), 24 (2009)
5. Huang, J.B., Kang, S.B., Ahuja, N., Kopf, J.: Image completion using planar structure guidance. ACM Trans. Graph. **33**(4), 1–10 (2014)
6. Yan, Z., Li, X., Li, M., Zuo, W., Shan, S.: Shift-Net: image inpainting via deep feature rearrangement. In: Ferrari, V., Hebert, M., Sminchisescu, C., Weiss, Y. (eds.) Computer Vision – ECCV 2018. LNCS, vol. 11218, pp. 3–19. Springer, Cham (2018). https://doi.org/10.1007/978-3-030-01264-9_1
7. Ronneberger, O., Fischer, P., Brox, T.: U-Net: convolutional networks for biomedical image segmentation. In: Navab, N., Hornegger, J., Wells, W.M., Frangi, A.F. (eds.) MICCAI 2015. LNCS, vol. 9351, pp. 234–241. Springer, Cham (2015). https://doi.org/10.1007/978-3-319-24574-4_28

8. Pathak, D., Krahenbuhl, P., Donahue, J., Darrell, T., Efros, A.A.: Context encoders: feature learning by inpainting. In: Proceedings of the IEEE Conference on Computer Vision and Pattern Recognition, pp. 2536–2544 (2016)

9. Iizuka, S., Simo-Serra, E., Ishikawa, H.: Globally and locally consistent image completion. ACM Trans. Graph. **36**(4), 1–14 (2017)

10. Song, Y., et al.: Contextual-based image inpainting: infer, match, and translate. In: Ferrari, V., Hebert, M., Sminchisescu, C., Weiss, Y. (eds.) ECCV 2018. LNCS, vol. 11206, pp. 3–18. Springer, Cham (2018). https://doi.org/10.1007/978-3-030-01216-8_1

11. Song, Y., Yang, C., Shen, Y., Wang, P., Huang, Q., Kuo, C.C.J.: SPG-Net: segmentation prediction and guidance network for image inpainting. arXiv preprint arXiv:03356 (2018)

12. Jo, Y., Park, J.: SC-FEGAN: face editing generative adversarial network with user's sketch and color. In: Proceedings of the IEEE/CVF International Conference on Computer Vision, pp. 1745–1753 (2019)

13. Yu, J., Lin, Z., Yang, J., Shen, X., Lu, X., Huang, T.S.: Free-form image inpainting with gated convolution. In: Proceedings of the IEEE/CVF International Conference on Computer Vision, pp. 4471–4480 (2019)

14. Xiao, Q., Li, G., Chen, Q.: Deep inception generative network for cognitive image inpainting. arXiv preprint arXiv:01458 (2018)

15. Nazeri, K., Ng, E., Joseph, T., Qureshi, F.Z., Ebrahimi, M.: EdgeConnect: generative image inpainting with adversarial edge learning. arXiv preprint arXiv:00212 (2019)

16. Liu, G., Reda, F.A., Shih, K.J., Wang, T.-C., Tao, A., Catanzaro, B.: Image inpainting for irregular holes using partial convolutions. In: Ferrari, V., Hebert, M., Sminchisescu, C., Weiss, Y. (eds.) ECCV 2018. LNCS, vol. 11215, pp. 89–105. Springer, Cham (2018). https://doi.org/10.1007/978-3-030-01252-6_6

17. Vaswani, A., et al.: Attention is all you need. In: Advances in Neural Information Processing Systems, pp. 5998–6008 (2017)

18. Xiao, Z., Li, D.: Generative image inpainting by hybrid contextual attention network. In: Lokoč, J., Patras, I. (eds.) MMM 2021. LNCS, vol. 12572, pp. 162–173. Springer, Cham (2021). https://doi.org/10.1007/978-3-030-67832-6_14

19. Xie, C., et al.: Image inpainting with learnable bidirectional attention maps. In: Proceedings of the IEEE/CVF International Conference on Computer Vision, pp. 8858–8867 (2019)

20. Yu, J., Lin, Z., Yang, J., Shen, X., Lu, X., Huang, T.S.: Generative image inpainting with contextual attention. In: Proceedings of the IEEE Conference on Computer Vision and Pattern Recognition, pp. 5505–5514 (2018)

21. Mohite, T.A., Phadke, G.S.: Image inpainting with contextual attention and partial convolution. In: 2020 International Conference on Artificial Intelligence and Signal Processing (AISP), pp. 1–6. IEEE (2020)

22. He, X., Cui, X., Li, Q.J.I.A.: Image inpainting based on inside-outside attention and wavelet decomposition. IEEE Access **8**, 62343–62355 (2020)

23. Qiu, J., Gao, Y.: Position and channel attention for image inpainting by semantic structure. In: 2020 IEEE 32nd International Conference on Tools with Artificial Intelligence (ICTAI), pp. 1290–1295. IEEE (2020)

24. Wu, H., Zhou, J.: IID-Net: image inpainting detection network via neural architecture search and attention. IEEE Trans. Circ. Technol. Syst. Video (2021)

25. Wang, C., Wang, J., Zhu, Q., Yin, B.: Generative image inpainting based on wavelet transform attention model. In: 2020 IEEE International Symposium on Circuits and Systems (ISCAS), pp. 1–5. IEEE (2020)

26. Li, J., Wang, N., Zhang, L., Du, B., Tao, D.: Recurrent feature reasoning for image inpainting. In: Proceedings of the IEEE/CVF Conference on Computer Vision and Pattern Recognition, pp. 7760–7768 (2020)
27. Wang, N., Ma, S., Li, J., Zhang, Y., Zhang, L.J.P.R.: Multistage attention network for image inpainting. Pattern Recognit. **106**, 107448 (2020)
28. Huang, L., Wang, W., Chen, J., Wei, X.Y.: Attention on attention for image captioning. In: Proceedings of the IEEE/CVF International Conference on Computer Vision, pp. 4634–4643 (2019)
29. Song, L., et al.: Unsupervised domain adaptive re-identification: theory and practice. Pattern Recognit. **102**, 107173 (2020)
30. Liu, H., Jiang, B., Xiao, Y., Yang, C.: Coherent semantic attention for image inpainting. In: Proceedings of the IEEE/CVF International Conference on Computer Vision, pp. 4170–4179 (2019)
31. Chen, B., Li, P., Sun, C., Wang, D., Yang, G., Lu, H.: Multi attention module for visual tracking. Pattern Recogn. **87**, 80–93 (2019)
32. Uddin, S., Jung, Y.J.: Global and local attention-based free-form image inpainting. Sensors **20**(11), 3204 (2020)
33. Jiao, L., Wu, H., Wang, H., Bie, R.: Multi-scale semantic image inpainting with residual learning and GAN. Neurocomputing **331**, 199–212 (2019)
34. Zheng, C., Cham, T.J., Cai, J.: Pluralistic image completion. In: Proceedings of the IEEE/CVF Conference on Computer Vision and Pattern Recognition, pp. 1438–1447 (2019)
35. Zeng, Y., Fu, J., Chao, H., Guo, B.: Learning pyramid-context encoder network for high-quality image inpainting. In: Proceedings of the IEEE/CVF Conference on Computer Vision and Pattern Recognition, pp. 1486–1494 (2019)
36. Vitoria, P., Sintes, J., Ballester, C.: Semantic image inpainting through improved Wasserstein generative adversarial networks. arXiv preprint arXiv:01071 (2018)
37. Yeh, R.A., Chen, C., Yian Lim, T., Schwing, A.G., Hasegawa-Johnson, M., Do, M.N.: Semantic image inpainting with deep generative models. In: Proceedings of the IEEE Conference on Computer Vision and Pattern Recognition, pp. 5485–5493
38. Qiu, J., Gao, Y., Shen, M.: Semantic-SCA: semantic structure image inpainting with the spatial-channel attention. IEEE Access **9**, 12997–13008 (2021)
39. Zhang, F., Wang, X., Sun, T., Xu, X.: SE-DCGAN: a new method of semantic image restoration. Cogn. Comput. **13**, 1–11 (2021)
40. Zhang, H., Hu, Z., Luo, C., Zuo, W., Wang, M.: Semantic image inpainting with progressive generative networks. In: Proceedings of the 26th ACM International Conference on Multimedia, pp. 1939–1947 (2018)
41. Wang, W., Gu, E., Fang, W.: An improvement of coherent semantic attention for image inpainting. In: Sun, X., Wang, J., Bertino, E. (eds.) ICAIS 2020. CCIS, vol. 1252, pp. 267–275. Springer, Singapore (2020). https://doi.org/10.1007/978-981-15-8083-3_24
42. Yang, W., Li, X., Zhang, L.: Toward semantic image inpainting: where global context meets local geometry. J. Electron. Imaging **30**(2), 023028 (2021)
43. Ciobanu, S., Ciortuz, L.: Semantic image inpainting via maximum likelihood. In: 2020 22nd International Symposium on Symbolic and Numeric Algorithms for Scientific Computing (SYNASC), pp. 153–160. IEEE (2020)
44. Shen, Z., Lai, W.S., Xu, T., Kautz, J., Yang, M.H.: Deep semantic face deblurring. In: Proceedings of the IEEE Conference on Computer Vision and Pattern Recognition, pp. 8260–8269 (2018)

45. Yang, C., Lu, X., Lin, Z., Shechtman, E., Wang, O., Li, H.: High-resolution image inpainting using multi-scale neural patch synthesis. In: Proceedings of the IEEE Conference on Computer Vision and Pattern Recognition, pp. 6721–6729 (2017)

46. Ma, B., An, X., Sun, N.: Face image inpainting algorithm via progressive generation network. In: 2020 IEEE 5th International Conference on Signal and Image Processing (ICSIP), pp. 175–179. IEEE (2020)

47. Xiong, W., et al.: Foreground-aware image inpainting. In: Proceedings of the IEEE/CVF Conference on Computer Vision and Pattern Recognition, pp. 5840–5848 (2019)

48. Zeng, Yu., Lin, Z., Yang, J., Zhang, J., Shechtman, E., Lu, H.: High-resolution image inpainting with iterative confidence feedback and guided upsampling. In: Vedaldi, A., Bischof, H., Brox, T., Frahm, J.-M. (eds.) ECCV 2020. LNCS, vol. 12364, pp. 1–17. Springer, Cham (2020). https://doi.org/10.1007/978-3-030-58529-7_1

49. Yen, S.H., Yeh, H.Y., Chang, H.W.: Progressive completion of a panoramic image. Multimedia Tools Appl. **76**(9), 11603–11620 (2017)

50. Karras, T., Aila, T., Laine, S., Lehtinen, J.: Progressive growing of GANs for improved quality, stability, and variation. arXiv preprint arXiv:10196 (2017)

51. Guo, Z., Chen, Z., Yu, T., Chen, J., Liu, S.: Progressive image inpainting with full-resolution residual network. In: Proceedings of the 27th ACM International Conference on Multimedia, pp. 2496–2504 (2019)

52. Huang, Z., Qin, C., Liu, R., Weng, Z., Zhu, Y.: Semantic-aware context aggregation for image inpainting. In: ICASSP 2021–2021 IEEE International Conference on Acoustics, Speech and Signal Processing (ICASSP), pp. 2465–2469. IEEE (2021)

53. Li, J., He, F., Zhang, L., Du, B., Tao, D.: Progressive reconstruction of visual structure for image inpainting. In: Proceedings of the IEEE/CVF International Conference on Computer Vision, pp. 5962–5971 (2019)

54. Zamir, S.W., et al.: Multi-stage progressive image restoration. In: Proceedings of the IEEE/CVF Conference on Computer Vision and Pattern Recognition, pp. 14821–14831 (2021)

55. Yang, Y., Guo, X., Ma, J., Ma, L., Ling, H.: LAFIN: generative landmark guided face inpainting. arXiv preprint arXiv:11394 (2019)

56. Gao, W., et al.: The CAS-PEAL large-scale Chinese face database and baseline evaluations. IEEE Trans. Syst. Man Syst. Cybernet. Part A Hum. **38**(1), 149–161 (2007)

57. Deng, J., Dong, W., Socher, R., Li, L.J., Li, K., Fei-Fei, L.: ImageNet: a large-scale hierarchical image database. In: 2009 IEEE Conference on Computer Vision and Pattern Recognition, pp. 248–255. IEEE (2009)

58. Le, V., Brandt, J., Lin, Z., Bourdev, L., Huang, T.S.: Interactive facial feature localization. In: Fitzgibbon, A., Lazebnik, S., Perona, P., Sato, Y., Schmid, C. (eds.) ECCV 2012. LNCS, vol. 7574, pp. 679–692. Springer, Heidelberg (2012). https://doi.org/10.1007/978-3-642-33712-3_49

59. Yi, D., Lei, Z., Liao, S., Li, S.Z.: Learning face representation from scratch. arXiv preprint arXiv (2014)

60. Zhou, B., Lapedriza, A., Khosla, A., Oliva, A., Torralba, A.: A 10 million image database for scene recognition. IEEE Trans. Pattern Anal. Intell. Mach. **40**(6), 1452–1464 (2017)

61. Liu, Z., Luo, P., Wang, X., Tang, X.: Large-scale CelebFaces attributes (CelebA) dataset. Retrieved August **15**, 11 (2018)
62. Wang, Z., Bovik, A.C., Sheikh, H.R., Simoncelli, E.P.: Image quality assessment: from error visibility to structural similarity. IEEE Trans. Image Process. **13**(4), 600–612 (2004)

Cloud Architecture and Challenges
in Real-World Use

Layered Service Model Architecture for Cloud Computing

Vishal Kaushik, Prajwal Bhardwaj, and Kaustubh Lohani[✉]

School of Computer Science, University of Petroleum and Energy Studies, Dehradun 248007,
India
vkaushik@ddn.upes.ac.in, kaustubhlohani25@gmail.com

Abstract. The National Institute of Standards and Technology defined three services models for cloud computing in 2011, namely IaaS, PaaS, and SaaS. Since
then, a decade has passed, and cloud delivery methodologies have evolved, and
newer ways of delivering cloud services have emerged. As a result of these new
methodologies, lines between traditional service models are constantly fading, and
new subcategories are emerging with totally different approaches to tackle cloud
service delivery. This paper introduces a layered cloud service model to replace the
three-category approach suggested by the NIST (IaaS, PaaS, and SaaS) in 2011.
Moreover, we also discuss the existing approaches prevalent in the industry and
the need for a new approach. Furthermore, we have mapped the existing services
in the industry are mapped on the proposed architecture.

Keywords: Cloud service delivery model · Cloud computing · IaaS · PaaS ·
SaaS · Cloud definition · NIST definitions

1 Introduction

In the late 1990s internet was booming; consequently, several products and services were
being created specifically for the internet. Hosting all of these products onto the internet
meant leasing out servers. This proved expensive and inefficient as the organization had
to pay for the leased servers even if they were not used. Cloud computing emerged as
a cost-effective way for the digitalization of organizations by enabling computational
resource sharing [11, 12, 15].

In 2011 NIST formally defined cloud computing and introduced three service models
to offer cloud computing services based on business requirement, functionality, and
control offered to the consumer. The three models are Infrastructure-as-a-Service (IaaS),
Software-as-a-Service (SaaS), and Platform-as-a-Service (PaaS). A decade has passed
since the introduction of these three service models, and since then, newer technologies
like containers and serverless computing have come up that are not fitting in the categories
of IaaS, PaaS, and SaaS [16].

Serverless computing provides a feature list that combines IaaS, PaaS, and SaaS;
consequently, classifying serverless as one of the NIST service models is incorrect.

© ICST Institute for Computer Sciences, Social Informatics and Telecommunications Engineering 2022
Published by Springer Nature Switzerland AG 2022. All Rights Reserved
M. R. Khosravi et al. (Eds.): CloudComp 2021, LNICST 430, pp. 91–106, 2022.
https://doi.org/10.1007/978-3-030-99191-3_8

Similarly, containers are considered as an IaaS offering because both of them seem to abstract the underlying computational layers. This argument breaks apart once we consider that IaaS virtualizes over the underlying hardware using a hypervisor. In contrast, containers abstract over the underlying operating system deployed over the hardware using a container engine, making them slightly different from the IaaS service model.

A slight change in approach by contemporary cloud service models is creating new categories of delivery methods that are not falling entirely in a single category of services defined by the NIST (IaaS, PaaS, and SaaS) in 2011. Soon more contemporary delivery methodologies like these may be introduced, further blurring the lines between rigidly defined NIST service models. Thus, a novel service model architecture is the need of the hour that accommodates the exceptions of NIST architecture at the same time should be scalable to accommodate future delivery methodologies.

Unfortunately, not many such approaches are being developed actively. Johan Den Haan proposed one such framework in 2013 [1]. Johan suggested seven categories starting from bare metal and going up to SaaS applications. Another such approach actively utilized in the current industry to categorize cloud services is anything-as-a-service (XaaS). XaaS refers to any service delivered over the internet through the cloud, previously delivered through on-site methods. Both these approaches try to propose a way out of the NIST models; however, they have some shortcomings which we try to address with our proposed architecture.

In this paper, first, we describe the challenges posed by serverless and container, which prompts the need to think beyond NIST service models. Furthermore, we outline the existing approaches along with their shortcomings. Next, we introduce the proposed architecture. Moreover, we plot the current services offered by various CSPs onto our model. Finally, we highlight future research directions and potential challenges.

2   Important Terms and Definitions

2.1   Cloud Computing

NIST defines cloud computing as a "computing model that enables ubiquitous, convenient and on-demand access to a shared pool of computing resources (e.g., servers, storage, networks, applications) that can be rapidly provisioned and released with minimal effort from the consumer or the CSP" [2].

2.2   Cloud Service Provider or CSP

CSPs are organizations that provide on-demand cloud services to their clients. These services can provide computing power or infrastructure, a platform to execute application libraries and code, or an application to satisfy a business requirement. Moreover, CSPs also establish and manage public, private, and hybrid clouds [3].

Some examples of prominent CSPs are Google Cloud, Microsoft Azure, and Amazon AWS.

2.3   Infrastructure as a Service or IaaS

NIST defines IaaS as a service that provides the consumer with the ability to choose the required amount of computational resources – in the form of processing power, storage, and networks – upon which the consumer can run any software such as the operating system [2].

In IaaS consumer does not manage or control the underlying cloud infrastructure, including the hardware in the server farm on which the IaaS services are provisioned. Popular IaaS offerings include Amazon EC2, Google Compute Engine (GCE), and Azure Virtual Machines.

2.4   Platform as a Service or PaaS

According to NIST, the PaaS service model provides the consumer with the capability to directly deploy a custom application or acquired application on the cloud infrastructure using the programming languages, libraries, tools, and services provided by the CSP [2, 18].

In PaaS, consumer does not manage underlying cloud infrastructure. Moreover, the consumer is not concerned with computational resources, network, storage configurations, and operating systems. However, the consumer controls the hosting environment and hosted application code and execution [2].

Popular PaaS offerings include AWS-Elastic Beanstalk, Microsoft Azure, and Redhat Openshift.

2.5   Software as a Service or SaaS

NIST defines SaaS as a service model where the CSP provides the consumer with ready-to-use applications on the cloud infrastructure. These applications are accessible through several client interfaces such as a web browser or a program interface [2].

In SaaS consumer neither controls the underlying cloud setup nor the computational, network, or storage resources. Further, the control of the operating system and other such software capabilities resides with the CSP. However, in some cases, the consumer has limited control to alter some user-specific settings [17].

Popular SaaS offerings include Microsoft Office 365, Salesforce.com, and Google applications such as Gmail or Google Drive.

2.6   Serverless Computing

A cloud computing service model in which CSP allocates the computing resources as per the consumer demand, moreover maintaining the servers on behalf of the consumer. Serverless provides the consumer with the convenience to deploy application code or external libraries without the hassle of maintaining the underlying servers. Consequently, the client does not need to worry about keeping the server configurations up to date with the latest offerings and security patches; the CSP takes care of all of this. Moreover, serverless also provides the user with immense flexibility and scalability with features like auto-scaling, which translates to scaling up the resources as the demand increases [10].

Some popular serverless hosting providers: AWS Lambda, Google Cloud Functions, IBM Openwhisk.

2.7   Containers and Containers as a Service (CaaS)

A container is an executable unit of a pre-defined or customized container image that generally encompasses one or more software programs to deliver an application or service [4]. A container is virtualized instance over the operating system created with the help of a container engine such as Docker.

CaaS or container as a service aims at providing users with services and tools to create, manage and organize container instances.

Some popular CaaS providers include Amazon EC2 Container Service, Azure Container Service, and Google Container Engine.

3   Need to Think Beyond IaaS, PaaS, and SaaS

As discussed in the introduction section above, contemporary technologies such as serverless and containers cannot fit in the NIST service models. Serverless and containers provide a slightly fundamentally different approach to the NIST-defined models in architecture, control, scalability, and cost.

3.1   Serverless vs IaaS, PaaS, and SaaS

Both serverless and PaaS attempt to hide the back-end for a more straightforward service model. In the case of PaaS, users are expected to manage the hosting environment – keeping the hosting environment up to date with the latest feature set – along with the deployed applications. However, as described above in Sect. 2.6 in serverless computing, the users are only expected to manage the deployed application with CSP taking up the responsibility of managing the servers and in turn executing the application code uploaded by the client, taking the control away from the client and placing it in the hands of CSP, consequently making the PaaS model more controllable for the client. Moreover, in serverless features, the pay-as-you-go subscription model where the client only needs to pay for the resources utilized by them as opposed to paying for the whole platform in the case of PaaS. Furthermore, Serverless supports auto-scaling, which means that the client automatically gets additional computational resources as the processing need increases; further, the allocated resources are taken back to the CSP pool once the need has gone down. Whereas PaaS usually does not feature auto-scaling and any jump in the requirement of the computational resources has to be taken up with the CSP, which will manually allocate the additional resources, however in most cases, there is no provision to take back once provisioned resources after the demand has decreased [13, 14].

Serverless is very different from the SaaS service model. Serverless provides the clients with the feature of executing application code on the cloud with the flexibility of CSP managing their servers, while SaaS is a whole end-to-end product offering over the cloud. In serverless, the client can code, compile, and execute their application, giving the client control over the application and its configuration. In contrast, SaaS is a product that is in a ready-to-use state from the moment the subscription starts. Further, in a SaaS offering client only controls certain user-specific settings.

IaaS is an infrastructure offering that gives the client complete control over the processing, networking, and storage aspects. In contrast, serverless takes away most of the control offered by the IaaS for a more straightforward approach providing clients with a more flexible and scalable approach without worrying about maintaining the underlying servers. Moreover, IaaS gives the client freedom of choosing the operating system and altering its settings. In contrast, in serverless, the client is provided a bundles package that contains all the software and the dependencies required to smoothly run the application making the client responsible only for the application code, and CSP takes care of executing the application on their servers.

3.2 CaaS vs IaaS, PaaS, and SaaS

PaaS can be considered a complete application delivery system encompassing application development and delivery in a single package. Here, the CSP provides the user with the platform bundled with the required specifications allowing the client to deploy application code and execute it. In contrast, CaaS is a different service approach that provides the clients with a service to create, organize and manage containers using tools such as Docker, a container image, an orchestrator, and infrastructure to deploy. Essentially, CaaS provides clients with just a container service on which they can set up their hosting environment comprising of calibrating hardware configurations, required software like an operating system, and external dependencies or libraries. After setting up the hosting environment, the client can deploy application code to be executed via the software packages installed by the client.

On the other hand, PaaS is sort of like a bundled package in which the hosting environment setup is taken care of by the CSP according to the specifications set by the user, and the user can focus on application development and delivery. Consequently, CaaS as a service generally offers more control when compared with PaaS. Generally, CaaS and PaaS are used hand in hand, PaaS for the application development and CaaS for application deployment, making this system CaaS-PaaS hybrid [9].

On the other hand, if the service approach, feature set, and control offered are considered, SaaS and CaaS can be thought of as opposite poles of a magnet. SaaS is a complete ready-to-use (from the moment subscription starts) application used by the organizations for its functionality and benefits them in conducting their business, such as an electronic-mail service. In contrast, CaaS is a container service on which a hosting environment can be set up, and a custom-made application can be developed and delivered through it.

Finally, CaaS has a fundamentally different approach to providing service compared with IaaS, resulting in a difference in control offered by both the services; consequently, classifying CaaS same as IaaS will not be entirely correct. Both of these technologies use the technique of virtualization for service delivery. However, the difference is that IaaS virtualizes on operating system placed over the data center hardware and creates VMs (Virtual Machines) whereas, CaaS uses a container engine to virtualize over the operating system, which is generally placed over an IaaS service. Using a container engine provides the client with easier horizontal scaling, meaning they can create additional containers without involving the CSP. In contrast, initializing more VMs in IaaS requires assistance from the CSP's end. However, since there is an additional layer involved in CaaS before the virtualization happens, which is absent in the virtualization process of IaaS, the level of control offered is more in IaaS.

4   Existing Approaches and the Need for New Approach

As discussed previously in the introduction section, very few novel frameworks talk about replacing the prevailing NIST system. However, people like Johan Den Haan [1] and Christine Miyachi [5] are suggesting changes since 2013. Furthermore, since the NIST system is ambiguous, the industry has decided to take a whole new approach wherein they categorize services based on the functionality they offer; for example, according to this system, a platform that provides disaster recovery tools and services is called DRaaS (Disaster Recovery as a Service) rather than PaaS. The model where categorizing services basis their functionality is done is referred to as XaaS (Anything as a Service). This section tries to explain the existing approaches (other than NIST service models), their shortcomings, and the need for another novel approach.

4.1   XaaS (Anything as a Service)

An approach used widely in recent times by CSPs is XaaS. XaaS refers to any service delivered over the internet that was previously delivered through physical means.

Naming a service on the lines of XaaS has gained popularity among the CSPs due to the marketing clarity it provides to their offering [6]. For example, a "Privacy as a Service (PRaaS) solution to take care of your privacy needs based on the geography" seems lucid than something like "Web-based SaaS for taking care of your privacy needs based on the geography."

Another factor contributing to organizations not using NIST service models to label their cloud offerings is the broad qualification parameters associated with each service. As time passed and new delivery methodologies came, these defined parameters became more outdated, leading to oversimplification of the features offered in a product. Essentially, the cloud technology matured, giving rise to novel service models such as serverless and containers. These novel delivery methods provided features that were a little different than those defined for IaaS, PaaS, and SaaS. So, if a CSP decided to label their product as per the NIST model, prospective clients could assume it provides the features described by the NIST and not further explore the product features, proving detrimental for the CSP's business.

At first, XaaS seems like a potential replacement for the NIST model. However, XaaS methodology solely focuses on the functionality to name service, meaning that there might be several variations to categorize the same service. For example, a service such as HaaS or "Healthcare as a Service" can also be called "Medicare on Demand as a Service." This variation might be legal as per the XaaS framework. However, multiple variations of the same service cause ambiguity. Essentially, XaaS is confusing and unintentionally unclear as the "aaS" suffix could potentially refer to anything other than cloud services too (Fig. 1).

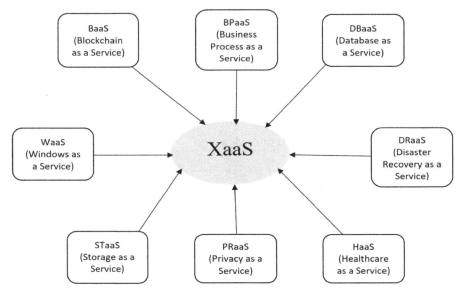

Fig. 1. Examples of anything as a Service (XaaS) offerings

4.2 Johan Den Haan Framework for Categorizing Cloud Services

In the article written in October 2013, Johan argues that "saying that I work for a PaaS company is as broad as saying that I work for a software company." Furthermore, he says, "The lines between IaaS, PaaS, and SaaS are blurring, and subcategories are emerging within these categories that describe a different range of approaches" [1].

Johan Den Haan, in his article, suggested a seven-layer model as shown in Table 1; starting with the bare-metal hardware (data centers) and defining each additional layer as an abstraction over the hardware layer until he gets the final layer where applications are used to execute the cloud service model.

The main advantage of this framework is the clear segregation of cloud services without overlapping between categories. For example, Serverless computing can now be considered as a separate service model as opposed to it previously being categorized simply as PaaS. However, CaaS is not included as a separate layer in this framework; instead, it is included in layer 2 (Foundational PaaS).

Foundational PaaS bears slight differences when compared with CaaS. Foundational PaaS is the layer on top of the infrastructure layer that gives the developer pre-packaged tools and a ready-to-use hosting environment [7]. In contrast, CaaS uses a container engine that virtualizes on the operating system deployed on the infrastructure; in CaaS, the CSP provides tools to manage these containers instead of a pre-packaged development environment, in case of CaaS how the organizations set up these containers to

Table 1. Johan Den Haan framework to categorize cloud services [1] further modified by Christine Miyachi [5]

S.No.	Layer name	Potential users
Layer 6	SaaS	End users
Layer 5	App services	Citizen developers
Layer 4	Model-driven PaaS	Rapid developers
Layer 3.5	Serverless computing	Speed developers
Layer 3	PaaS	Developers/Coders
Layer 2	Foundational PaaS	DevOps
Layer 1	Software-defined data centre	Infrastructure engineers
Layer 0	Hardware	–

deploy their application is not the concern of the CSP. Due to the slight architectural differences between CaaS and Foundational PaaS, CaaS generally offers more control than Foundational PaaS.

Essentially Foundational PaaS is a bigger umbrella under which many types of similar services come; CaaS could be one. According to Gartner, by 2022, more than 75% of applications will be running on containers instead of less than 30% today [8]. This stat by Gartner shows that the technology is not yet peaked; if the technology keeps on growing, the approach of delivering CaaS services may change and consequently bear less and less resemblance with Foundational PaaS, which would again prompt for the model to be updated. Thus, we believe that CaaS should receive its own category.

5   Proposed Architecture

5.1   Preview

The proposed service model classification architecture comprises eight primary layers starting from layer 1 to layer 8. Compute, network, and storage or CNS are the building blocks of the model.

Layer 0 denotes the hardware layer onto which further abstractions are constructed to create other layers (layer 1 till layer 8). Layer 0 represents on-site deployment or data centers set up by the CSPs and is included to provide a clear baseline for the above layers. Layer 0 is not a cloud service model; rather, it represents the fundamental building blocks of further layers. Layer 1 till Layer 8 represent delivery methodologies.

Abstraction over a layer signifies an additional software deployment on the said layer. This software deployment essentially gives the product situated in the said layer the features of a cloud service model. Abstraction encapsulates the layer within a custom software, enabling the CSP to modify the feature set of the layer on which it is deployed, consequently changing how the service is offered on that layer. Hence, creating a new cloud delivery model with a different feature set and control offered to the client. For example, a container engine – a software – if deployed on top of Layer 1 changes the fundamental characteristics of the Layer 1 service model. Thereby creating a new layer comprising of CaaS or container services (layer 2).

Furthermore, we have divided the layers into three categories on the lines of the NIST model for easy understanding and to enable seamless between the proposed architecture and the NIST model. These categories are:

1. Basic Infrastructure: Includes layers that deal primarily with offerings that give some form of hardware with or without the abstraction.
2. Platform: Includes layers that offer a platform for development and application to the clients.
3. Application: The application category contains layers that offer products pre-packaged as applications.

5.2 Design Methodology and Trends

The model has been designed with CNS (Compute, Network, and Storage) as the fundamental components. Any level of abstraction or encapsulation onto CNS components of a layer creates a new layer on top of the previous layer.

We have constructed the architecture such that the level of control over CNS given to the client decreases as the layer number increases. So, layer 1 offers the maximum control over CNS, and layer 8 offers the least.

Furthermore, as the layer number increases, the control of CSP over the product increases. Essentially, the CSP manages most part of the products placed on layer 8, including the underlying infrastructure.

5.3 Architecture Explanation

The architecture is represented as shown in Fig. 2; here, the layers are marked along the vertical direction, and the components (CNS) are shown along the horizontal direction. The intersection of layers with the fundamental components (CNS) clarifies the product's functionality and is represented with a symbol. Cloud services or products offered by the CSPs are placed at a suitable layer with coordinates of suitable intersection determined by the product purpose or functionality.

For example, According to the proposed architecture matrix, Amazon EC2 is a service suitable for layer 1 at coordinates [1, C].

The layers, as shown in Fig. 2, are as follows:

- Layer 0: Physical Hardware
- Layer 1: Virtualized Hardware
- Layer 2: CaaS
- Layer 3: Foundational PaaS
- Layer 4: PaaS
- Layer 5: Serverless Computing
- Layer 6: Built-up PaaS
- Layer 7: Application Services
- Layer 8: SaaS

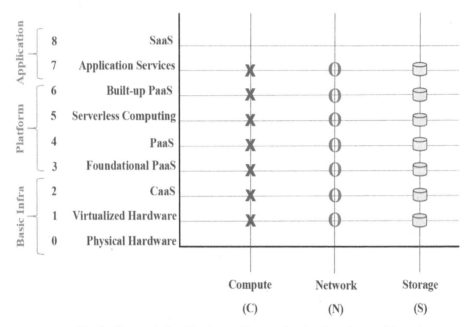

Fig. 2. Proposed classification architecture for cloud service models

5.4 Layers Explanation and Criteria

Layer 0 – Physical Hardware

This layer is the physical layer and is placed for setting a baseline on which abstractions could be placed to create cloud offerings. Independently this layer can be considered as an on-site setup which is opposite to cloud computing.

Abstractions over the CNS components of this layer create different feature sets, thereby creating additional layers.

Since this layer is entirely set up on the organization's premises, it offers maximum control over the CNS components. Physical data centers can be considered as part of this layer.

Layer 1 – Virtualized Hardware

This layer comprises virtual machines, networks, or virtual storage created using abstracting over the physical hardware using something like hypervisors by the CSP.

The products at this layer offer virtualized hardware components that can be utilized the same as regular hardware. Hardware virtualization is more efficient and is also less costly than actual physical hardware deployment. Also, hardware virtualization offers almost a similar level of control as physical hardware, but at the same time, it is more reliable than using physical systems.

Organizations use the products at this layer, but mostly hardware virtualization is the primary way used by the CSP to deliver customized platforms and software. Further abstracting this layer creates customized cloud solutions that come under the platform and application category.

The primary criteria for a product to be placed in this layer are that it offers physical hardware components via placing an additional virtualization layer upon it.

Layer 2 – CaaS or Container as a Service

This layer comprises container management products and products that virtualize upon hardware using an additional layer of container engine over the host operating system that can be possibly placed on virtualized hardware.

This layer is an abstraction over layer 1 (Virtualized Hardware Layer). This layer provides the consumers with container management systems that can create, manage, and organize containers. The clients are given complete control of the containers that they create. Moreover, the user can customize the container environment to suit their application development; this customization includes installing required OS, libraries, tools, and additional dependencies.

This layer offers control over the OS as opposed to the virtualized hardware layer, which focuses more on the infrastructure layer.

We have added a separate layer for CaaS services instead of including it in the foundational PaaS as the level of control offered here is more when compared with foundational PaaS (Layer 3).

Layer 3 – Foundational PaaS

This layer comprises products that offer the client a platform for their development tasks. The provided platform contains pre-installed libraries and dependencies according to the specifications provided by the client. However, the client is given the freedom to deploy additional libraries as the need arises.

The compute vertical on this layer focuses on services like DevOps, where a custom platform is provided to ensure compliance with DevOps. However, the user can modify the platform and include additional dependencies to cater to their organization's specific requirements. The network vertical deals with solutions that cater to communications inside and outside the platform, ensuring intelligent load balancing, scheduling, and queuing the incoming application access requests. Finally, the storage vertical deals with something like object storage.

The level of control offered here is the most among the platform category, with features like the inclusion of custom dependencies absent in further layers of the platform category.

Layer 4 –PaaS

The PaaS layer includes products that provide the consumer with a platform as per the specifications required by the client to facilitate application development and deployment. However, offerings at this layer offer less control than platform offerings at layer 4. Essentially, if a client purchases a PaaS product from the CSP, they will get a platform that will be pre-equipped to perform the required task and managed and maintained by the CSP. Products in this layer do not give the user control to deploy libraries other than those provided by the CSP. Essentially, if a client purchases a PaaS product for SQL Database they will get a platform with pre-installed libraries to facilitate just the

SQL development ultimately; the user will not get any feature to install libraries for MongoDB in the same product, for that they will need to purchase a different platform. However, the users can manage and control the code execution over the servers.

This layer offers specific language compilers such as java or python deployed over a container in the compute vertical. The communicate vertical encompasses products that facilitate communication among applications deployed over the cloud and applications deployed on-site. The storage vertical offers specialized storage solutions provided as a platform and uses a popular database technology like SQL or DynamoDB to store the inserted data.

Products at this layer should provide a specialized platform for a specific task – such as code execution and deployment, communication between applications, and storage solutions – with the condition that the provided platform will perform the said task with the pre-installed libraries and no libraries could be added that are not in the bracket of requirements to perform the said task.

Layer 5 – Serverless Computing

This layer comprises products that offer a platform for carrying out application development and deployment. However, like other platform category layers, products at this layer do not let the users control their execution servers. The CSP manages everything after uploading the code and pressing execute. Furthermore, products at this layer offer the clients to only pay for the time they have engaged the servers and not for the whole platform as in products at other platform category layers.

Products at this layer come as a platform equipped with all necessary libraries for the task chosen by the client. The client controls the application code and application deployment, but the servers for code execution are controlled by the CSP and not by the client.

Layer 6 – Built-up PaaS

Products at this layer can be best described as drag and drop PaaS. The product offered at this layer specifically targets rapid developers. Rapid developers are developers who want to develop an application but do not have an in-depth knowledge of various technologies required to do so. So, products offered at this layer provide such developers with a platform containing ready-made parts which they can assemble as per their application requirements. They do not need to make changes to these ready-made components. However, products at this layer provide the functionality to customize a read-made offering according to their use-case.

For example, a built-up PaaS product to develop a website rapidly would have ready-made HTML form plug-ins, design plug-ins to customize the look and feel of the web-page, and authentication systems already available to be used off the shelf as per the developer's will. The developer can utilize these off-the-shelf components directly or make adjustments to them to suit the application better.

The product at this layer offer platform control to the client to some extent. Moreover, the freedom to change the default offerings to suit a specific application better is also provided. However, the developer cannot control the code execution and the basic infrastructure settings like the operating system and language libraries; the user has to work with the libraries and languages provided by the platform and cannot install external libraries. Essentially, this layer is the result of amalgamating the features of platform category layers with application category layers which in turn means that products at this layer will have more control than application category layers but the least level of control among platform category layers.

Layer 7 – Application Services

The products at this layer offer developers an application that provides off-the-shelf services that can be repackaged to become a part of a customized application according to a client-specific use case.

At first, the products at this layer may seem the same as those on the previous layer (Layer- 6: Built-up PaaS), but the crucial difference lies in controlling and customizing the ready-to-use components. In this layer, the products offer a choice to create a final application by repackaging numerous ready-made components. In contrast, the products on the Built-up-PaaS layer offer the developers control to choose from the components and customize those components according to a specific use-case by uploading custom code in the language supported by the product. Control to customize every component and then repackage those customized components as an application is absent in the products offered at this layer. Product at this layer offers control only to repackage the already available components as they are provided inside the product offered by the CSP.

However, the depth of control while repackaging can vary, which means that users can select a single feature inside a particular component to include in their application and ignore the rest. However, what the user cannot do is add a feature of their own inside the component. For example, in Application Services for privacy, the client can select if they want the feature to "automatically create privacy policy documents" after they answer a "questionnaire" from the "Generate Documentation Module." However, the client cannot modify the "privacy policy generator" and include additional code that outputs an additional line as per the data in the questionnaire.

Layer 8 – SaaS

The last layer contains products that are ready-to-use applications in which the user can make customizations that only affect themselves or their organizations, such as company geographical location changes.

Among all the layers, SaaS offers the least amount of control to the client, and almost all the management is taken care of by the CSP.

Products classified as SaaS are essentially pre-packaged software delivered through the cloud and are used by the organizations for the functionality it provides rather than creating or hosting their application.

In SaaS services, each of the CNS components' involvement cannot be determined separately as the level of abstraction is relatively high, and the underlying configurations are invisible to the user. Thus, there are no intersections shown in Fig. 2 on layer 8.

The primary criteria for a product to be classified as SaaS are that it should be a pre-packed software delivered over the cloud that serves a particular purpose and offers no environmental or infrastructure control, meaning almost all of the components are controlled by the CSP rather than the client.

6   Plotting Cloud Products in the Proposed Architecture

In this section, we have mapped the prevalent cloud product of popular CSPs. According to our understanding, the services are mapped as follows (Table 2):

Table 2. Mapping popular cloud products on the proposed architecture

CSP	Product	Co-ordinates
Amazon	Amazon EC2 (Elastic Compute Cloud)	1, (C)
Amazon	Amazon RDS (Relational Database Services)	4, (S)
Amazon	Amazon S3 (Simple Storage Service)	3, (S)
Amazon	Amazon Lambda	5, (C)
Amazon	Amazon CloudFront	8
Amazon	Amazon Glacier	
Amazon	Amazon SNS (Simple Notification Service)	8
Amazon	Amazon Elastic load balancing	3, (N)
Amazon	Amazon Kinesis	8
Amazon	Amazon IAM (Identity and Access Management)	8
Amazon	Amazon Elastic Beanstalk	4, (C)
Amazon	Amazon Redshift	4, (S)
Amazon	Amazon Cloudwatch	8
Microsoft	Azure DevOps	3, (C)
Microsoft	Virtual Machines	1, (C)
Microsoft	Azure Active Directory	8
Microsoft	Azure Logic Apps	6, (C)
Microsoft	Azure Site Recovery	7, (C,N,S)
Microsoft	Azure Bots	4, (C)
Microsoft	Office 365	8
Docker	Container	2, (C)
Docker	Docker Swarm	3, (N)
Salesforce	Salesforce.com	7, (C,N,S)
Google	Google Compute Engine	1, (C)
Google	Google Container Engine	2, (C)
Google	Google Cloud Functions	5, (C)

7   Future Research Directions

The proposed model would work for the foreseeable innovations in cloud service methodology. Nevertheless, after a while, the number of layers might increase to a number beyond manageable. Another dimension could be added to the framework that could take care of minor fluctuations in the delivery approach.

In the subsequent papers, we will look at exact parameters for the third dimension. Moreover, we would look at how another dimension could change the proposed framework and the number of layers.

Finally, we would like to suggest the following research directions that can be pursued to improve the proposed architecture:

- Addition of another dimension that can take care of minor fluctuations in the delivery approach resulting in a cleaner model.
- We have considered CNS (Compute, Network, and Storage) as the means of cloud service delivery; however, there might be more ways of delivering cloud services that remain to be explored.
- The criteria to place a product on a service layer are by no means concrete or complete, and there might be other parameters that should be included to make the architecture more relevant. These additional parameters remain to be explored.

8   Conclusion

NIST service models were defined a decade ago, and since then, cloud delivery systems have evolved a lot, and many novel service methodologies have emerged, such as Serverless Computing and CaaS are widening the cracks in the NIST-defined service models.

In this paper, we have tried to address the issue of NIST service models categorization getting outdated by proposing a layered architecture. We proposed a nine-layer framework with each layer defining a separate service model. We have also tried to shed light on the topic, why we should update the NIST model. We argued that technologies like Serverless and CaaS use a fundamentally different approach due to which a different level of control is offered by them, which makes it difficult to place in the buckets of IaaS, PaaS, and SaaS, which are again defined by NIST based on control given to the client. Finally, we have placed cloud services currently prevalent in the industry onto our model.

NIST models might be losing industry significance, but they still do a great job introducing the cloud delivery methodology to a novice in this field. Thus, we believe that the NIST models should introduce a novice to the field, but a more comprehensive model should be utilized for industry usage.

References

1. Haan, J.D.: The cloud landscape Described, categorized, and compared. The cloud landscape described, categorized, and compared, October 2013. http://www.theenterprisearchitect.eu/blog/2013/10/12/the-cloud-landscape-described-categorized-and-compared/. Accessed 10 Aug 2021

2. Mell, P., Grance, T.: The NIST definition of cloud computing. NIST (2011). https://doi.org/10.6028/nist.sp.800-145

3. Red Hat. What are cloud service providers? https://www.redhat.com/en/topics/cloud-computing/what-are-cloud-providers. Accessed 10 Aug 2021

4. Erl, T., Mahmood, Z., Puttini, R.: Cloud Computing: Concepts, Technology, & Architecture. Prentice Hall, Hoboken (2014)

5. Miyachi, C.: What is "Cloud"? It is time to update the NIST definition? IEEE Cloud Comput. 5(3), 6–11 (2018)

6. Simmon, E.: Evaluation of cloud computing services based on NIST SP 800–145. NIST Spec. Publ. 500, 322 (2018)

7. Mendix: What is platform as a service (paas)? Mendix, January 2013. https://www.mendix.com/blog/making-sense-of-paas/. Accessed 10 Aug 2021

8. Gartner: Gartner forecasts strong revenue growth for Global container management software and services through 2024. Gartner, June 2020. https://www.gartner.com/en/newsroom/press-releases/2020-06-25-gartner-forecasts-strong-revenue-growth-for-global-co. Accessed 10 Aug 2021

9. Pahl, C.: Containerization and the PaaS cloud. IEEE Cloud Comput. 2(3), 24–31 (2015)

10. Castro, P., Ishakian, V., Muthusamy, V., Slominski, A.: The rise of serverless computing. Commun. ACM 62(12), 44–54 (2019)

11. Sosinsky, B.: Cloud Computing Bible. Wiley Publication, Hoboken (2011)

12. Buyya, R., Broberg, J., Andrzej, G.: Cloud computing: Principles and paradigms. Wiley, Hoboken (2011)

13. Van Eyk, E., Toader, L., Talluri, S., Versluis, L., Uță, A., Iosup, A.: Serverless is more: from PaaS to present cloud computing. IEEE Internet Comput. 22(5), 8–17 (2018)

14. McGrath, G., Brenner, P.R.: Serverless computing: design, implementation, and performance. In: 2017 IEEE 37th International Conference on Distributed Computing Systems Workshops (ICDCSW), pp. 405–410. IEEE, June 2017

15. Bahga, A., Madisetti, V.: Cloud Computing: A Hands-on Approach. Universities Press, Lanham (2014)

16. Gibson, J., Rondeau, R., Eveleigh, D., Tan, Q.: Benefits and challenges of three cloud computing service models. In 2012 Fourth International Conference on Computational Aspects of Social Networks (CASoN), pp. 198–205. IEEE, November 2012

17. Sowmya, S.K., Deepika, P., Naren, J.: Layers of cloud–IaaS, PaaS and SaaS: a survey. Int. J. Comput. Sci. Inf. Technol. 5(3), 4477–4480 (2014)

18. Mohammed, C.M., Zebaree, S.R.: Sufficient comparison among cloud computing services: IaaS, PaaS, and SaaS: a review. Int. J. Sci. Bus. 5(2), 17–30 (2021)

KPG4Rec: Knowledge Property-Aware Graph for Recommender Systems

Hao Ge[1], Qianmu Li[1,2(✉)], Shunmei Meng[1], and Jun Hou[3]

[1] Nanjing University of Science and Technology, Nanjing, China
{2429642242,qianmu,mengshunmei}@njust.edu.cn
[2] Intelligent Manufacturing Department, Wuyi University, Nanping, China
[3] School of Social Science, Nanjing Vocational University of Industry Technology, Nanjing, China

Abstract. The collaborative filtering (CF) based models have the powerful ability to use the interaction of users and items for recommendation. However, many existing CF-based approaches can only grasp the single relationship between users or items, such as item-based CF, which utilizes the single relationship of similarity identified from user-item matrix to compute recommendations. To overcome these shortcomings, we propose a novel approach named KPG4Rec which integrates multiple property relationships of items for personalized recommendation. In the initial step, we extract properties and corresponding triples of items from an existing knowledge graph, and utilize them to construct property-aware graphs based on user-item interaction graphs. Then, continuous low-dimensional vectors are learned through node2vec technology in these graphs. In the prediction phase, the recommendation score of one candidate item is computed by comparing it with each item in the user history preference sequence, where the pretrained embedding vectors of items are used to take all the properties into consideration. On the other hand, Locality Sensitive Hashing (LSH) mechanism is adopted to generate brand new preference sequences of users to improve the efficiency of KPG4Rec. Through extensive experiments on two real-world datasets, our approach is proved to outperform several widely adopted methods in the Top-N recommendation scenario.

Keywords: Knowledge graph · Property-aware graph · Semantic information · Recommendation system

1 Introduction

Existing methods for recommender systems (RS) can be divided into two categories in general: collaborative filtering and content-based model. CF-based methods [1–3] find items that users may like through their historical behavior and then filter out items that is not worth being recommended. According to the metadata of the item or content, content-based methods [4, 5] recommend similar items to a user based on the correlation of the items. In recent decades, many different methods have been derived based on the idea of

M. R. Khosravi et al. (Eds.): CloudComp 2021, LNICST 430, pp. 107–122, 2022.
https://doi.org/10.1007/978-3-030-99191-3_9

CF. Sarwar et al. [6] proposed Item-based CF to calculate the similarity between items by counting the co-occurrence times, and recommends the most similar items to users. Matrix factorization [7] characterizes both items and users with vectors of factors for recommendation. BPRMF [8] is directly optimized for ranking and NMF [9] is designed to solve CF problems subject to the constraint of non-negativity.

To deal with the limitations in traditional CF-based methods, researchers have proposed incorporating side information into RS. During many kinds of side information, knowledge graph (KG) contains the most abundant semantic information. Over the past years, several typical KGs have been constructed such as DBpedia, YAGO and Satori which aim to describe all kinds of items or concepts and their relationships in the real world. Thus, making good use of KG has beneficial effects on recommendation results. Personalized Entity Recommendation (PER) [10] combines the heterogeneous relationship information of each user differently to provide high-quality recommendation results. FMG [11] integrates meta-graph into the HIN-based recommendation system.

Inspired by the widely use of KG and its abundant semantic information, we explore an approach to calculate the property similarities between items. In order to fully take advantage of the semantic information, we restructure the user-item bipartite graph by adding property edges between items. So, not only the semantic information is contained in our graphs, collaborative signals of user-item interaction are also considered. Then, node representations are gain by simulating random walks on these graphs. Like the method in [12], the LSH technique is also adopted for the real-time optimization. At last, we compute the final recommended score through aggregating semantic similarities. Experiments are conducted on two real-world recommendation datasets and the results show the efficacy of our model.

2 Preliminary and Overview

2.1 Knowledge Graph (KG)

A classical KG is a kind of directed heterogeneous graph like Fig. 1. It consists of massive triples and these triples are represented as (h, r, t). Here h, r, and t denote the head entity, relation and tail entity respectively.

2.2 Node2vec Mechanism

Node2vec [13] generates sequences of nodes by simulating random walks on a given graph, and then these sequences are fed into a neural language model to learn the embedding vectors. The probability of walking from node v to x is:

$$P(c_i = x | c_{i-1} = v) = \begin{cases} \frac{\pi_{vx}}{Z} & \text{if } (v, x) \in E \\ 0 & \text{otherwise} \end{cases} \tag{1}$$

where π_{vx} is the unnormalized transition probability between node v and x, Z is the normalizing constant. With the introduced parameters, π_{vx} can be computed through

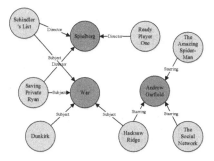

Fig. 1. A simple illustration of KG. The orange nodes represent head entities and the green nodes represent tail entities. Relations such as subject and director are formed as directed edges. (Color figure online)

$\pi_{vx} = \alpha_{pq}(v, x) \cdot w_{vx}$, w_{vx} is the weight of edge (v, x) and α_{pq} is defined as:

$$\alpha_{pq}(v, x) = \begin{cases} \frac{1}{p} & \text{if } d_{vx} = 0 \\ 1 & \text{if } d_{vx} = 1 \\ \frac{1}{q} & \text{if } d_{vx} = 2 \end{cases} \tag{2}$$

where d_{vx} denotes the shortest path distance between node v and node x. Then, a mapping function $f(v) \to R^d$ is learned for a given graph G by optimizing the object function of Node2vec:

$$\max_f \sum_{v \in G} \left[-\log Z_v + \sum_{n_i \in N_s(v)} f(n_i) \cdot f(v) \right] \tag{3}$$

where v refers to one node, R represents the embedding of v, d is the dimension. $Z_v = \sum_{e \in G} \exp(f(v) \cdot f(e))$ is the per-node partition function which is approximated by negative sampling. $N_s(v)$ is the neighbors of v defined by random walks.

2.3 Locality Sensitive Hashing (LSH)

The LSH mechanism [14] is described as follow: After passing two adjacent points through same hash functions, the possibility that the two points are still adjacent is high. For these, hash functions need to meet the conditions follow:

Condition 1. If $d(x, y) \leq d_1$, then the probability of $h(x) = h(y)$ is at least p_1;
Condition 2. If $d(x, y) \leq d_2$, then the probability of $h(x) = h(y)$ is at most p_2;

where $d(x, y)$ represents the distance between data x and y, $d_1 < d_2$, $h(x)$ and $h(y)$ represent the hash transformation of x and y respectively. The LSH technique can also be used in the field of security [15]. In recent years, researchers have also incorporated the LSH technology into recommender systems in order to improve the efficiency of models, such as the method proposed in [16].

2.4 Problem Formulation

The formulation of the recommendation problem in this paper is given as follows. Like many of others [17, 18], the sets of users and items are denoted by $U = \{u_1, u_2, u_3...u_M\}$ and $V = \{v_1, v_2, v_3...v_N\}$ respectively. M and N represent the number of users and items. The matrix of user-item interaction is defined as Y, where

$$Y_{ij} = \begin{cases} 1 \text{ if user } i \text{ interacted with item } j \\ 0 \text{ otherwise} \end{cases} \quad (4)$$

If user u_i has an implicit interaction with an item v_j before, such as behaviors of browsing or clicking, then Y_{ij} equals to 1, otherwise 0. Given a user u_i, we denote his or her history preference sequence l_i as $\{v_1, v_2, v_3...v_{N_i}\}$ and N_i is the number of interacted items. In addition to Y, a knowledge graph KG is also available. With different properties extracted from KG, property-aware graphs G_p of the corresponding property p can be constructed. The goal of our model is to predict whether a user will like an item which he or her has not noticed before. The framework of KPG4Rec is illustrated in Fig. 2. It takes one recommended user u_i and one candidate item v_c as input, and output is the probability score s that u_i like v_c.

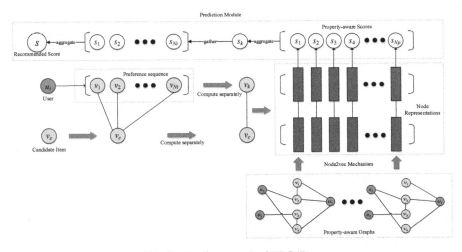

Fig. 2. The framework of KPG4Rec.

3 Methodology

3.1 Construction of Property-Aware Graphs

In order to get the semantic information of an item, we utilize knowledge graph as the side information to assist our recommendation task. KG usually consists of fruitful facts and connections among entities (see Fig. 1). The semantic properties of an entity can be queried through its corresponding (h, r, t) triples, where r refers to the relationships of properties we need. An item in RS usually has a matched entity in KG, thus the semantic information of the item is equal to its mapped entity and they can be extracted as the supplementary of our model. What follows in this paper, the proper noun item represents both the item in RS and its mapped entity in KG.

Apart from KG, we can also construct the user-item interaction graph (u-i graph) from the interaction matrix Y (see Fig. 3 left). Note that this type of graph is the representation of user-item interaction information, so there are only explicit collaborative signals contained. In this work, semantic information is integrated into u-i graphs by adding relationships among items. We can extract these relationships from KG by simplifying pairs of triples. Intuitively, two items could be linked up directly in the graph through their common ground (see Fig. 3 right). For instance, two nodes representing movies will be connected if they have the same director. By linking up all items with common ground in KG based on the u-i graph, a brand-new graph named property-aware graph is generated. In KPG4Rec, we construct several different property-aware graphs under corresponding relationships.

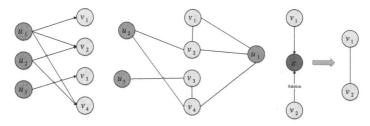

Fig. 3. The user-item interaction graph (left) and property-aware graph (mid).

3.2   Generation of Property-Aware Vectors

When considering different aspects, items could have different degrees of divergence. So, it is necessary to take all the properties of items into consideration. Aiming to learn different vector representations of each item in all of the property-aware graphs, we adopt the efficient random walk algorithm Node2vec to deal with this task. Node2vec works in our model by simulating random walks on the property-aware graphs. Sequences of items are generated and then fed into a neural language model Word2Vec [19] to learn the vector representations. Then, the proposed approach is that for each property-aware graph G_p generated in Sect. 3.1, we learn a mapping function $f^p(v) \rightarrow R^d$ where v refers to an item, R represents the vector representation of v in G_p and d is the dimension, by optimizing the object function of Node2vec:

$$\max_{f^p} \sum_{v \in G_p} \left[-\log Z_v + \sum_{n_i \in N_s(v)} f^p(n_i) \cdot f^p(v) \right] \tag{5}$$

$Z_v = \sum_{e \in G_p} \exp(f^p(v) \cdot f^p(e))$ is the per-node partition function and Eq. 5 is optimized by SGD. Through the above steps, an item v_j can be expressed by representation of vectors R_j in all the property-aware graphs:

$$R_j = \{R_1, R_2, R_3 \cdots R_{N_p}\} \tag{6}$$

N_p is the number of property-aware graphs and $R_k (k = 1, 2 \ldots N_p)$ is the vector representation of v_j in graph G_k. With these vectors, the similarities of items under different properties can be separately and easily computed through vector computed measures.

3.3 Regeneration of User Preference Sequence with LSH

In real application scenarios, a user may have purchased a huge amount of items during the accumulated time. The calculation of property similarities between the candidate item and each of all the interacted items would consume too much resources. In consideration of the real time requirements in recommender systems, we adopt the LSH mechanism in two different forms which are termed as Local-LSH and Global-LSH respectively. The basic idea of our LSH mechanism is to hash similar items into a same "bucket" with a high probability of collision. Since a large number of irrelevant items are filtered out, the cost of property similarities calculation is reduced reasonably. Details of Local-LSH and Global-LSH mechanism in KPG4Rec are described as follows.

Local-LSH. Given a complete sequence l_i of items liked by the user u_i, calculating the semantic similarities of all items in l_i and items in the candidate set will consume a huge amount of time. Note that in these items, many of them have similar properties. So, it is feasible to cluster the sequence l_i before making prediction. We use the first form of LSH called Local-LSH to separate all items in l_i into different buckets, and items with similar properties will be placed in the same bucket. Since using one single hash function for bucketing is prone to lead decreased accuracy, a group of k hash functions are selected randomly and uniformly to ensure similar items more likely to fall into the same bucket. The group of functions is formed as:

$$G = \{f(v) : R^d \rightarrow R^k\} \tag{7}$$

where v is the particular item in l_i and

$$f(v) = (h_1(v), h_2(v) \ldots h_k(v)) \tag{8}$$

where $h(v)$ is a hash function. In this work, we hash all items in l_i through G. Each hash function $h(v)$ maps the origin item into two different data spaces and a total of 2^k buckets are generated since there are k functions. Each bucket represents a class of items which are similar in some respects. Thus, we select one item from each bucket as a representative, and then a new preference sequence l_i' is obtained by combining representatives in all the buckets.

Global-LSH. Note that in the actual recommendation scenario, items with higher similarity to the candidate items often have a greater influence on the user's decision. We adopt Global-LSH to quickly find the neighbors of the candidate item and effectively reduce the time overhead. Similar to Local-LSH, Global-LSH also use a group of functions $G = \{f(v): R^d \rightarrow R^k\}$ to hash the original data. The difference is that in this approach, the candidate item is also hashed by G. After this operation, items in each bucket can be seen as the most similar items in the global state. Thus, all the items in the bucket where the candidate item is located are selected to form a new preference sequence l_i'.

In order to improve the efficiency of our model, both the sequence l_i' generated from Local-LSH and Global-LSH can be used to replace the sequence l_i in the prediction module.

3.4 Prediction Module

Aiming to recommend a list of items to a target user, each candidate item will get a score calculated in the prediction module. All of the candidate items are ranked then, and items with the highest N scores would be recommended.

In the recommender system, a user could have lots of interacted items. We extract these items of one user as an interaction sequence in order to fully discover the user's preference. Given user u_i and candidate item v_c, we use l_i to represent the interaction list of u_i. In order to improve the efficiency of our approach, l_i can also be replaced with sequence l_i' which is described in Sect. 3.3, and the performance of different sequences would be discussed in the experimental part. Each item $v_j (j = 1, 2...N_i)$ in l_i and the candidate item v_c are able to be denoted by vector representations. Thus, given the pair of items v_j and v_c in our model, the score s_p which is termed as property-aware score between them under the property p can be calculated by cosine similarity with the vector representations generated from $f^p(v) \rightarrow R^d$:

$$s_p = \frac{\sum_{m=1}^{d} (f_m^p(v_j) \times f_m^p(v_c))}{\sqrt{\sum_{m=1}^{d} (f_m^p(v_j))^2} \times \sqrt{\sum_{m=1}^{d} (f_m^p(v_c))^2}} \tag{9}$$

Note that there are a total of N_p property-aware graphs, the property-aware scores between v_j and v_c can be expressed by the set S_p as follow:

$$S_p = \{s_1, s_2, s_3 \cdots s_{N_p}\} \tag{10}$$

where $s_k (k = 1, 2 ... N_p)$ is the property-aware score between v_j and v_c under graph G_k. Get the scores of semantic relationships, we aggregate them to get the final similarity score of v_j and v_c which could be calculated by a pooling operation, such as taking the average or the maximum value. In our model, softmax weighted average operation is adopted in order to fully reflect the most similar semantic relationship between items. The final similarity measure score s_j of item v_j and v_c is defined as:

$$s_j = \sum_{s_k \in S_p} \left(\frac{\exp(s_k)}{\sum_{s_m \in S_p} \exp(s_m)} \cdot s_k \right) \tag{11}$$

Extend the situation of one single item v_j to the complete sequence, each item in l_i could get a similarity score by computing with the candidate item. Thus, scores between each item in l_i and the target item can be given in the form of set S_i:

$$S_i = \{s_1, s_2, s_3 \ldots s_{N_i}\} \tag{12}$$

Where N_i is the length of l_i. Similar to Eq. 11, the recommended score s of a candidate item v_c for the specific user is calculated by:

$$s = \sum_{s_k \in S_i} \left(\frac{\exp(s_k)}{\sum_{s_m \in S_i} \exp(s_m)} \cdot s_k \right) \tag{13}$$

After sorting all candidate items according to the final score s, items with N highest scores are recommended to the user u_i.

4 Experiments

4.1 Datasets

In this section, our proposed model KPG4Rec is evaluated on two real-world datasets. The first we utilized is MovieLens-1M which contains 1,000,209 anonymous ratings made by 6,040 users on 3,952 movies. In this experiment, items rated by users are taken as positive feedback to construct user-item interaction graphs. The second dataset is LastFM from the online music system Last.fm. LastFM contains 92,834 implicit feedback of 1,892 users on 17,632 musical artists.

Items in MovieLens-1M and LastFM can be mapped to the corresponding DBpedia entities in a previous work [20]. By using these Linked Open Data, we build a KG and construct property-aware graphs based on u-i graphs. Note that not every item in the datasets can correspond to a DBpedia entity, we kick out items with no matched or multiple matched entities for simplicity. In order to fully reflect the importance of user history preferences, users with no more than ten interactions are also excluded. After the above two operations, the number of items and ratings of MovieLens-1M becomes 3,226 and 948,976 respectively; the number of users and musical artists of LastFM attenuates to 1,865 and 9,765, the number of feedback tags reduce to 78,633 at the same time. For each dataset, we divide training, evaluation and test set according to the ratio of 7:1:2. The three parts are used to represent the user's historical behavior, determine the hyperparameters and evaluate KPG4Rec respectively.

4.2 Evaluation Metrics

Evaluation metrics occupies a pivotal position in the recommendation system. Since our recommendation task is a Top-N recommendation based on the click-through rate, methodologies which are based on error metrics (such as RMSE and MAE) are not appropriate for evaluating our model [21]. In this work, we take two classification accuracy measures Precision and Recall, the average of which are defined as follows:

$$\text{Precision}@k = \frac{\sum_{u \in U} \sum_{i=1}^{k} \frac{\text{hit}(u, v_i)}{k}}{|U|} \cdot \text{Recall}@k = \frac{\sum_{u \in U} \sum_{i=1}^{k} \frac{\text{hit}(u, v_i)}{l(u)}}{|U|}$$

where k is the number of items to be recommended, $\text{hit}(u, v_i) = 1$ if the recommended item v_i is in user u's interaction list of the test set, otherwise 0, and $l(u)$ is the length of the interaction list. In order to determine the hyperparameters in KPG4Rec, F1 score which is the comprehensive consideration of precision and recall is also adopted:

$$F1@k = \frac{2 \times \text{Precision}@k \times \text{Recall}@k}{\text{Precision}@k + \text{Recall}@k}$$

4.3 Impact of Parameters

Aiming at constructing property-aware graphs, we select the most frequently occurring properties from the DBpedia Ontology and extract all triples from KG for the corresponding property. Then, we look for items which connected to the same entity through SPARQL queries, and link them up directly in u-i graphs under the particular property. In our experiment, hyperparameters in Node2vec are set as follows. Number of walks per entity $n = 50$, length of each walk $l = 100$, the return hyperparameter $p = 1$ and the in-out hyperparameter $q = 1$, the dimension of vector embedding $d = 200$, context size for optimization is 30 and number of epochs in SGD is 5.

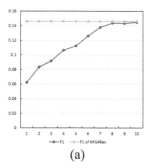
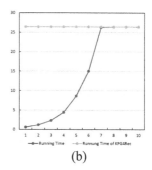

(a)   (b)

Fig. 4. Effect of parameter k on MovieLens-1M. The value of the x-axis refers to k, the orange line refers to the evaluation of KPG4Rec without LSH. (a) shows the effect of our model under different k values and (b) shows the running time.

Another important hyperparameter is the number k of hash functions. In order to select the appropriate k based on the time consumption and F1 value, KPG4Rec with Local-LSH is evaluated on the evaluation set of MovieLens-1M and LastFM. Precision@5 and Recall@5 are used to compute the F1 value and results are shown in Figs. 4 and 5.

It can be clearly found that as the value of k increases, the model effect and running time are increasing simultaneously. Our requirement for selecting k is to minimize the running time while maintaining the original efficiency without too much fluctuation. For the reason that the F1 value only changes less than 0.02 while the running time is reduced to nearly half, we choose 6 as the number of hash functions in Local-LSH for MovieLens-1M. This configuration also means that there is a total of 64 buckets and the length of the user preference sequence is 64. For KPG4Rec with Global-LSH, we choose 4 as the value of k to ensure that the length of the user preference sequence is consistent with that in Local-LSH. Similar to MovieLens-1M, we choose 4 and 1 respectively as the number of Local-LSH and Global-LSH hash functions for the dataset LastFM.

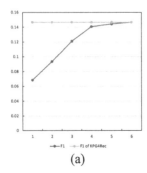
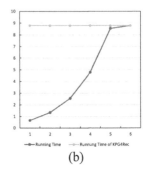

(a)   (b)

Fig. 5. Effect of parameter k on LastFM. The value of the x-axis refers to k, the orange line refers to the evaluation of KPG4Rec without LSH. (a) shows the effect of our model under different k values and (b) shows the running time.

4.4 Performance Evaluation

In this subsection, we evaluate our novel model KPG4Rec and compare it against the following baselines:

BPRMF: A matrix factorization recommendation algorithm optimized by Bayesian Personalized Ranking.

ItemKNN: A classic CF recommendation algorithm based on item similarity.

NMF: A Non-negative Matrix Factorization-based approach to perform collaborative filtering and implement recommendations.

SLIM [22]: A sparse linear method (SLIM) which generates Top-N recommendations through aggregating from user purchase profiles.

SpectralCF [23]: A deep recommendation model which is able to explore deep connections between users and items.

TopPop: A recommendation strategy which recommends top-N items with the highest popularity.

In addition to the baselines mentioned above, we also take KPG4Rec with Local-LSH and Global-LSH into consideration which are termed as **KPG4Rec(L)** and **KPG4Rec(G)** respectively. Figure 6 shows the performance of different methods on MovieLens-1M, and Fig. 7 shows that on LastFM.

It can be seen from the experimental results significantly that our proposed model performs much better than the other methods in both MovieLens-1M and LastFM. In addition, as the number N changes, our model can still maintain the best performance. In the comparison of KPG4Rec and its two variants, KPG4Rec (L) has a slightly worse performance while KPG4Rec (G) performs best of all the three models. The reason is that the buckets generated from the hash function in Local-LSH are not the most accurate

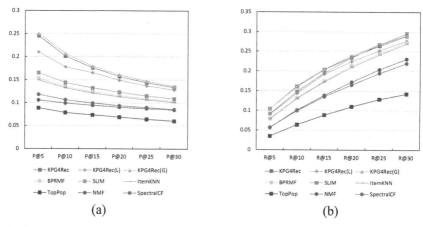

Fig. 6. Precision@*N* (a) and Recall@*N* (b) of Top-*N* recommendation for MovieLens-1M.

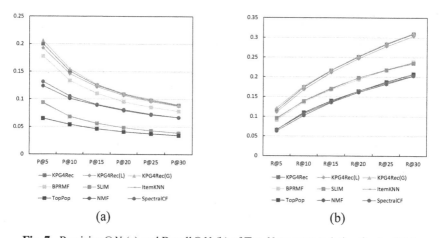

Fig. 7. Precision@*N* (a) and Recall@*N* (b) of Top-*N* recommendation for LastFM.

classification of each item in the user's preference sequence. Different from this, the hash functions in Global-LSH map a candidate item and its similar items to a same bucket. The outstanding performance of KPG4Rec with Global-LSH could reflect a fact: items that are similar to the candidate item usually occupy an important position in the user's decision-making consideration.

4.5 Evaluation of Different Properties

Since our recommendation is based on the semantic information, the effect of using only one single property-aware graph in KPG4Rec will be discussed in this subsection. In order to fully explore the semantic relevance between items, we select the nine most frequently occurring properties from the DBpedia Ontology to construct property-aware graphs. Aiming at discovering the differences among different semantic properties, one single graph is used in KPG4Rec(G) to make prediction in this part. Results are shown in Table 1 and Table 2. It is not difficult to find that using only one single property-aware graph for recommendation is also very effective. Note that the property-aware graph contains not only the semantic information of items, but also the interactive information between users and items. Thus, the collaborative signals of user-item interaction considered when constructing property-aware graphs play a vital role in our proposed model KPG4Rec.

In the movie recommendation scene, using the graph constructed under the single property of MusicComposer, Subject or Distributor has a higher recommendation significance. This means that when a user chooses to watch a movie, the music, theme, and other factors play a more important determinant. Similar to the movie field, music subjects and genres are more considered by the users which can be inferred from Table 2. By using the semantic information of items, the recommendation results are also interpretable for ordinary users. Give a simple example, a movie is recommended to a user because it has the same subject or the same director as movies the user has watched before.

Table 1. Evaluation of using one single property in KPG4Rec(G) on MovieLens-1M.

Property	P@5	P@10	P@15	R@5	R@10	R@15
Director	0.2376	0.1975	0.1719	0.0985	0.1564	0.1959
Starring	0.2281	0.1899	0.1662	0.0944	0.1484	0.1886
Distributor	0.2413	0.1963	0.1711	0.1008	0.1557	0.1968
Writer	0.2344	0.1939	0.1681	0.0973	0.1537	0.1941
MusicComposer	0.2435	0.2002	0.1739	0.1019	0.1584	0.1997
Producer	0.2377	0.1961	0.1689	0.0982	0.1544	0.1918
Cinematography	0.2395	0.1986	0.1733	0.1001	0.1574	0.1995
Editing	0.2370	0.1945	0.1697	0.0991	0.1536	0.1949
Subject	0.2404	0.1995	0.1735	0.1003	0.1560	0.1961
KPG4Rec(G)	0.2503	0.2068	0.1791	0.1037	0.1625	0.2045

Table 2. Evaluation of using one single property in KPG4Rec(G) on LastFM.

Property	P@5	P@10	P@15	R@5	R@10	R@15
Genre	0.1937	0.1458	0.1221	0.1126	0.1691	0.2129
RecordLabel	0.1977	0.1501	0.1242	0.1147	0.1741	0.2162
Hometown	0.1932	0.1456	0.1216	0.1113	0.1679	0.2101
AssociatedBand	0.1890	0.1442	0.1185	0.1099	0.1674	0.2060
AssociatedMusicalArtist	0.1867	0.1434	0.1193	0.1084	0.1665	0.2075
BirthPlace	0.1913	0.1429	0.1196	0.1103	0.1650	0.2071
BandMember	0.1807	0.1367	0.1145	0.1046	0.1574	0.1981
FormerBandMember	0.1812	0.1373	0.1148	0.1046	0.1578	0.1984
Subject	0.1988	0.1511	0.1279	0.1161	0.1766	0.2238
KPG4Rec(G)	0.2064	0.1544	0.1262	0.1214	0.1771	0.2174

5 Related Work

5.1 Random Walk Algorithm

In recent years, some models in the natural language processing (NLP) field are utilized in random walk algorithms to extract the structural features of graphs. Nodes in graphs are represented by low dimensional continuous vectors which can be used for downstream tasks then. Word2Vec [19] is an efficient NLP model which can capture a large number of precise syntactic and semantic word relationships by learning high-quality distributed vector representations (Skip-gram). DeepWalk [24] aims at learning latent representations of vertices in a network like graphs. These latent representations can be easily exploited by NLP models for the reason that they encode social relations in a continuous vector space. Node2vec [13] adjusts the weight of random walk to control the tendency of BFS or DFS based on DeepWalk. Due to its high performance, Node2vec technique is adopted in KPG4Rec.

5.2 Recommendations Using Knowledge Graph

Recently, the usage of the KG in RS is attracting increasing attention and has shown the effectiveness already. For example, DKN [25] is a news recommendation model which utilizes knowledge graph representation and deep networks. KGCN [26] captures relatedness of items by mining their associated semantic relationships in KG, and the model is learned through an end-to-end way. CKAN [27] proposes a natural method of combining collaborative signals which are encoded by collaboration propagation with semantic associations contained in KG together. In this paper, we utilize multiple property relationships of items extracted from KG for personalized recommendation.

6 Conclusion

In this paper, we propose a novel model KPG4Rec with the enhancement of a knowledge graph for Top-N recommendation. Our approach aims to make better use of the semantic information of items. Following this destination, we first construct several property-aware graphs which contain both the collaborative signals and the semantic information. Next, a random walk algorithm of graph Node2vec is adopted on these graphs to generate item vector representations under different properties. Then these representations are used to make the final prediction. In addition, we also use the LSH technique to reduce the time overhead and improve the accuracy of our model. Extensive experiments have been conducted on two real-world datasets, and the effectiveness of our KPG4Rec framework is validated. For future work, we plan to (1) apply graph mining methods to our property-aware graphs to better explore user's potential interests; (2) utilize the recently popular deep networks for a more efficient recommendation like [28, 29].

Acknowledgement. This work is supported in part by the Fundamental Research Fund for the Central Universities (30920041112, 30919011282), the National Key R&D Program of China (Funding No. 2020YFB1805503), Jiangsu Province Modern Education Technology Research Project (84365); National Vocational Education Teacher Enterprise Practice Base "Integration of Industry and Education" Special Project (Study on Evaluation Standard of Artificial Intelligence Vocational Skilled Level). the Postdoctoral Science Foundation of China (2019M651835), National Natural Science Foundation of China (61702264).

References

1. Bell, R.M., Koren, Y.: Improved neighborhood-based collaborative filtering. In: KDD Cup Workshop 13th ACM SIGKDD International Conference on Knowledge Discovery, pp. 7–14. ACM, San Jose (2007)
2. Wang, F., Zhu, H., Srivastava, G., Li, S., Khosravi, M.R., Qi, L.: Robust collaborative filtering recommendation with user-item-trust records. IEEE Trans. Comput. Soc. Syst. 1–11 (2021)
3. Li, B., Zhu, X., Li, R., Zhang, C.: Rating knowledge sharing in cross-domain collaborative filtering. IEEE Trans. Cybern. **45**(5), 1054–1068 (2015)
4. Linden, G., Smith, B., York, J.: Amazon. com recommendations: item-to-item collaborative filtering. IEEE. Internet. Comput. **7**(1), 76–80 (2003)
5. Liu, J., Dolan, P., Pedersen, E.R.: Personalized news recommendation based on click behavior. In: ACM 15th International Conference Intelligence User Interfaces, pp. 31–40. ACM, Hong Kong (2010)
6. Sarwar, B., Karypis, G., Konstan, J., Riedl, J.: Item-based collaborative filtering recommendation. In: 10th International Conference World Wide Web, pp. 285–295. ACM, Hong Kong (2001)
7. Koren, Y., Bell, R.M., Volinsky, C.: Matrix factorization techniques for recommender systems. Computer **42**(8), 30–37 (2009)
8. Rendle, S., Freudenthaler, C., Gantner, Z., Schmidt-Thieme, L.: BPR: Bayesian personalized ranking from implicit feedback. In: 25th Conference Uncertainty Artificial Intelligence, pp. 452–461. UAI 2009 (2009)
9. Luo, X., Zhou, M., Xia, Y., Zhu, Q.: An efficient non-negative matrix-factorization-based approach to collaborative filtering for recommender systems. IEEE Trans. Ind. Inform. **10**, 1273–1284 (2014)

10. Yu, X., et al.: Personalized entity recommendation: A heterogeneous information network approach. In: WSDM 2014 - Proceedings of 7th ACM International Conference Web Search Data Mining, pp. 283–292. ACM, New York (2014)

11. Zhao, H., Yao, Q., Li, J., Song, Y., Lee, D.L.: Meta-graph based recommendation fusion over heterogeneous information networks. In: ACM SIGKDD International Conference on Knowledge Discovery Data Mining, pp. 635–644. ACM, Halifax (2017)

12. Xu, X., Huang, Q., Zhang, Y., Li, S., Qi, L., Dou, W.: An LSH-based offloading method for IoMT services in integrated cloud-edge environment. ACM Trans. Multimed. Comput. Commun. **16**(3), 1–19 (2021)

13. Grover, A., Leskovec, J.: Node2Vec. In: KDD 2016: Proceedings of the 22nd ACM SIGKDD International Conference on Knowledge Discovery and Data Mining, pp. 855–864. ACM, San Francisco (2016)

14. Datar, M., Indyk, P., Immorlica, N., Mirrokni, V.S.: Locality-sensitive hashing scheme based on p-stable distributions. In: Annual Symposium on Computational Geometry, pp. 253–262. ACM, Brooklyn (2004)

15. Xu, X., et al.: Secure service offloading for internet of vehicles in SDN-enabled mobile edge computing. IEEE Trans. Intell. Transp. Syst. **22**(6), 3720–3729 (2021)

16. Qi, L., Wang, X., Xu, X., Dou, W., Li, S.: Privacy-aware cross-platform service recommendation based on enhanced locality-sensitive hashing. IEEE Trans. Netw. Sci. Eng. **8**, 1145–1153 (2020)

17. Wang, H., et al.: RippleNet: propagating user preferences on the knowledge graph for recommender systems. In: International Conference on Information and Knowledge Management Proceedings, pp. 417–426. ACM, Torino (2018)

18. Wang, H., Zhang, F., Zhao, M., Li, W., Xie, X., Guo, M.: Multi-task feature learning for knowledge graph enhanced recommendation. In: Web Conference on 2019 - Proceedings of World Wide Web Conference, pp. 2000–2010. ACM, San Francisco (2019)

19. Mikolov, T., Sutskever, I., Chen, K., Corrado, G., Dean, J.: Distributed representations of words and phrases and their compositionality. In: Advances in Neural Information Processing Systems 26, pp. 3111–3119. NIPS (2013)

20. Ostuni, V.C., Di Noia, T., Mirizzi, R., Di Sciascio, E.: Top-N recommendations from implicit feedback leveraging linked open data. In: CEUR Workshop Proceedings, pp. 20–27. ACM, Hong Kong (2014)

21. Cremonesi, P., Koren, Y., Turrin, R.: Performance of recommender algorithms on top-N recommendation tasks. In: RecSys 2010 – Proceedings of 4th ACM Conference on Recommendation Systems, pp. 39–46. ACM, Barcelona (2010)

22. Ning, X., Karypis, G.: SLIM: sparse linear methods for top-N recommender systems. In: IEEE International Conference Data Mining, ICDM, pp. 497–506. IEEE, Vancouver (2011)

23. Zheng, L., Lu, C.T., Jiang, F., Zhang, J., Yu, P.S.: Spectral collaborative filtering. In: RecSys 2018 - 12th ACM Conference on Recommendation Systems, pp. 311–319. ACM. Vancouver (2018)

24. Perozzi, B., Al-Rfou, R., Skiena, S.: DeepWalk: Online learning of social representations. In: ACM SIGKDD International Conference Knowledge Discovery and Data Mining, pp. 701–710. ACM, New York (2014)

25. Wang, H., Zhang, F., Xie, X., Guo, M.: DKN: Deep knowledge-aware network for news recommendation. In: Web Conference on 2018 – Proceedings of World Wide Web Conference WWW 2018, pp. 1835–1844. ACM, Lyon (2018)

26. Wang, H., Zhao, M., Xie, X., Li, W., Guo, M.: Knowledge graph convolutional networks for recommender systems. In: Web Conference on 2019 – Proceedings of World Wide Web Conference WWW 2019, pp. 3307–3313. ACM, San Francisco (2019)

27. Wang, Z., Lin, G., Tan, H., Chen, Q., Liu, X.: CKAN: collaborative knowledge-aware attentive network for recommender systems. In: SIGIR 2020 – Proceedings of 43rd International ACM SIGIR Conference on Research and Development in Information Retrieval. pp. 219–228. ACM, Virtual Event (2020)
28. Xu, X., et al.: Edge content caching with deep spatiotemporal residual network for IoV in smart city. ACM Trans. Sens. Netw. **17**(3), 1–33 (2021)
29. Liu, Y., et al.: An attention-based category-aware GRU model for the next POI recommendation. Int. J. Intell. Syst. **36**, 3174–3189 (2021)

ERP as Software-as-a-Service: Factors Depicting Large Enterprises Cloud Adoption

Juha Kinnunen(⊠) ⓘ

University of Jyväskylä, PO Box 35, 40014 Jyväskylä, Finland
juha.a.kinnunen@jyu.fi

Abstract. Cloud computing has shifted the paradigm from developing enterprise software to acquiring it as a service. While supportive information systems have rapidly transformed to Software-as-a-Service (SaaS) solutions, mission-critical ERP's largely remain in more conventional operation models. Especially with SAP ERP systems utilized by large enterprises, adoption to public cloud-based SaaS ERP has been slow and on-premise ERP is still thriving. Based on a multi-case study interviewing six large enterprises, we identified four elementary factors which affect cloud adoption for mission-critical ERP's. The findings indicate that service quality and costs are the most significant factors influencing SaaS adoption, while technical limitations and cloud characteristics are also identified as key factors.

Keywords: Software-as-a-Service · SaaS · Enterprise resource planning · Cloud computing · Cloud transformation · SAP · ERP

1 Introduction

Cloud computing offers a novel approach to the utilization and ownership of information systems (IS) and the use of cloud solutions has increased rapidly during the past decade. Cloud computing has practically revolutionized the way software is utilized by enabling the use of information technology as a commodity [1, 2]. Software-as-a-service (SaaS) cloud service model offers many benefits, the vendor installs the software on its own equipment and is fully responsible for updates and development efforts. Essentially, cloud computing transforms software acquisition into service acquisition [3] where cloud computing resembles software renting instead of purchasing [4].

Whether an information system is implemented as a traditional on-premise system or acquired as a service from the cloud, the company's requirements for the system should remain the same. ERP systems play a very central role in business operations, as they are responsible for day-to-day operational activities [5]. For business customers, the cloud seems like an attractive solution. Cloud computing promises a fully outsourced, elastic service model which can be priced according to use [6, 7]. This may be easier and more cost-effective especially for SMEs. While small companies are more flexible in their needs, large companies typically require tailored solutions, especially if they are

M. R. Khosravi et al. (Eds.): CloudComp 2021, LNICST 430, pp. 123–142, 2022.
https://doi.org/10.1007/978-3-030-99191-3_10

replacing mission-critical systems [8]. ERP systems are also impacted with high switching costs between software vendors, which can also help to protect a SaaS providers position and pricing [4, 18]. Cloud has some limitations due to its nature, e.g. privacy concerns can prevent adoption as a company's sensitive business data would be entirely on the responsibility of the cloud service provider [9, 12], also software customizing options can be limited [12]. Cloud technology migration may also involve significant costs for enterprises [10].

Although cloud computing has been on the rise for the past decade within many areas, SaaS ERP solutions for large enterprises core systems is still a recent phenomenon. Previous research on cloud computing has shown little interest in ERP specific factors that would apply to the cloud paradigm [11]. Some academic researchers suggest that cloud ERPs could benefit from lower implementation costs, faster deployment, usability, availability of new technology, as well as frequently deployed upgrades and version changes [12]. Others have shown inconsistencies between the findings of different researchers; for example, performance and security issues were seen in other studies as risk factors for cloud computing [13], in some studies these factors are an explicit benefit to the cloud [14]. It has been suggested that SaaS ERP will eventually be implemented by large companies [26], yet this still seems waiting for realization.

We thus identify a research gap in previous literature on explaining why large enterprises still seem reluctant to move their mission-critical SAP ERP systems to public cloud SaaS, especially when SME's SaaS ERP adoption rates are high. Thus, the research question for this article is defined as "Which factors affect large enterprises SaaS ERP adoption for mission-critical systems?" This article seeks to clarify these issues and contribute to the IS field of research by exploring how large enterprises are operating SaaS ERP solutions as compared to traditional on-premise solutions. The aim of this study is also to understand whether the transition to a SaaS ERP also realizes the benefits that are generally presented for cloud services. While there are different delivery models for cloud services, such as public and private cloud for the deployment model or infrastructure-as-a-service and platform-as-a-service for cloud service models [6], we specifically focus this research on public cloud SaaS ERP systems to understand their significant differences to the currently exploited service models of large companies on-premise ERP systems.

2   Literature Review

To form a basis for the empirical research, we conducted a literature review with systematicity and rigor [40] on previous research in order recognize the describing factors between public cloud SaaS ERP and the traditional on-premise service models. Based on the synthesis of existing literature we construct a simplified framework of the defining areas between these service models, in order to adopt our empirical analysis on SaaS for large companies. Existing literature was systematically searched from the academic databases ACM Digital Library and IEEE Xplore, while Google Scholar search engine was also used in a supportive role. We used search terms such as "cloud computing", "cloud ERP" and "SaaS ERP", all relevant papers and articles were reviewed rigorously to improve quality [41].

On-premise systems are information system which are installed and managed by the customer, through internal or external resources. A company must acquire all the required infrastructure, the determining factor being that the management of the system is in the company's own hands. Service production can be outsourced, but ultimately the company decides how it will develop the system [15]. In public cloud SaaS systems, the company leases the information system. The service provider acquires the infrastructure and implements the information system for the use of the customer, who pays a monthly rent to utilize the system. The fee includes license, i.e. access to the system, as well as to the infrastructure under it [3, 32]. The acquisition or development of an on-premise system requires a large initial investment, e.g. in the infrastructure whereas in the cloud, the system is subscribed as a service [16].

Traditionally ERP systems have been installed as on-premise systems, running and operated on conventional data centers close to the organization [19]. The acquisition or development of an on-premise system requires a large initial investment in e.g. the underlying infrastructure, whereas in the cloud the system is made available as a service [16]. SaaS vendors acquire the required infrastructure and implement the system, where customers pay subscription fees for usage [3, 31]. Some of the perceived risks associated with using SaaS cloud services are related to security [9, 33], especially with ERP systems as they contain sensitive business data. The technical implementation of security measures is increasingly in the responsibility of the cloud service provider. SaaS service providers also share resources between several different clients, which propose new challenges to the traditional concept of security [17, 20].

From a cost perspective, cloud services are expected to be more affordable due to the economies of scale that the service providers can pass on to their customers. However, large companies might not benefit from this as they have specific and complex needs [21]. Cloud services provide continuous development in the form of software updates [3], which should be noted when considering the total cost of ownership for IS [22]. Licensing models also differ between on-premise and cloud systems. On-premise software licenses are typically perpetual by nature, while SaaS licenses are subscriptions that are valid for as long as the customer keeps paying for the monthly fees. Lifecycle investments also follow a different approach, on-premise systems require recurring investments in version upgrades and new infrastructure, while these are all covered by SaaS subscriptions in the cloud [3, 11, 23]. ERP customization options are a key issue from the business process perspective. Typically customizing options are more extensive with on-premise systems, where SaaS systems only offer limited customizing possibilities [24, 25].

Cloud performance and availability may also differ from an on-premise system. Previous research has shown conflicting results in this regard, as some see performance and availability as an advantage for the cloud while others view this as a risk [9, 13, 14, 30]. One of the characteristics of cloud service is the continuous development, which brings new functionalities to the customer. New innovations are frequently rolled out to the system, customers no longer need to conduct technical version upgrades [3].

The most mission critical IS are usually reluctant to move to the cloud. Cloud solutions per se should not be a self-sufficient solution, but cloud migrations are expected to produce concrete benefits [5]. Business applications which are not mission critical are usually seen as a more natural choice for cloud migration [15]. Business applications like

CRM and office suites are already showing high SaaS adoption rates for small and large companies [27]. Even specialized niche market software has increased interest in consuming SaaS model [34], but SaaS ERP adoption remains low [27]. While the existing literature has widely studied SaaS ERP adoption for SMEs [8, 28–30], similar studies for large enterprises distinct adoption are sparse. Some researchers suggest that large enterprises SaaS ERP adoption may be hindered by complex implementations [4, 21, 27], expensive subscription fees due to large user base and multiple modules [21], organizational resistance [21] or security and reliability issues [21, 27]. Previous research also identifies the need for more in-depth studies specifically on large companies SaaS adoption [21].

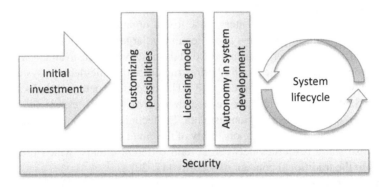

Fig. 1. Framework for on-premise IS and SaaS IS differences.

SaaS services thus have certain, clearly distinguishable characteristics from on-premise systems (Fig. 1). This provides benefits to the customer, but it can also be a limitation for companies that need precisely tailored solutions for their own business processes. SaaS and on-premise systems therefore have their own potentials, strengths and weaknesses. We propose a framework for describing the essential characteristics between on-premise IS and SaaS IS. Implementing an information system begins with an *initial investment*, where on-premise IS typically require a more substantial investment due to hardware purchases and system installations. SaaS vendors provide all the required components as a service, leading to a smaller initial investment [3, 15, 16, 31, 32].

The characteristics depict how the system is utilized and operated by the customer. *Customizing possibilities* reflect the flexibility of the system and how individually it can be configured to respond to distinct business demands. On-premise systems typically have a high amount of customizing possibilities, where the system can be tailored to be fit-for-purpose. SaaS vendors limit the customizing options in order to provide a more limited IS template for multiple customers, while still following industry best-practices for business processes [24, 25]. *Licensing model* differentiates the system operational models as well. On-premise systems are commonly following a perpetual licensing model, where customers can use the purchased software for as long as they want to. SaaS systems, however, are based on a subscription licensing model where the customer is renting the software for a specific amount of time. While the SaaS system is being utilized, the monthly licensing costs keep adding up [3, 11, 23].

Autonomy in systems development is describing how the IS development itself can be controlled by the customer. On-premise systems give more autonomy as a service model, where customers can decide to develop new features and operate the system solely through their own resources or outsource these tasks to an external service provide. SaaS vendors, on the other hand, are more independently developing the system for multiple customers simultaneously, who have less autonomy to align on the development of new features [16, 19].

System Lifecycle refers to the maintenance of the IS, such as commencing version upgrades, updating the system and performance tuning. On-premise systems typically embrace heavy and expensive upgrade projects, which are executed rarely or infrequently due to their size and the involved costs. SaaS systems incorporate these as part of the service model, upgrades are more frequent and require less effort, thus the customer can benefit from continuous digital innovations [3, 12, 16].

Finally, *Security* is a crucial part of any IS regardless of their service models, which should be considered in all parts of IS. Again, on-premise systems require the customer to apply frequent security patches on many different components, while SaaS vendors are responsible for the majority of these requirements in the cloud. On the other hand, SaaS customers are typically sharing at least certain underlying resources which presents different technical security aspects as well as concerns for potential security breaches [9, 17, 20, 33].

3   Research Method

As the research question was defined to focus on large enterprises cloud ERP adoption, we selected a case study research method for this paper. Case studies examine real events and obtain a wide range of information for this purpose, their strength is in explaining how or why a phenomenon has occurred [35, 36]. The research was conducted as a multiple case study as the phenomena was seen diverse by nature, requiring cross-case comparison between different enterprises [37]. We interviewed six different persons from six large companies, where the common denominator was a large implementation of SAP ERP on-premise systems responsible for the company's core business processes, but also experiences from SAP's SaaS cloud services. The interviewees were randomly selected from the participants of a technology seminar, the selection criteria required practical experiences from transferring on-premise SAP systems to a SaaS-based cloud service, so that the collected data would be able to answer the research question. The sample provided a diverse view of the experiences of large companies utilizing SAP ERP as their mission-critical IS.

Interviews were conducted both face-to-face and via Teams, following a semi-structured interview format. The list of interview questions was provided to the participants for prior acquaintance by e-mail so that everyone had the opportunity to prepare for the topics of the interview. Notes were handwritten and transcribed immediately after the interview. The transcribed interviews were subsequently sent to the interviewees by e-mail, giving participants the opportunity to correct any errors or misunderstandings.

About half of the interviewees returned to these and made minor edits to the transcribed text, which helped increase the validity of the material. The actual interviews lasted 30–60 minutes per interviewee. Following the semi-structured formula, ten questions were discussed with the interviewees, allowing further questions to be clarified according to the answers as well as sprawling outside the question area. A total of 24 pages of transcribed data was collected. In the analysis phase, the data was coded while reflecting on the research questions. The analysis of the data was following a three-step model, by first reducing the data, creating displays of the data, then drawing conclusions and verifications [42, 43]. Computer assistance was utilized to organize and code the data in support of the analysis [38]. Analysis was carried out by coding the material initially in a word processor, then running a Python script which extracted all the codings into a spreadsheet program [39]. This was continued by organizing the material and deriving themes from it.

All interviewees had long work experience in the IT industry, as well as several years of experience in utilizing cloud services. The interviewees had served in various roles during their careers, for example as developers, project managers and architects. Their views provided a diverse picture of large companies' business-critical systems with recent experiences on utilizing cloud services on a large scale. The interviewees details are described in Table 1 below.

Table 1. Background information for the interviewees.

Interviewee	Work experience	Cloud experience	Industry	Company size (employees)	ERP role
A	15 years	3 years	Manufacturing	>5 000	Client
B	16 years	4 years	Manufacturing	>15 000	Client
C	25 years	5 years	Manufacturing	>15 000	Client
D	20 years	3 years	Public sector	>5 000	Client
E	20 years	3 years	Public sector	>5 000	Client
F	25 years	7 years	Consulting	>100	Partner

The role of the company describes the relationship with SAP. All of the companies utilized SAP systems in their core business and where perceived as customers for SAP. However, interviewee F represented a consulting partner for SAP that implemented SAP systems and provided consulting to client companies. The experiences of interviewees A-E were thus based on customer role for SAP ERP and the day-to-day operational use of the system, while the experiences of interviewee F were based on the expert experience from numerous different customer implementation projects.

4   Results

Based on the analysis of the data, four topics were formed to describe the main factors affecting SaaS ERP adoption: service quality, costs, technical limitations and cloud characteristics. Service quality was considered to include features which were influencing business continuity via the information system. The topics reflected the differences between on-premise and SaaS ERP systems, while also answering why large enterprises continue running their mission-critical systems on-premises. The analysis implied these as the most important factors, as depicted in Fig. 2 below.

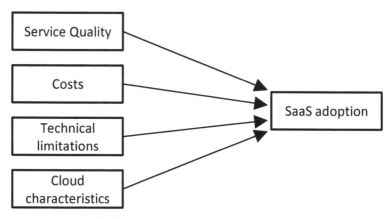

Fig. 2. Factors affecting SaaS ERP adoption.

4.1 Service Quality

The service quality of mission-critical systems is fundamentally important, as large enterprises are utilizing IS in their core operations. There were mixed experiences with the service quality and reliability of SaaS ERP between the interviewees, where the majority felt that the level of service and reliability had deteriorated significantly when compared to the on-premise system while some saw the SaaS system as stable and reliable. This was dependent on the experienced service level of the previous on-premise system: companies which were unhappy with the preceding systems quality were content with SaaS service quality, and vice versa. If the old on-premise system had been unstable, the customer may experience even a small improvement as a major benefit that was achieved via SaaS adoption. However, large companies tend to have made major investments in the service quality of their business-critical on-premise ERP systems in order to maximize availability. Thus, the quality of service in a SaaS system may appear to be significantly lower for them. Overall, the results indicate that service quality for SaaS ERP systems may be lower than what large companies are accustomed to with their on-premise systems.

> *"The quality of service has sometimes varied. There has been some more downtime, but the system has also recovered quickly."* (Interviewee E)

> *"Some customers have criticized cloud performance ... SaaS has had worse performance than on-premise systems. Most of the time the applications have functioned at least satisfactorily, but the problem is that there is no recipient for performance problems when they have occurred."* (Interviewee F)

On-premise systems were hence seen as more reliable than their cloud counterparts. However, in terms of incident handling and application support, SAP's own service level was perceived to be similar in both systems. Issues which required SAP's direct input were thus equal by nature. Regarding vendor related issues, personal support was seen as an advantage of on-premise systems because the enterprise knows which data centre their systems are physically located in but also who actually maintains them. There can even be personal relations and familiar support personnel to call in case of a n problem, instead of a faceless incident handling process:

> *"On-premise has been more stable on these ... SAP's support services for the cloud itself are exactly the same as for on-premise products: you create a ticket for a problem and hope that someone will handle it."* (Interviewee B)

> *"With traditional on-premise models, the customer has a personal relationship to the operator. The company usually knows who to contact if things don't work out, which makes corrections faster."* (Interviewee F)

SaaS ERP may not be suitable for all enterprise customers, but the transition of services to the cloud could still be an otherwise ongoing trend. The service model for future information systems may possibly reside in hybrid models, where some of the systems are acquired as ready-made services while some core system functionalities are kept more in self-managed or hosted on-premise solutions:

> *"SaaS will never work for all companies, it will fit some better than the others. A full cloud transition is unlikely to ever happen."* (Interviewee F)

The service quality of mission-critical information systems is strongly influenced by the content of service level agreements (SLA), which determine the availability of the system and the possible sanction for breaching the SLA. In this regard, SaaS SLAs were seen as too weak for large companies' mission-critical systems. Unplanned downtime of SaaS was seen as a clear barrier to adoption, while vendor support from SAP was also seen too weak for a critical system. This indicates that the quality of service of the SaaS system is an important factor which influences large companies' business-critical SaaS ERP adoption. SaaS ERP was seen as more suitable for SMEs, or to information systems which are running non-urgent supportive functions. In the current state, the quality of the SaaS ERP service provided by SAP is not sufficient.

> *"Based on my experiences, I would see that unplanned downtime and monitoring issues are the main reasons why this is not fit for mission-critical applications."* (Interviewee B)

> *"The quality of the service largely depends on how well the service level agreement is defined on paper."* (Interviewee C)

> *"Service level agreements are too lax, and most users are probably already aware of the challenges with SAP support. In my view, at least these factors have the greatest impact on why business-critical applications will not move to the cloud in the near future."* (Interviewee E)

4.2 Costs

The second topic that emerged from the interviews were information system costs. This includes costs incurred in different ways that directly or indirectly affect the total cost of ownership. Information system costs were seen to include e.g. licenses, personnel costs, consulting costs, hardware, system deployment, development upgrades, and testing. Cost structures were reflected from the SaaS systems which were used by the interviewees, while comparing to their preceding on-premise counterparts.

SaaS costs were considered to include the costs related to the implementation, operation and development of the system. Directly involved costs were estimated to be at approximately the same level in SaaS systems when compared to the preceding on-premise system. The implementation effort of deploying the system was also seen to be at the same level as in the old system, as SaaS ERP needs to be configured to the company's requirements. Deployment costs are also case-specific and depend on the enterprise specific requirements, meaning that these costs may move in either direction when compared to on-premise. The implementation effort in a SaaS system was seen to be different by nature but involving an equal amount of time and matter. For example, system installation work is minimal and technical deployment is fast but deploying business process specific functionalities requires an equal amount of workshops and requirement planning as previously.

"There was no large difference in the amount of work for implementing the system when compared to the implementation of the on-premise system ... The costs have supposedly remained the same." (Interviewee A)

"We didn't need to do any installations by ourselves. For servers, this was cheaper. ... I've operated the previous on-premise version and this is much easier in the cloud, where all basic configurations were ready out-of-the-box ... On our usage level the total costs have virtually remained unchanged." (Interviewee B)

SaaS may not be a cost-effective alternative either to running an own data centre solution or to a hosted Infrastructure-as-a-Service solution. If a company has already invested extensively in its own servers and infrastructure or in an IaaS provider, similar costs in SaaS may even be much higher. Focusing and tendering large platform contracts may give more significant overall discounts due to economies of scale, than what is realizing to the customer side from SaaS ERP. SaaS cost benefits are more present in the amount of required consulting hours for functional development. Thus, SaaS cloud systems have some advantages in terms of investment planning and the amount of required labour:

"As an investment, the cloud has been much clearer. In my opinion the investment plans have been more accurate than with on-premise... I would say that the difference is really noticeable in how much the system requires outsourced consultants or our own work. The cloud is therefore clearly producing results in this respect." (Interviewee D)

In general, comparing the operating costs between on-premise and SaaS systems is not easy due to the differences in their characteristics. The systems are developed through different models, so the cost benefits depend partially on exploiting each models' benefits. The operating costs of a SaaS ERP may still be higher for large enterprises than with an on-premise system.

> *"The cost of operating a cloud ERP will eventually reach the same level, even if it doesn't require an initial investment. However, there is no single answer to which one is more cost efficient as a whole ... It's difficult to say whether cloud is actually able to save on costs, because it's hard to compare to on-premise costs."* (Interviewee F)

Comparing the total cost of cloud to that of an on-premise system is, in many respects, difficult. For many large companies, SaaS ERP's experiences are limited in both time and quantity. Additionally, past on-premise costs have often not been tracked at an exact level, such as the tracking the accumulated personnel and server costs. This also makes it difficult to compare total costs between these systems. On the other hand, the mere cost of SaaS and on-premise should not be directly compared because the service model itself is different:

> *"Admittedly, it is difficult to compare these because we have had many more on-premise systems and they have contained more functionality."* (Interviewee D)

> *"It may be a little difficult to compare the costs when they are so different ... However, this is not just about the costs, but about a different model of service production."* (Interviewee E)

The meaningfulness of cost comparison is affected by the fundamental difference between a SaaS system and an on-premise system. SaaS is intended to be implemented in a more standardized format, while on-premise systems have been freely customizable by the customer. However, free customization possibilities are not just a positive thing:

> *"This is really a question about comparing apples to oranges. Traditionally customers on-premise SAPs have been fully tailored to meet customer specific needs, which in turn has led to implementation projects reaching a certain size and appearance."* (Interviewee F)

4.3 Technical Limitations

SaaS also has certain technical limitations. Because various technical components of the public cloud service are entirely in the hands of the supplier, the customer does not always have the possibility to influence all the relevant functions which they have come accustomed to. Network latency was seen as one of the potentially limiting factors, as the data centres operating the cloud services platform are usually farther away from the customer than the customer's own data centres. This can pose challenges for industrial automation systems, for example, whose latency requirements can be very stringent:

> *"Latency problems are also a major problem because large companies have a network of systems which produce their core functionalities. If ERP is in the cloud*

and the legacy systems remain on-premise, the latency can be intolerable especially with business-critical integrations" (Interviewee C)

"*SAP has decided in all their wisdom that the session timeout is 20 minutes which cannot be changed. Then there are tasks that take longer to complete, but the application discards the data if the session has expired.*" (Interviewee B)

The customizing capabilities of the cloud service is one common limitation for customers, which is also widely identified in the previous literature. The customizability of a SaaS system is more limited than in an on-premises because the same system is offered to multiple customers. This is especially significant for large companies, who have widely customized solutions fit for their specific business processes.

"*At least one vast problem that we have encountered is with customizations.*" (Interviewee B).

"*Certain things could not be implemented in the cloud, so we decided to utilize a hybrid model and implement these things on the on-premise side ... Otherwise, the functionalities could be implemented from the service as-is, we use these processes now in for example induction.*" (Interviewee D)

Although limited customization appears to be a restriction for SaaS ERP, it can also be seen as an advantage specifically in leveraging industry standard best-practice business processes, rather than tailoring the system extensively to fit self-developed requirements.

"*The implementation of a cloud system is first and foremost about the organizational change processes and what the company wants to do in terms of its own business processes. In other words, will the information system be adapted to fit the business processes, or the processes themselves adapted to standard solutions that are readily available in the system.*" (Interviewee A)

"*The implementation of a SaaS system requires the company to make both process changes and changes in various operational methods. It requires a completely different way of working, not just moving from on-premise to the cloud ... Operatively it isn't sustainable if a large number of tailoring is desired.*" (Interviewee F)

The fitness for purpose of the information system is important for customers, i.e. how well the system meets the company's requirements. This is not just a question of the system's customizability, but more generally about the functionalities contained in the system and the flexibility of implementation. From an ERP perspective, a SaaS solution may not be suitable for the mission-critical system of large enterprises due to the limitations in customization capabilities. SaaS ERP can be seen as more suitable as an SME solution for which standard solutions are more likely to be sufficient. In practice, a SaaS ERP system is not able to provide sufficiently flexible solutions for specialized industries. Above all, there is a lack of flexibility and the system is not able to meet the requirements. These technical limitations of SaaS ERP are therefore preventing adoption for large companies.

"*For a small company SaaS is a good solution, as long as you can suffice to a standard solution and configurations. However, for the core business of large companies this is not yet mature, I don't see that a global ERP system could be completely provided from cloud."* (Interviewee C)

"For our business-critical systems, I don't see this as possible. They are just too industry-centric." (Interviewee D)

Information security is an integral part of the service production of enterprise information systems, both in SaaS and on-premise systems. Security requirements have also been presented in previous literature as a restriction on the adoption of SaaS ERP. However, the interviewees did not perceive security issues as a major concern or a preventing factor. The companies had a high level of confidence in the supplier's expertise in proper technical information security. Security practices were seen as part of normal system development, which is addressed as a separate part of the implementation project. The amount of work required on information security in utilizing a SaaS service may depend on the degree of maturity of the solutions used by a company. Many large companies have already done numerous evaluations and preparations in advance, in order to understand what technical measures are required from them to utilize SaaS systems.

"We have done a lot of work regarding information security. This has been contingency planning and investigating different solutions which has been carried out both in-house and via benchmarking." (Interviewee D)

Security issues were seen as important technical aspects on leveraging a SaaS system, this perspective is slightly different for customers than with on-premise systems previously. In on-premise systems, security requires more investments in physical and technical components, these are typically elements inside a company's own intranet. With SaaS systems, security is more as an application-side factor for the customers as technical security features will be administered by the vendor.

"For browser-based applications the security measures are provided by the SaaS vendor. Typically, investments in security are physical things like firewalls and technical hardenings, but these differ from application security." (Interviewee F)

4.4 Cloud Characteristics

SaaS end-user satisfaction is clearly a positive factor. Also, SaaS systems can be further customized by in-house super users without external consultant resources. Ease of use and new technological benefits, such as mobile use of the system, are the most common benefits of cloud ERP. In this sense business applications start to resemble consumer applications, where usability improvements are frequent.

"The most important aspects which have brought user satisfaction are accessibility, mobile applications, and ease of use. Our business has been satisfied with the system and its processes, although it has had to modify its own processes." (Interviewee C)

"The new system has been very beneficial and easy to use. This is primarily due to the fact that there was previously no desire to upgrade our on-premise system earlier. With cloud ERP, the newer version was inevitably available. The newer

version has introduced welcome improvements for business, for example in the form of ready-made automation or user-friendly interfaces." (Interviewee F)

One part of cloud characteristics are system upgrades. With on-premise systems, upgrades and version changes require extensive work and are heavier by nature than with SaaS. Upgrades are more frequent in SaaS ERP, allowing new features to be more readily available. As more frequent system upgrades are perceived as a strength for SaaS, the overall view of this is positive for customers:

"The system is upgraded frequently which is good, there's no need to pay for version changes separately as in the old system." (Interviewee A)

"New innovations in the system are more seen as positive than negative." (Interviewee D)

In addition to the perceived benefits of frequent technical updates, this also has its own challenges. The release cycle for SAP's cloud ERP system upgrades is usually four times a year, which many find unnecessarily frequent. Depending on the SaaS implementation, customers may be able to postpone upgrades up to a certain point. However, in some SaaS ERP systems the customers can't influence the upgrade schedules and they are forced to be rolled out to the customer systems via a predefined schedule. Practices vary between different products. This may also present a risk factor if frequent upgrades are combined with extensive customizations or extensions:

"Upgrades to the SaaS system are frequent, for example quarterly. Any organization will be in trouble if it makes overly customized processes in the system." (Interviewee C)

An important aspect on technical upgrades is in the service delivery model of cloud ERP: there is a significant difference in terms of upgrades between public cloud and private cloud implementations. Companies face very differing options here, for example, in the ability to postpone upgrades or freedom on customizations which has a major impact on the customer experience also. Some customers have decided not to upgrade their private cloud environments at all because the service provider is not forcing these customers to do so. Business continuity is again important in this regard, which is why upgrades can also be seen as a risk:

"On-premises upgrades can often be delayed because they are not mandatory ... The business continuity of any company itself is obviously more important than a single cloud application. The benefit of frequent upgrades is really case-specific." (Interviewee F)

The challenge of frequent upgrades is that their effects are reflected in the core functionalities utilized by the company. The upgrade must not break any core functionality, which may be more challenging with customer modifications in the cloud and external system integrations. This requires extensive testing from the customer side as companies need to validate their own critical functionalities affected by the cloud upgrades. This is easier to manage if the implementation of the system is as standard as possible and testing efforts are properly resourced. Integrations are particularly crucial: if the cloud is integrated into an on-premise system, this part must always be tested simultaneously with cloud upgrades. The need for extensive testing due to technical cloud upgrades can thus be surprisingly wide, which can also generate excessive testing costs. Thus, the role of automated testing should be evaluated with SaaS ERP implementations. Workloads resulting from testing efforts were therefore perceived as a negative issue that was increasing with cloud ERP:

> "*We are forced to do extra work four times per year due to upgrades, which is perceived negatively. This means, for example, testing.*" (Interviewee D)

> "*All your own extensions and integrations are always required to be tested. The amount of testing has increased slightly.*" (Interviewee E)

The interviews were altogether reflecting well on the distinct requirements that large companies possess on their mission-critical ERP systems. Each recognized category was showing how these companies utilize information systems and which factors are relevant when considering SaaS adaption. Service quality, costs, technical limitations and cloud characteristics are all factors that need to be addressed by the SaaS vendor to support adoption or face the risk that SaaS ERP will remain as an SME specific phenomenon.

5 Discussion and Conclusions

As large enterprises rely their daily operations on these mission-critical systems, service quality is expected to be high. The availability of the cloud platform needs to match that of an on-premise system, while also service level agreements must convince large companies so that they are able to trust the service quality will fulfil their requirements. Experiences for the level of vendor support on incidents and the personality of support are also affecting the service quality, as previous negative experiences on vendor support can undermine SaaS adaption for mission-critical systems. The findings indicate that system availability is currently perceived higher in on-premise systems where large companies have made significant investments to guarantee high availability, while the having experienced SAP's SaaS ERP services to be more commonly plagued with unplanned downtime and subliminal support. Cloud ERP SLA's were implied to be inferior, while trust in the level of support from SAP was perceived as inflexible and anonymous. As business continuity was indicated of being one of the most important factors for large enterprises mission-critical ERP systems, the perceived service quality of SaaS ERP is currently preventing adoption for these companies. Previous literature has identified system availability and reliability as a challenge in implementing SaaS ERP [see e.g. 30], our research shows that large enterprises consider this as a key factor which affects SaaS adoption for mission-critical ERP systems. Supportive systems, such as HCM or CRM, may tolerate lower service quality as they are typically non-critical systems with lower impact on business continuity. As large enterprises have already widely adopted systems such as cloud CRM but remain reluctant on adopting core ERP as SaaS [27], these findings also help to explain this phenomenon.

Costs were the second identified factor in this paper. Comparing the costs between on-premise and SaaS ERP systems was noted to be difficult, as they are different by nature and direct comparisons are not always possible. However, the overall indication was that SaaS ERP will not bring any cost benefits for large companies: even with no upfront investments in SaaS ERP the total cost of ownership is expected to remain on the same level as with on-premise systems. Over time SaaS ERP may even cost more, as the higher monthly payments accumulate. Thus, any cost benefit that has been suggested for cloud ERP by previous research [5] was absent in this study. Some academics have also proposed that SaaS ERP may be more expensive for large enterprises as they use multiple modules and have a large number of users [21]. We agree that expensive costs are an adoption factor here but also conclude that this is more related to SaaS pricing strategies than the amount of use. None of the interviewed companies were using a pay-per-use model, as they had negotiated longer contracts with larger discounts based on their business volume. Still, the costs were indicated to be at least on the same lever or even higher over time than operating similar functions and user volumes in an on-premise system. As most of the interviewed companies were outsourcing their on-premise systems operations to external partners, this would indicate that either IT companies which offer SAP platform operations are able to provide customer exclusive ERP systems more cost-effectively than SAP's public cloud offerings, or that SAP is charging a significantly higher profit margin for cloud capacity. Whatever cost benefits there might exist from the economies of scale behind SAP's vast cloud operations capacity, it seems to be not passing on to the customers side. The results also indicated that SaaS ERP implementation is comparably large as an effort to an on-premise ERP implementation. This affects vendor lock-in as depicted by [4], since cloud ERP is not practical to be rented for a short time at least in the scope of large enterprises.

Technical limitations are also a key factor which affects SaaS ERP adoption. For example, network latency is a clearly measurable technical limitation that may prevent SaaS adoption. Especially large enterprises utilize certain information systems that require low latency, such as systems that control heavily automated assembly lines or warehouses. Thus, latency can be a direct obstacle which prevents a company from adopting SaaS ERP, as latency sensitive systems like on-site automation devices may restrict how far away the ERP system can physically be located. While network latency is relatively easy to measure and define a technical requirement that a SaaS system must meet, customization limitations may be much harder to evaluate. Although customization possibilities are clearly more limited with public cloud SaaS ERP than in on-premise, these processes are based on industry best-practices while on-premise systems are typically more tailored to customers own process definitions [24]. Customization limitations should also be considered as a question of how the company is able to leverage competitive advantage from heavily tailored ERP processes. A generic SaaS ERP template will better fit processes where heavy customization would only bring low added value or differentiation from competitors. This may also help to explain why SME's have more widely adapted SaaS ERP, as they may be more content with the out-of-the-box business processes. Large enterprises views are thus somewhat different on SaaS ERP adoption than SME's, which is natural as their requirements and resources are considerably different. SaaS adoption for large enterprises may be a more peculiar phenomenon, as the companies are mostly running on-premise systems which are tailored to create added value and competitive advantages for their core business processes. When a company is already running their own streamlined business processes in a tailored ERP system, it can be perceived as a significant risk to change the way of working in order to fit the predefined processes of SaaS ERP. We conclude that for large companies, SaaS ERP may be more suitable on business processes that are not mission-critical or providing a competitive advantage for the company.

Information security is also a technical limitation that can affect cloud adoption [9, 21], however our results indicate that large companies seem well prepared for cloud related security challenges and their trust in cloud vendors technical capabilities are high. Security was perceived as part of the implementation phase, which needs to be addressed with rigor like any other technical area. While some researchers have proposed cloud insecurity of being the main concern for large companies preventing cloud ERP adoption [21], we perceive security issues as technical tasks which are covered before or during the system implementation. From a technical point of view, large companies possess the resources for ensuring cybersecurity, but this is equally complementing SaaS adoption as the companies can understand their technical security requirements and appreciate the SaaS vendors competencies.

Finally, cloud characteristics was recognized as the fourth factor which affects SaaS ERP adoption for large companies. The essential characteristics – such as mobile access, improved user interfaces, and continuous technical innovations [3, 21] – are indeed desirable features for ERP systems. These might also moderate on the other factors: for example, if cloud characteristics are valued highly, it may help adoption even if the costs of the system would increase. However, from an adoption point-of-view some of these characteristics can also prevent the cloud ERP adoption of large companies. Frequent upgrades cause extensive testing efforts especially for large companies, as they require their own extensions and vast integrations to external systems. SMEs rarely have similar requirements, which is yet another difference to large companies on SaaS ERP adoption. While the promise of continuous new innovations to a SaaS ERP system may initially sound appealing, the reality of the required testing workload may hinder adoption. ERP upgrades in general require rigorous and costly testing efforts [44, 45]. As the research results also indicate that large companies are hesitant to upgrade their current on-premise ERP systems, the frequent upgrades and their required testing efforts can be seen as a disadvantage of SaaS ERP. These results and their properties are summarized in Table 2 below.

Although currently these factors are preventing a full-scale adoption of public cloud SaaS ERP for large companies, this may very well change in the near future. As cloud services evolve, their technical maturity will help to address some important factors, such as guaranteeing business continuity. This study is contributing to the field of information systems research by helping to fill the gap on which factors affect large companies SaaS ERP adoption. It highlights the differing requirements of large companies when compared to SME's, while helping to understand how cloud vendors could be fulfilling their specific needs. We recognize that the research has some limitations, as it is only focused on one SaaS ERP vendor and large companies that are based on a single country, even though their operations are international. Further research could be conducted on evaluating how different cloud vendors are able to answer these requirements, as well

Table 2. Factors affecting SaaS ERP adoption.

Factor	Properties	Main drivers for large companies
Service quality	System availability	System needs to be available during critical business hours, SLA's need to guarantee sufficient availability and compensation for breach
	Support transparency	Trustworthiness of support process, companies require incidents to be handled and communicated visibly
	Personality of support	Familiar experts who the company can contact immediately, instead of an anonymous incident channel
Costs	Implementation effort	Amount of time and money required to install and configure the system
	Operational costs	Required fees and labor hours to operate the system
	Total Cost of Ownership	The total costs for the complete lifecycle of the system, including implementation, operation and decommissioning
Technical limitations	Network latency	Latency challenges between on-prem legacy system integrations or on-site systems, such as automation lines
	Customizing capabilities	Amount of customizing that can be performed in the information system
	Flexibility	How well the predefined, best-practices business processes are fit for the company and how much they can be enhanced
	Information security	Technical information security, required amount of security enhancements, or the perceived security threats with cloud systems
Cloud characteristics	Ease of use	New applications and user interfaces enhancing end user experience
	Ubiquitous access	Access the cloud system widely and easily, e.g. without connecting VPN
	Mobile applications	Specific mobile friendly applications available on handheld devices
	Frequent upgrades	System upgrades providing the latest innovations while also requiring constant testing of e.g. integrations and customer enhancements

as in various companies in different geographical areas to understand the phenomenon more deeply.

Acknowledgements. We would like to thank Pasi Tyrväinen and Mirja Pulkkinen for their valuable and constructive comments that helped to improve this research paper. We would also like to give a special thank you to Mari Kinnunen for her suggestions and encouragement during the research.

References

1. Buyya, R., Yeo, C.S., Venugopal, S., Broberg, J., Brandic, I.: Cloud computing and emerging it platforms: vision, hype, and reality for delivering computing as the 5th utility. Futur. Gener. Comput. Syst. **25**(6), 599–616 (2009)
2. Buyya, R., et al.: A manifesto for future generation cloud computing: research directions for the next decade. ACM Comput. Surv. **51**(5), 1–38 (2018)
3. Choudhary, V.: Comparison of software quality under perpetual licensing and software as a service. J. Manag. Inf. Syst. **24**(2), 141–165 (2007)
4. Ojala, A.: Adjusting software revenue and pricing strategics in the era of cloud computing. J. Syst. Softw. **122**, 40–51 (2016)
5. Johansson, B., Ruivo, P.: Exploring factors for adopting ERP as SaaS. Procedia Technol. **9**(2013), 94–99 (2013)
6. Mell, P., Grance, T.: The NIST Definition of Cloud Computing. National Institute of Standards and Technology. Special Publication, pp. 800–145 (2011). doi:https://doi.org/10.6028/NIST. SP.800-145
7. Marston, S., Li, Z., Bandyopadhyay, S., Zhang, J., Ghalsasi, A.: Cloud computing—the business perspective. Decis. Support Syst. **51**(1), 176–189 (2011)
8. Karabek, M.R., Kleinert, J., Pohl, A.: Cloud services for SMEs–evolution or revolution? Business+ Innovation **1**, 26–33 (2011). https://doi.org/10.1365/s35789-011-0005-4
9. Peng, G.C.A., Gala, C.: Cloud ERP: a new dilemma to modern organisations? J. Comput. Inf. Syst. **54**(4), 22–30 (2014)
10. Boillat, T., Legner, C.: From on-premise software to cloud services: the impact of cloud computing on enterprise software vendors' business models. J. Theor. Appl. Electron. Commer. Res. **8**(3), 39–58 (2013)
11. Scavo, F., Newton, B., Longwell, M.: Choosing between cloud and hosted ERP, and why it matters. Comput. Econ. Rep. **34**(8), 1–12 (2012)
12. Abd Elmonem, M.A., Nasr, E.S., Geith, M.H.: Benefits and challenges of cloud ERP systems– a systematic literature review. Future Comput. Inf. J. **1**(1–2), 1–9 (2016)
13. Lenart, A.: ERP in the cloud–benefits and challenges. In: Wrycza, S. (ed.) EuroSymposium on Systems Analysis and Design, pp. 39–50. Springer, Berlin (2011). https://doi.org/10.1007/978-3-642-25676-9_4
14. Castellina, N.: SaaS and Cloud ERP Trends, Observations, and Performance 2011. Analyst Insight (2011). https://www.meritsolutions.com/resources/whitepapers/Aberdeen-Research-SaaS-Cloud-ERP-Trands-2011.pdf
15. Bibi, S., Katsaros, D., Bozanis, P.: Business application acquisition: on-premise or SaaS-based solutions? IEEE Softw. **29**(3), 86–93 (2012)
16. Vithayathil, J.: Will cloud computing make the Information Technology (IT) department obsolete? Inf. Syst. J. **28**(4), 634–649 (2017)

17. Dillon, T., Wu, C., Chang, E.: Cloud computing: issues and challenges. 2010 24. In: IEEE International Conference on Advanced Information Networking and Applications, pp. 27–33. IEEE (2020)
18. Brydon, M., Vining, A.R.: Adoption, improvement, and disruption: predicting the impact of open source applications in enterprise software markets. J. Database Manage. **19**(2), 73–94 (2008)
19. Orosz, I., Selmeci, A., Orosz, T.: Software as a service operation model in cloud based ERP systems. In: 2019 IEEE 17th World Symposium on Applied Machine Intelligence and Informatics (SAMI), pp. 345–354. IEEE (2019)
20. Saa, P., Moscoso-Zea, O., Costales, A.C., Luján-Mora, S.: Data security issues in cloud-based Software-as-a-Service ERP. In: 2017 12th Iberian Conference on Information Systems and Technologies (CISTI), pp. 1–7. IEEE (2017)
21. Johansson, B., Alajbegovic, A., Alexopoulo, V., Desalermos, A.: Cloud ERP adoption opportunities and concerns: the role of organizational size. In: 2015 48th Hawaii International Conference on System Sciences, pp. 4211–4219. IEEE (2015)
22. Martens, B., Walterbusch, M., Teuteberg, F.: Costing of cloud computing services: a total cost of ownership approach. In: 2012 45th Hawaii International Conference on System Sciences, pp. 1563–1572. IEEE (2012)
23. Ojala, A.: Software renting in the era of cloud computing. In: 2012 IEEE Fifth International Conference on Cloud Computing, pp. 662–669. IEEE (2012)
24. Mijac, M., Picek, R., Stapic, Z.: Cloud ERP system customization challenges. In: Central European Conference on Information and Intelligent Systems, pp. 132–141 (2013)
25. Hustad, E., Haddara, M., Kalvenes, B.: ERP and organizational misfits: an ERP customization journey. Procedia Comput. Sci. **100**, 429–439 (2016)
26. Hofmann, P.: ERP is dead, long live ERP. IEEE Internet Comput. **12**(4), 84–88 (2008)
27. Gallardo, G., Hernantes, J., Serrano, N.: Designing SaaS for enterprise adoption based on task, company, and value-chain context. IEEE Internet Comput. **22**(4), 37–45 (2018)
28. Rodrigues, J., Ruivo, P., Johansson, B., Oliveira, T.: Factors for adopting ERP as SaaS amongst SMEs: the customers vs. Vendor point of view. Inf. Resour. Manage. J. **29**(4), 1–16 (2016)
29. Seethamraju, R.: Adoption of software as a service (SaaS) enterprise resource planning (ERP) systems in small and medium sized enterprises (SMEs). Inf. Syst. Front. **17**(3), 475–492 (2015)
30. Lewandowski, J., Salako, A.O., Garcia-Perez, A.: SaaS enterprise resource planning systems: challenges of their adoption in SMEs. In: 2013 IEEE 10th International Conference on e-Business Engineering, pp. 56–61. IEEE (2013)
31. Sánchez, J.L., Yagüe, A.: Competitive advantages of the ERP: new perspectives. In: Proceedings of the 11th International Conference on Product Focused Software, pp. 108–109, June 2010
32. Wu, L., Garg, S.K., Buyya, R.: SLA-based resource allocation for software as a service provider (SaaS) in cloud computing environments. In: 2011 11th IEEE/ACM International Symposium on Cluster, Cloud and Grid Computing, pp. 195–204. IEEE, May 2011
33. Rad, B.B., Diaby, T., Rana, M.E.: Cloud computing adoption: a short review of issues and challenges. In: Proceedings of the 2017 International Conference on E-commerce, E-Business and E-Government, pp. 51–55, June 2017
34. Frank, L., Luoma, E., Mazhelis, O., Pulkkinen, M., Tyrväinen, P.: Software business in the telecommunications sector. Telecommun. Econ. **7216**, 148–155 (2012)
35. Yin, R.K.: Case Study Research: Design and Methods, 3rd edn. SAGE Publishing, Thousand Oaks (2003)
36. Eisenhardt, K.M.: Building theories from case study research. Acad. Manag. Rev. **14**(4), 532–550 (1989)

37. Darke, P., Shanks, G., Broadbent, M.: Successfully completing case study research: combining rigour, relevance and pragmatism. Inf. Syst. J. **8**(4), 273–289 (1998)

38. Tracy, S.J.: Qualitative Research Methods: Collecting Evidence, Crafting Analysis, Communicating Impact. John Wiley & Sons, West Sussex (2013)

39. Knoch, C.: Qualitative data analysis with Microsoft Word comments & Python (updated) (2020). https://carstenknoch.com/2020/02/qualitative-data-analysis-with-micros oft-word-comments-python-updated/

40. Rowe, F.: What literature review is not: diversity, boundaries and recommendations (2014)

41. Templier, M., Paré, G.: A framework for guiding and evaluating literature reviews. Commun. Assoc. Inf. Syst. **37**(1), 6 (2015)

42. Miles, M.B., Huberman, A.M.: Qualitative Data Analysis: An Expanded Sourcebook. Sage (1994)

43. Frechtling, J.A., Sharp, L.M. (eds.): User-Friendly Handbook for Mixed Method Evaluations. Diane Publishing (1997)

44. Beatty, R.C., Williams, C.D.: ERP II: best practices for successfully implementing an ERP upgrade. Commun. ACM **49**(3), 105–109 (2006)

45. Ng, C.S.P., Gable, G.G.: Maintaining ERP packaged software–a revelatory case study. J. Inf. Technol. **25**(1), 65–90 (2010)

Design of an Evaluation System of Limb Motor Function Using Inertial Sensor

Chengqian Wang[1], Liang Lu[2], Peng Zhang[2], Mingxu Sun[1], Tingting Wang[1], and Xuqun Pei[3](✉)

[1] University of Jinan, Nanxinzhuangxi Road 336, Jinan 250022, Shandong, China
[2] Jinan Minzu Hospital, Wenhuaxi Road 125, Shandong 250012 Jinan, China
[3] Jinan Central Hospital, Jiefang Road 105, Jinan 250013, Shandong, China
13370582962@163.com

Abstract. Tailoring the training process according to recovery potentials has gained importance in the process of training. Nowadays, the intelligent hospital is coming into sight, and the traditional rehabilitation assessment has been unable to meet the development of the times. In order to meet the demand, a dynamic assessment of the performance of the recovery process is required. Cloud computing can calculate and store massive data, and its application in the evaluation system of limb motor function using inertial sensor can meet the requirements of hospitals for data security, resource sharing, maintainability and so on. In order to accurately assess rehabilitation for the upper limb, the inertial sensors are used to collect the real-time limb movement data of patients. In the next steps, an evaluation of the patients rehabilitation exercises results is presented, saved and statistically analyzed. The assessment can help achieve more individualized patient care. Therefore, this paper designs an evaluation system of limb motor function using inertial sensor, which effectively improves the efficiency of rehabilitation assessment. The evaluation system increases the real-time action display on the screen to improve the practicability of the evaluation system. At present, the evaluation system is in the development stage, and a lot of data and work are still needed to improve the evaluation system.

Keywords: Rehabilitation assessment · Inertial sensor · Cloud computing

1 Introduction

In the process of rehabilitation assessment, the majority of rehabilitation assessments are carried out manually by rehabilitation physicians, which is highly susceptible to subjective factors that can lead to inaccurate assessment results. Accurate and reliable results of rehabilitation assessment play an important role in the rehabilitation of limb motor dysfunction patients [1]. The dynamic movement evaluation of limb motor dysfunction patients is helpful to provide customized rehabilitation training plan [2]. After rehabilitation training, limb motor dysfunction patients pay more and more attention to accurate rehabilitation assessment results.

© ICST Institute for Computer Sciences, Social Informatics and Telecommunications Engineering 2022
Published by Springer Nature Switzerland AG 2022. All Rights Reserved
M. R. Khosravi et al. (Eds.): CloudComp 2021, LNICST 430, pp. 143–148, 2022.
https://doi.org/10.1007/978-3-030-99191-3_11

In recent years, with the increasing of population aging, the number of limb motor dysfunction patients are also increasing, and the collected rehabilitation assessment data is also increasing. Wearable sensors increasingly being used for human movement analysis [3]. Therefore, a evaluation system of limb motor function using inertial sensor is designed. The evaluation system measures the limb movement information of patients in real time using inertial sensors, and then calculates and stores the results of the rehabilitation assessment. Rehabilitation physicians can use the results of rehabilitation assessment calculated by the evaluation system as a reference for formulating rehabilitation training plans.

2   Design of the Rehabilitation Assessment Module

2.1   General Structure Design

The evaluation system of limb motor function using inertial sensor is a data acquisition and display system combining software and hardware. The hardware of the evaluation system is inertial sensor, and unity3d is used as the data display and processing platform in PC. After a systematic requirement analysis, the general structure of the evaluation system for limb motor dysfunction based on inertial sensor is shown in Fig. 1.

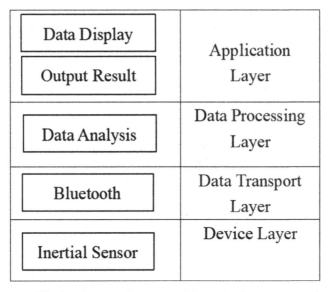

Fig. 1. The general structure of the evaluation system.

Device Layer. The device layer is located at the bottom of the evaluation system and is the foundation of the whole system. The hardware device used in the device layer is inertial sensor, which is used to measure the limb movement information of patients during rehabilitation assessment. Quaternion is used to describe the attitude information of the inertial sensor in reference coordinate system.

Data Transport Layer. The data transport layer is located in the upper layer of the device layer. The main function of the transport layer is to transmit the data collected by the device layer to the computer through Bluetooth.

Data Processing Layer. The data processing layer is located in the upper layer of the data transport layer. The data processing layer receives the data transmitted by the data transport layer. After the received data is processed by the data processing layer, more accurate rehabilitation assessment data can be obtained. Finally, the results of the rehabilitation assessment were calculated.

Application Layer. The application layer is at the top of the whole system. The application layer includes two modules for the data display and the output result. The application layer receives the rehabilitation assessment data and results processed by the data processing layer. The evaluation system drives the human model for real-time movement simulation based on rehabilitation assessment data and presents The results of rehabilitation evaluation in the form of line chart.

2.2 Realization of Upper Limb Real Time Motion Simulation

Human joint motion data is an important parameter for rehabilitation assessment [4]. So the inertial sensor is used to measure the motion data of the joint. The real-time motion simulation of upper limb involves many degrees of freedom of joints, so it is the most important part of human motion analysis. The upper limb consists of the shoulder joint, the elbow joint and the wrist joint. The shoulder joint has three degrees of freedom. The elbow has one degree of freedom. The wrist has two degrees of freedom.

Wearing of Sensor. Before the rehabilitation data is measured, the inertial sensor should be worn in the corresponding position, and ensure that each inertial sensor is on the same horizontal plane. The wearing of inertial sensor is shown in Fig. 2. The inertial sensors are attached to the body with straps.

As shown in Fig. 3. The positions of shoulder joint, elbow joint and wrist joint are A_1, A_2 and A_3 in the global coordinate system. The four-dimensional vectors of upper arm is $\overrightarrow{A_1A_2}(0, 0, 0, -len_{A_1A_2})$. The four-dimensional vectors of fore arm is $\overrightarrow{A_2A_3}(0, 0, 0, -len_{A_2A_3})$.

Measurement of Shoulder Range of Motion. The range of motion of shoulder joint was measured by adduction, abduction, flexion, extension, internal pronation and external pronation. To define $\overrightarrow{A_1A_2}^*$ as a vector of $\overrightarrow{A_1A_2}$. The subscript u indicates that the motion data of the upper arm is calculated. The x_u indicates the motion data of the upper arm in the x-axis direction. The y_u indicates the motion data of the upper arm in the y-axis direction. The z_u indicates the motion data of the upper arm in the z-axis direction. The $q_{u(t)}$ represents the upper arm motion data measured at moment t and expressed as a quaternion. Using the following (1):

$$\overrightarrow{A_1A_2}^* \, (0, x_u, y_u, z_u) = q_{u(t)} \otimes \overrightarrow{A_1A_2} \otimes q_{u(t)}^{-1} \tag{1}$$

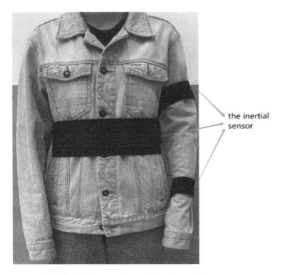

Fig. 2. The wearing of the inertial sensor.

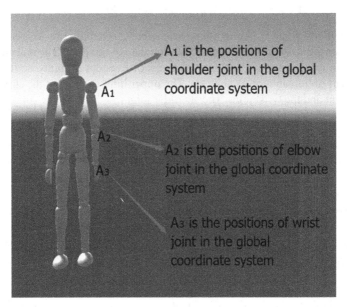

Fig. 3. The character model.

The real-time position of the upper arm in the global coordinate system is calculated as following (2):

$$P_u = (x_u, y_u, z_u) \tag{2}$$

The P_u indicates the position of the upper arm in the global coordinate system.

The real-time motion simulation of shoulder joint range of motion is shown in Fig. 4.

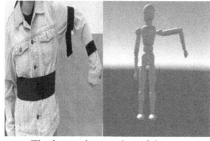

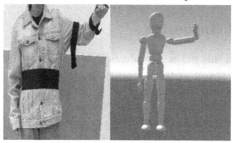

a. The flexion of the shoulder joint.

b. The extension of the shoulder joint.

c. The internal pronation of the
shoulder joint.

d. The external pronation of the
shoulder joint.

Fig. 4. The real-time motion simulation of shoulder joint range of motion measurement.

Measurement of Elbow Range of Motion. The range of motion of the elbow joint is measured by flexion and extension. To define $\overrightarrow{A_2A_3}^*$ as a vector of $\overrightarrow{A_2A_3}$. The subscript u indicates that the motion data of the fore arm is calculated. The x_f indicates the motion data of the fore arm in the x-axis direction. The y_f indicates the motion data of the fore arm in the y-axis direction. The z_f indicates the motion data of the fore arm in the z-axis direction. The $q_{f(t)}$ represents the fore arm motion data measured at moment t and expressed as a quaternion. Using the following (3).

$$\overrightarrow{A_2A_3}^*(0, x_f, y_f, z_f) = q_{f(t)} \otimes \overrightarrow{A_2A_3} \otimes q_{f(t)}^{-1} \tag{3}$$

The real-time position of the forearm in the global coordinate system is calculated as following (4):

$$P_f = (x_f, y_f, z_f) \tag{4}$$

The P_f indicates the position of the fore arm in the global coordinate system.

The real-time motion simulation of elbow joint activity measurement is shown in Fig. 5.

a. The flexion of the elbow joint.   b. The extension of the elbow joint.

Fig. 5. The real-time motion simulation of elbow joint range of motion measurement.

3   Discussion

In this paper, a evaluation system that uses inertial sensors to measure rehabilitation assessment data and output rehabilitation assessment results is presented. The evaluation system still needs a lot of comparative experiments to improve the accuracy of the rehabilitation assessment results output by the evaluation system. A large amount of data was generated during the rehabilitation assessment. Cloud computing can effectively handle the huge amounts of data generated in healthcare [5]. In the future, it is expected that the evaluation system will be deployed on cloud computing platforms, making it possible to benefit more users.

4   Conclusion

The effective management of rehabilitation assess process is helpful to improve the work efficiency of rehabilitation physicians. In the boring process of rehabilitation, the character model of real-time simulation on the screen also improves the rehabilitation enthusiasm of patients. The evaluation system of limb motor function using inertial sensor can provide rehabilitation assessment for limb motor dysfunction patients and save these rehabilitation data. Rehabilitation physicians can log in to the evaluation system at any time to view the rehabilitation data, which reflects the good application effect of the evaluation system.

References

1. Zhang, M., Sun, J., Wang, Q., Liu, D.: Walking rehabilitation evaluation based on gait analysis. J. Biosci. Med. **8**(6), 215–223 (2020)
2. Meziani, Y., Morère, Y., Hadj-Abdelkader, A., Benmansour, M., Bourhis, G.: Towards adaptive and finer rehabilitation assessment: a learning framework for kinematic evaluation of upper limb rehabilitation on an Armeo Spring exoskeleton. Control Eng. Pract. **111**, 104804 (2021)
3. Chander, H., et al.: Wearable stretch sensors for human movement monitoring and fall detection in ergonomics. Int. J. Environ. Res. Public Health **17**(10), 3554 (2020)
4. Xiong, B., et al.: Determining the online measurable input variables in human joint moment intelligent prediction based on the hill muscle model. Sensors **20**(4), 1185 (2020)
5. Rajabion, L., Shaltooki, A.A., Taghikhah, M., Ghasemi, A., Badfar, A.: Healthcare big data processing mechanisms: the role of cloud computing. Int. J. Inf. Manage. **49**, 271–289 (2019)

Towards a GPU-Accelerated Open Source VDI for OpenStack

Manuel Bentele[✉], Dirk von Suchodoletz, Manuel Messner,
and Simon Rettberg

Computer Center, University of Freiburg, Freiburg im Breisgau, Germany
{manuel.bentele,dirk.von.suchodoletz,
manuel.messner,simon.rettberg}@rz.uni-freiburg.de
https://www.rz.uni-freiburg.de

Abstract. Starting from summarizing preexisting work and technologies, this paper introduces the necessary considerations and steps to develop a fully Open Source Virtual Desktop Infrastructure (OSVDI) on top of OpenStack. Unlike other already available open-source solutions, a Virtual Desktop Infrastructure (VDI) with access for 3D or video rendering using Graphics Processing Units (GPUs) caters to various use cases like GPU-accelerated desktop environments, remote visualization, or large-scale desktop virtualization. Such use cases require the integration of special-purpose hardware in cloud servers and the sharing of devices as well as resource scheduling, a user interface for session or resource selection, and efficient remote transport. The envisioned OSVDI is yet in its infancy growing from previous work to provide efficient large-scale remote access to existing PC pools in the bwLehrpool service for various teaching and learning environments. This preliminary cloud provides insights and experience to design the necessary (additional) OpenStack components and configurations.

Keywords: VDI · OpenStack · Desktop virtualization · Remote access

1 Motivation

Like other IT services, the traditional desktop computer and workstations are getting centralized and cloud-operated as well. This paradigm shift supersedes decentralized, distributed machine deployment and operation. The advantages cover flexible provisioning of a wide range of software environments, reduced administration, better access control, higher security to more efficient and flexible hardware and software utilization as well as fostering of green IT efforts. Plus, it caters to the expectations of modern home office schemes offered by an increasing number of employers.

The modern-day term widely used for this kind of machine operation is Virtual Desktop Infrastructure (VDI). In an abstract and generic view, a VDI is

M. R. Khosravi et al. (Eds.): CloudComp 2021, LNICST 430, pp. 149–164, 2022.
https://doi.org/10.1007/978-3-030-99191-3_12

composed of a set of interlinked components, requiring a (virtual) machine or compute node with graphic rendering capabilities (software rendering or dedicated GPU). For scalable infrastructures, the focus lies on Virtual Machines (VMs) since they allow the most flexible deployments and allow the implementation of security designs as well as the separation of different access and data domains. Further components provide the preprocessing of rendered desktop content: Grab a framebuffer from a VM, encode it as a video stream, and transport video streams to the remote (thin) client over the LAN. To host multiple clients, various management and multiplexing services are required. Finally, modules for authentication, Quality of Service (QoS) for networks, or stream encryption may play a role as well, but will not be covered in this paper. Any VDI requires an interplay of several components and building blocks in hardware and software. Typically, the commercial vendors bundle those modules and attach a label to it to market them as a product.[1] There is no direct equivalent in the open-source domain but a range of components that could be combined to achieve similar objectives are mostly there [17]. Often these approaches lack seamless integration and ease of setup.

The authors got involved with the VDI topic when developing remote access to original (emulated) computer environments [19] or when providing remote access to hundreds of PC pool machines offering a wide range of teaching and learning software environments provided through the bwLehrpool service [2]. The latter provides a perfect baseline and playground to discuss and develop ideas for an OSVDI. Further use cases can profit from an OSVDI. This includes remote teaching scenarios on standard IT setups, access to high-performance analysis workstations for graphical workflows in various domains in science, as well as standard desktop environments in labs and offices. Additionally, the typical remote visualization scenarios in High Performance Computing (HPC) clusters would profit, where VirtualGL[2] lacks appropriate support. A VDI provides a building block to (re)centralize computer infrastructures and allow a much more flexible utilization of resources. Further, we got involved in the PePP project,[3] promoting the idea of using controlled IT environments in electronic assessments requiring VDI solutions to host up to several hundred students in parallel.

The paper will be structured as follows. We will provide an updated overview on existing implementations of GPU virtualization, relevant aspects around remote access protocols, and desktop access including provided interaction and transport channels. From the summary of the state-of-the-art, we try to identify all relevant gaps and provide a first outline of the envisioned setup and structure of the OpenStack VDI extension to be developed.

---

[1] Desktop virtualization is dominated for the time being by Citrix or VMware products [6]. These commercial solutions are seldom attractive for research and education purposes as they involve proprietary components and come with significant costs.

[2] See https://www.virtualgl.org.

[3] Partnership for innovative E-Assessments – Joint Project of the Baden-Württemberg Universities, see https://www.hnd-bw.de/projekte/pepp.

2   Related Work

The general idea of remote access to desktop environments is nothing new, dating back to the era of X11/XDM, LTSP, Virtual Network Computing (VNC), XEN/Citrix, VMware, and the Windows Terminal Server. A couple of different implementations evolved to provide the graphical output of the desktop over LAN or WAN connections to the user and user input back to the central infrastructure. Depending on the actual protocol, additional channels like uni- or multi-directional audio, USB redirection, or optical drive access are implemented as well. Before suggesting further development and improvement of existing components, we summarize the state-of-the-art for relevant modules required for an OSVDI.

2.1   GPU Virtualization

Virtualization of GPUs has become mandatory, starting with the evolution of full machine virtualization to render and obtain a machine's graphical output. Nowadays, there are several approaches to virtualize GPUs for VMs as presented in [17,22,23] and depicted in Fig. 1. All these approaches aim to abstract GPUs either by emulation of full GPU hardware or by virtualization of GPUs.

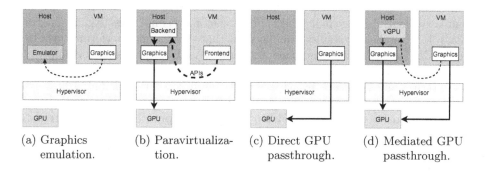

(a) Graphics emulation.   (b) Paravirtualization.   (c) Direct GPU passthrough.   (d) Mediated GPU passthrough.

Fig. 1. GPU virtualization approaches.

In the early beginning, the *emulation* of graphic devices, especially VGA adapters, evolved to provide virtual GPUs to VMs. Most virtualizer solutions, like Quick Emulator (QEMU), Virtualbox, or VMware Workstation, provide legacy support for graphics emulation according to the approach visualized in Fig. 1a. The graphics emulation is provided by an emulator on the host system that emulates a framebuffer for graphics rendering. The emulator does not require access to any physical GPU resulting in increased flexibility and scalability. However, the low graphics performance through missing GPU acceleration is a major limitation for graphics-intensive applications [22].

In order to improve the graphics performance, optimizations like *paravirtualization* (Fig. 1b) have been developed [8]. Paravirtualization improves the emulation approach by the use of predefined Application Programming Interfaces (APIs), which are exposed by the host system. Those APIs provide the functionality to offload graphic commands from a graphics frontend driver in a VM to a graphics backend on the host system (which is often referred to as API forwarding). The computation of graphic commands takes place in the graphics backend, which itself uses a GPU of the host system for GPU-accelerated rendering. GPU-accelerated rendering increases the overall graphics performance compared to pure emulation [8], but requires the host system to provide access to a physical GPU through a suitable graphics driver. This approach does not allow a VM to acquire a physical GPU directly.

To accelerate graphics performance further, a *direct GPU passthrough* can be implemented as shown in Fig. 1c. This approach allows a VM to directly access a physical GPU using hardware capabilities for direct assignment of I/O devices, e.g. an I/O Memory Management Unit (IOMMU). These capabilities provide a hardware-based memory address mapping to map GPU-related device addresses and interrupts into the memory space of a VM without the need for any software-based mapping implementation. A major advantage is the fast and transparent access to the entire GPU. Therefore, a VM is only required to use the native graphics driver to be able to directly access the physical framebuffer and rendering capabilities of the GPU. A drawback here is the fact that the GPU resources (e.g. framebuffer) are entirely and statically assigned to the VM and cannot be shared with the host system. This limitation can be circumvented explicitly using dedicated shared memory technologies (e.g. in *Looking Glass*[4]). Nevertheless, results from [3] show that the graphics performance of the direct GPU passthrough approach accelerates VDI performance and improves user experience.

A rather novel concept to achieve GPU resource sharing among a host system and several VMs while preserving direct access to the GPU is implemented as *gVirt*, also known as *Intel GVT-g* [22]. This approach is often referred to as *mediated GPU passthrough* and is visualized in Fig. 1d. Following this approach, resources of a physical GPU can be partitioned into Virtual GPU (vGPU) instances. Each of these vGPU instances is a fully virtualized GPU providing its own framebuffer and rendering capabilities. All vGPU instances are managed by the host system and can be acquired and accessed by any VM or the host system itself (e.g. to share a framebuffer). A VM has direct access to the physical GPU resources of its acquired vGPU. The partitioning can either take place temporal or spatial. Intel GVT-g implements temporal partitioning in a time-shared manner (scheduling), whereas the latest dedicated GPU products (e.g. A100 MIG) from Nvidia implement spatial partitioning without any scheduling. Both partitioning methods increase flexibility, scalability, and efficiency, especially for graphic workloads that do not fully saturate the entire compute capacity of a GPU. Besides flexibility, evaluation results for the mediated GPU passthrough approach show, that GPU workloads achieve almost native performance [22].

---

[4] See https://looking-glass.io.

2.2   Video Encoding and Decoding

Any graphics output of each VM as part of a VDI is available as a stream of images in a raw framebuffer format. Without proper preprocessing and compression, such a stream requires an increasingly high network bandwidth on an increasing resolution during the real-time transport to a remote thin-client (e.g. 3+ Gbit/s for Full HD). But network bandwidth is often limited in a WAN, even in a LAN, especially if the network requirements for a VDI are underestimated [16]. Therefore, a preprocessing and adjustable encoding of the framebuffer as a compressed video stream is necessary to lower the overall network throughput per virtual desktop instance while preserving a high display quality for an acceptable Quality of Experience (QoE).

While the traditional remote transport protocols mainly use variants of JPEG encoding, this is less suitable to encode fast-changing video or 3D content from a virtual desktop session [10]. For that purpose, variants of video encoding are used, most widely the Advanced Video Coding (AVC) [4] and the High Efficiency Video Coding (HEVC) [5]. AVC, also referred to as H.264 or MPEG-4 Part 10, is a video compression standard based on block-oriented, motion-compensated integer-DCT coding. HEVC, also known as H.265 and MPEG-H Part 2, is a video compression standard designed as part of the MPEG-H project as a successor to AVC, optimized for high resolutions beyond high definition video formats [20]. Both codecs achieve high compression rates resulting in low network bandwidth. Like many other codecs, AVC and HEVC can be configured and adjusted by several parameters. For example, there is a parameter for video quality that influences the network bandwidth and QoE.

For an OSVDI, it is important that there are free and open-source implementations of video codecs. The open-source library *libavcodec*[5] implements encoding and decoding for AVC and HEVC based on the *x264*[6] and *x265*[7] software library. In addition to that, libavcodec contains decoder and sometimes encoder implementations of several other proprietary codecs, for which no public specification has been released. As such, a significant reverse engineering effort is part of libavcodec development.

Video encoding could be sped up significantly involving specialized hardware, which can be utilized by libavcodec, too. Most GPUs on the market for the server-side, as well as the client-side, contain already one or several built-in video encoder and decoder units. These units perform video encoding or decoding based on AVC or HEVC without wasting compute capacity of a CPU. If further video codecs are considered for the development of an OSVDI, the hardware acceleration for that codec should be checked first on all intended VDI devices. This scrutiny ensures an efficient video encoding or decoding with a high QoE even on low-power remote (thin) clients. Alternatively, if hardware acceleration for a specific codec is missing, an automatic codec selection is conceivable. Such an automatism preserves compatibility, especially for legacy remote (thin) clients

---

[5] libavcodec is part of the FFmpeg project, http://ffmpeg.org.

[6] See https://www.videolan.org/developers/x264.html.

[7] See https://www.videolan.org/developers/x265.html.

as well as flexibility for different type of clients like browser-based or dedicated remote (thin) clients.

2.3 Remote Desktop Transport

Transport Protocols. Remote desktop transport protocols specify the communication between a remote (virtual) machine and a (thin) client. Such transport protocols have in common, that they establish a bi-directional communication for data exchanges. One direction of the communication is used to transfer graphic output from a desktop session on a remote (virtual) machine to a (thin) client for visualization purposes. The second direction is used to transfer user inputs (e.g. mouse and keyboard events) from a user's (thin) client to the remote (virtual) machine. Both directions of the communication allow a seamless remote desktop interaction while facing the challenge for a low latency to achieve an acceptable QoE.

Transport protocols for remote desktops can be characterized by their supported amount of graphics primitives for a transfer to a client. The VNC protocol [15] implements the Remote Framebuffer Protocol (RFB) [14]. RFB works at the framebuffer level and watches for bitmap changes on a (virtual) machine's framebuffer. Then, the protocol streams those bitmap updates block by block to the client. Therefore, RFB uses a single graphics primitive to update bitmaps on a certain screen location which results in high network bandwidth and poor video performance [12]. To improve video performance, a VNC setup can be extended with a VNC proxy accelerator as shown in [21]. The OpenStack cloud platform contains a built-in VNC implementation called *noVNC*.[8] noVNC provides a web client for VNC and performs worse than the external Guacamole VNC implementation [3].

A similar protocol to RFB is the Thin-Client Internet Computing (THINC) protocol. THINC implements more low level graphic primitives which improves RFB and results in a better video performance [1], which even outperforms older Remote Desktop Protocol (RDP) versions. RDP is an proprietary remote desktop transport protocol from Microsoft and supports a significant number of high-level graphic primitives including optimizations like caching of already transferred primitives or support for glyphs. These optimizations offer a high QoE while preserving low network bandwidth for normal productivity desktop work [12] compared to VNC [24].

The Simple Protocol for Independent Computing Environments (SPICE)[9] is an open-source alternative to the proprietary RDP. Similar to RDP, SPICE supports high-level graphic primitives and is intended and optimized for remote access to VMs. Other optimizations include an additional display mode to improve QoE [11] and further interaction features like audio support, folder sharing, USB redirection, and reduced response time [9].

---

[8] See https://novnc.com.

[9] See https://www.spice-space.org.

Both protocols, RDP and SPICE, benefit from the transport of high-level graphic primitives and the rendering of those primitives on the (thin) clients. However, this is problematic if a user interacts with a graphic-intense application but its (thin) client is not equipped with the required rendering capabilities [10, 13,17]. In addition to that, both protocols are not very suitable for large desktop screen areas which change rapidly (e.g. during video playback) [7,10]. Therefore, work in [7] improves the QoE of SPICE by a motion-based JPEG compression for high-resolution video playbacks while lowering network bandwidth.

A completely different approach [18] for optimizing video playbacks is the detection of video streams within a desktop session. The detected video streams are directly transferred to the (thin) client. On client-side, those video streams are decoded and visualized using hardware acceleration. Using this approach, the network bandwidth is limited drastically during video playback. A similar concept pushes the detection of video streams one step further and encodes the entire remote desktop screen with the AVC/H.264 codec as video stream [25]. Compared to VNC, THINC, and RDP, this enhancement achieved the lowest latency in WAN environments while preserving a high QoE, even for graphic-intensive multimedia applications. A full remote desktop screen encoding is available for SPICE, too. It can be enabled using the additional *SPICE Streaming Agent* (See footnote 9) which runs in a VM. The agent captures and encodes the entire screen for a subsequent transport via SPICE. As of the writing of this paper, the agent based approach is marked as experimental and requires the guest system to be prepared.

(Thin) Clients. The term client refers to a device that allows a user to interact with a remote (virtual) desktop session. Therefore, a client is equipped with an application to receive desktop content from a remote (virtual) machine and send user input back to this machine. Such an application implements one or several remote desktop transport protocols like VNC, SPICE, or proprietary protocols (e.g. RDP) and is often realized as a web application (e.g. noVNC) or as a native (standalone) program (e.g. *virt-viewer*[10] which implements VNC and SPICE).

A client device is mostly a PC optimized for remote interaction, but can be a laptop, mobile phone, tablet, or single-board computer, too. If such a device is a low-performance computer, we call this type of client a *thin client* (e.g. a low-power tablet). Nowadays, mobile devices are equipped with a web browser. Therefore, a browser-based solution (web application) supports more client devices, whereas dedicated (thin) clients provide more interactions features, like USB redirection and multi-directional audio exchange. Nevertheless, most client devices support hardware-accelerated decoding of video streams (e.g. AVC or HEVC) and 3D rendering capabilities.

---

[10] See https://virt-manager.org.

2.4   Preliminary Work in bwLehrpool

The current pandemic demonstrated the need for adequately scaling online desktop solutions and thus pushed the implementation of a remote access for the bwLehrpool service based on Guacamole/VNC for both remote teaching and electronic exams. As an ad-hoc solution, the existing computer labs—closed due to the pandemic—were re-purposed as tiny cloud nodes, hosting one student session each. This posed the challenge of adequately assigning resources to students depending on workload; it could not be done dynamically as is possible on large servers in a cloud environment, but must be decided beforehand, since scheduling a student requiring a 3D-intense environment on a small PC with integrated graphics would lead to a sub-par experience. The solution was to partition the available machines by their specifications, and prompting the student with a selection screen (see Fig. 2a) when logging into the service, optionally protecting the more capable systems with a password.

(a) Step 1: PC pool selection.   (b) Step 2: VM image selection.

Fig. 2. Central entry point to bwLehrpool remote access through the browser and consecutive selection of a desired software environment.

Moving parts of the PC lab infrastructure to the cloud offers an expanded service based on familiar and longer-established environments, but ensures business continuity after students return to the labs post-pandemic. Resources can be provided very quickly on an ad-hoc basis so that the requirements of courses and the needs of students can be matched more precisely. These developments allow for ubiquitous teaching in presence and at home. Lecturers could benefit significantly if computer-based teaching infrastructure could be provided on-demand and tailored to students at any time, not limited to on-campus PC labs. Triggered by the increasing demand for high-performance and easy-to-use GPU resources, the bwGPUL project[11] focused on extending the existing bwLehrpool setup to access General Purpose GPUs (GPGPUs) from within VMs for tools that require hardware acceleration in the field of artificial intelligence and machine learning.

---

[11] See https://www.bwlehrpool.de/bwgpul. The project focused on the utilization of existing hardware to avoid too expensive installations of special server hardware.

2.5   OpenStack – Basis and Missing Pieces

OpenStack is a free cloud platform, most commonly deployed as Infrastructure-as-a-Service and licensed under the Apache License 2.0. The platform is composed of several components and services. Each component and service is responsible for a certain set of tasks and provides a RESTful API for communication. OpenStack's main focus is to provide an infrastructure for VMs, their storage and their network. Although, there are many components which expand this functionality in adjacent areas, like container management or bare-metal computation (see Table 1).

Table 1. Important OpenStack components

Nova	Management of VMs	**Neutron**	Software Defined Networks
Keystone	Authentication	**Horizon**	Official dashboard
Cinder	Block Storage	**Glance**	Base images and metadata

Relevant for our considerations is Nova. It manages the lifecycle (including scheduling) of the single VMs and therefore uses many APIs of other components. Nova offers a backend with a common interface to various lower level technologies (e.g. libvirt with Kernel-based Virtual Machine (KVM) infrastructure, XEN and Hyper-V) for providing VMs.

An integration of the mediated GPU passthrough technology is part of the OpenStack platform since version Queens,[12] although it's listed as experimental until version Train.[13] But even in the most up-to-date version, as of this writing, this module has severe caveats and are only available for the libvirt/KVM backend of Nova. (See footnote 13) Besides the mediated GPU passthrough support in OpenStack, there are other frameworks and tools, such as *LibVF.IO*,[14] available to orchestrate VMs and vGPU instances. LibVF.IO automates the creation and configuration of VMs and vGPU instances, but cannot provide any resource scheduling for cloud computing as OpenStack does.

There are VDI plugins available for OpenStack, such as plugins for Citrix XenDestop, Microsoft RDS, or Apache Guacamole.[15] Most plugins only address commercial VDI solutions, or in the case of Apache Guacamole, just support the VNC or RDP transport protocol. Native GPU acceleration and SPICE support are missing while using these plugins.

---

[12] See https://docs.openstack.org/nova/queens/admin/virtual-gpu.html.

[13] See https://docs.openstack.org/nova/train/admin/virtual-gpu.html.

[14] See https://libvf.io.

[15] See OpenStack Summit – Boston, MA (2017): https://www.openstack.org/videos/summits/boston-2017/virtual-desktop-infrastructure-vdi-with-openstack.

3   Proposed System Architecture

A cloud-based desktop infrastructure is more efficient and flexible than the earlier presented approach using commodity hardware from (unused) computer labs, as it allows the assigning and sharing of system resources between multiple VMs. Only in rare cases, where students require comparatively expensive computing resources, a more careful approach to resource allocation must be taken, e.g. for GPGPU tasks that have high Video RAM (VRAM) requirements that could only be fulfilled by a few expensive, specially equipped cloud nodes. For this reason, relevant information is pinned as meta-data to the VM in question, and the student's session is scheduled to a node depending on its meta-data. In the first Guacamole-based implementation of the bwLehrpool remote access, this was simply not possible, as the workflow required the student to first select the machine type they wanted to use (Fig. 2a), and only then be presented with the list of available VM (Fig. 2b), due to technical reasons and time constraints. Our vision for the next version is to have a public VDI web application where users log in, select a VM they want to use, and finally be scheduled to an appropriate cloud node. Additional logic could be added, e.g. limiting or skipping the VM selection for a student or user group depending on the time of day, day of the week, etc. This can be useful for conducting cloud-based e-exams, to prevent students from selecting a wrong VM, and also preventing users not belonging to the group of examinees from booting into that VM.

Our focus is mainly on the mediated GPU passthrough for further development of an OSVDI because this approach combines the flexibility of emulation and paravirtualization with the performance boost of direct GPU passthrough. Since an OSVDI is built on open-source software, we use the Linux operating system on the host system. Linux already provides the *mdev* subsystem and tools for mediated devices (vGPUs) and their device drivers. Using this subsystem has the major advantage that the Linux host system can manage all vGPUs and mediate shared access. This shared access allows the Linux host to access the framebuffer of a vGPU directly in a read-only manner with low overhead and latency (e.g. with *dma-buf*), which does not work out well with the direct GPU passthrough approach as part of an OSVDI. The direct access to a framebuffer of a vGPU means in terms of an OSVDI that the Linux host system can obtain the graphics output of any VM (virtual desktop) and can control those output for further processing and transfer to remote (thin) clients.

Access to a VM session can then be implemented via two methods: A browser-based approach, using modern technologies like WebAssembly, WebUSB and MediaDevices, resulting in immediate access from a wide range of devices like laptops, tablets and mobile phones. Still, the alternative approach of using a dedicated native application the user has to install first can offer even greater integration with the user's system, as well as yielding better performance depending on its use case.

We see at least three distinct use cases for an OSVDI in conjunction with OpenStack supplied through a suitable orchestration framework:

1. OpenStack user dedicated interactive VM in stateful operation as already implemented to get started via the dashboard and either using the native noVNC or some guest system remote access built-in like VNC or RDP.
2. (Large scale) virtual PC pool setups like offered in stateless mode by the bwLehrpool service with remote access. Users do not have an associated project or personal VM in OpenStack and thus requiring a dedicated entry point (Fig. 2a) and the possibility to choose the desired VM (Fig. 2b) kicked-off from a template. This scenario matches to the objectives of the respective sub-project in PePP.
3. Special purpose (powerful) virtual workstations offering tools for interactive image analysis dedicated through a booking system preallocating resources upon request (no direct relation between OpenStack users and persons requiring such a VM). Those virtual workstations could be offered through a selection list and mapped into the project concept of OpenStack owned by the lab requiring such software environments.

The first use case is already available in the standard setup, but the other two need some consideration regarding scheduling, resource allocation and means of access. A VDI integration into OpenStack would require to implement two modules: A service for managing all relevant VDI aspects and a Nova plugin connecting Nova and the VDI service.

VDI Service. Like the other OpenStack services, the VDI service offers a RESTful API for inter-service-communication. It's task is to manage jobs, their requirements and the lifecycle of VDI VMs via Nova. This can be broken down further into different aspects as follows.

Reservations. A common problem in clouds used in teaching is that often VMs are started once, being used once a week for an hour and idle in the meantime. As GPUs are a comparable expensive resource, a job based scheduling scheme, like in HPC, is more efficient. So GPUs can be reused during the idle times by other jobs.

Priorities. When looking at jobs, there are jobs with user interaction (e.g. classes), thus having a time dependency and jobs that just have to calculate some results. The service's task would be to prioritize the first category over the second one and make sure all needed resources are available when e.g. classes start by killing or pausing lower priority VMs and rescheduling them after e.g. the class has finished.

Job Handling and Registration. The last job of the service would be to handle the different jobs. Some discussion is needed whether an existing job scheduler should be included, or whether it should be implemented from scratch. Also, the service would offer a usable interface for job administration, as well as, registration and for passing all relevant requirements. This can be extended and simplified with an user interface, e.g. a dashboard. It does not necessarily need to be included into Horizon, because the job based scheduling suggested here is orthogonal to the normal usage of VMs in OpenStack.

Nova Plugin. The second module would be a Nova plugin which connects Nova and the VDI service during the VM creation process. It's task is to provide the service with all relevant metadata and properties as well as to respect (upcoming) jobs during normal VM scheduling.

4   Work Program and Planned Efforts

For the imagined OSVDI we plan three to five major development cycles and a minimum viable product approach. In a precursor the existing Guacamole bwLehrpool remote access should get improved through hardware rendering and stream encoding deploying the Intel GVT-g desktop graphic architecture together with the KVM infrastructure as a Linux-based hypervisor and produce an assessment of ease to use and stability. This will get implemented as an enhanced bwLehrpool service and prove the capabilities of the existing kernel drivers regarding GPU virtualization and hardware partitioning. We will use the SPICE client and Looking Glass as a prove and performance measure when accessing the virtual framebuffer for AVC/H.264 encoding and transport. Upon this we will explore how to encode with low latency, and how to send it to browsers and display the content there with low latency. This provides a possible baseline to check certain expectations and features before delivering similar services like those for an OpenStack cloud.

In a second milestone, we focus on a basic VNC model (leaving further improvements of remote access to parallel or later developments) in the cloud including orchestration of resources which covers the scope of our contribution to the PePP project. This milestone starts to extend the OpenStack framework for missing components and modules. First, we develop concepts for PC pool scheduling on shared and non-shared hardware resources. Further, this milestone deals with the challenges of a suitable access broker to distribute users requesting certain types of desktops onto a suitable VM. The access broker includes the provisioning of basic interaction channels starting from a single PC pool setup.

While the previous step focused on a basic integration and the outline of strategic components the next milestone focuses on the special hardware virtualization and integration parts both from the viewpoint of the guest systems and as encoding devices from the host perspective (Fig. 3). The remote access should enjoy at least an enhanced hardware-backed video stream transport model for the remote visual cloud. Later milestones should deal with further remote interaction channels and further features and improvements for typical VDI setups like suspend and resume of interactive desktop sessions.

Starting during the second milestone measures should be taken to form a sustainable community and financing concept around the proposed service. Both ongoing support, code maintenance and future development are to be supported through some stable organizational structure.

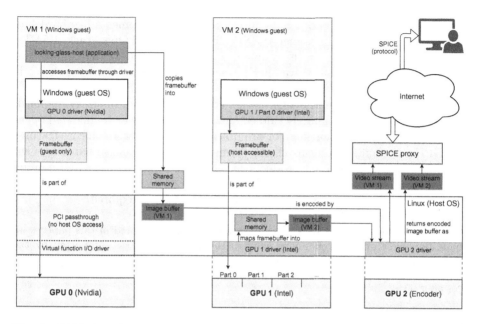

Fig. 3. GPU virtualization options and remote transport: direct GPU passthrough (left) or mediated GPU passthrough (middle) for windows guests, where a framebuffer (virtual desktop) of each windows guest is encoded as video stream (right), which is transferred to a remote client using the SPICE protocol.

5   Conclusion and Outlook

This paper intended not only to provide an exhaustive update on technology development around OSVDI but being at the same time a call for collaboration and feedback from further interested parties.[16] Up to now we were able to progress significantly in our first milestone exploring the foundations of the envisioned OSVDI. The bwLehrpool remote access including resource allocation upon demand runs smoothly with good user feedback. Starting into our new project on enabling large scale e-assessments we hope to run tasks in parallel to a certain degree to speed up development if resources permit. Certain tasks can get outsourced, e.g. the programming of well-defined software components, if additional funding is acquired. With the start of the PePP project we work on improving the project management wrt. an OSVDI solution by consolidating the code repository, pushing developments upstream to the benefit of the wider community including hardware vendors and software developers.

As a provider of large scale research infrastructures the computer center strives to integrate the activities into other evolving infrastructures like the German National Research Data Infrastructure (NFDI) and participates in further grant applications to bolster the efforts. Like in other software projects, we are

---

[16] See project information and resources at https://github.com/bwLehrpool/osvdi.

standing on the shoulders of giants and depend on developments like hardware virtualization in the Linux kernel, the SPICE protocol, and OpenStack. 1.5 FTE working at the endeavor at the moment and are financed for the coming two years. To gain sustainability, we offer proper support, maintenance of the code and collaboration with the relevant software projects and hardware vendors.[17]

On the hardware side, the VDI market strongly evolved around Nvidia hardware [17] which is unfortunately riddled with an incomplete or fragmented opensource Linux driver support and/or prohibitive software licenses on core features like GPU partitioning. A future chance stems from the tendency of hardware vendors to create more focused products for computational purposes and gaming or visualization. If there is e.g. a dedicated adapter just for video encoding this might simplify setups as no virtualization/partitioning is required.

Acknowledgments. Part of the activities and insights presented in this paper were made possible through preliminary work in the bwGPUL project supported by the Baden-Württemberg Ministry of Science, Research, and the Arts, the collaboration in the PePP project (FBM2020-VA-77-8-01241), and the German NFDI initiative (NFDI 7/1).

References

1. Baratto, R.A., Kim, L.N., Nieh, J.: THINC: a virtual display architecture for thin-client computing. In: Proceedings of the Twentieth ACM Symposium on Operating Systems Principles, SOSP 2005, pp. 277–290. Association for Computing Machinery, New York (2005). https://doi.org/10.1145/1095810.1095837

2. Bauer, J., Rettberg, S., Ritter, S., Rößler, C., von Suchodoletz, D., Münchenberg, J.: bwLehrpool - a jointly managed and financed inter-university it project. In: EDULEARN 2019 Proceedings. 11th International Conference on Education and New Learning Technologies, IATED, pp. 5548–5555 (2019). https://doi.org/10.21125/edulearn.2019.1360

3. Chang, C.H., Yang, C.T., Lee, J.Y., Lai, C.L., Kuo, C.C.: On construction and performance evaluation of a virtual desktop infrastructure with GPU accelerated. IEEE Access **8**, 170162–170173 (2020). https://doi.org/10.1109/ACCESS.2020.3023924

4. ITU-T: Advanced video coding for generic audiovisual services. Recommendation H.264 and ISO/IEC 14496-1. International Telecommunication Union (2003)

5. ITU-T: High efficiency video coding. Recommendation H.265 and ISO/IEC 23008-2. International Telecommunication Union (2013)

6. Jeong, D., Park, J., Lee, S., Kang, C.: Investigation methodology of a virtual desktop infrastructure for IoT. J. Appl. Math. **2015**, 1–10 (2015). https://doi.org/10.1155/2015/689870

7. Lan, Y., Xu, H.: Research on technology of desktop virtualization based on SPICE protocol and its improvement solutions. Front. Comput. Sci. **8**(6), 885–892 (2014). https://doi.org/10.1007/s11704-014-3410-5

---

[17] We try to open communication channels to the relevant hardware vendors through ongoing procurements for our cloud and high performance computing infrastructures.

8. Li, H., Jin, H., Liao, X.: Graphic acceleration mechanism for multiple desktop system based on virtualization technology. In: 2011 14th IEEE International Conference on Computational Science and Engineering, pp. 447–452 (2011). https://doi.org/10.1109/CSE.2011.82

9. Li, W., Wang, B., Yu, J., Zhu, C., Xiao, S., Sheng, J.: The optimization of transparent-desktop service mechanism based on SPICE. Concurr. Comput. Pract. Exp. **28**(18), 4543–4556 (2016). https://doi.org/10.1002/cpe.3858

10. Lin, Y., Kämäräinen, T., Di Francesco, M., Ylä-Jääski, A.: Performance evaluation of remote display access for mobile cloud computing. Comput. Commun. **72**, 17–25 (2015). https://doi.org/10.1016/j.comcom.2015.05.006

11. Liu, X., Zhu, M., Xiao, L., Jiang, Y.: A VM-shared desktop virtualization system based on OpenStack. AIP Conf. Proc. **1955**(1), 040137 (2018). https://doi.org/10.1063/1.5033801

12. Magaña, E., Sesma, I., Morató, D., Izal, M.: Remote access protocols for Desktop-as-a-Service solutions. PLoS One **14**(1), 1–28 (2019). https://doi.org/10.1371/journal.pone.0207512

13. Nehra, S., Kumar, C.: Enterprise virtual desktop infrastructure architecture on OpenStack cloud with lightweight directory access protocol. In: 2020 8th International Conference on Reliability, Infocom Technologies and Optimization (Trends and Future Directions) (ICRITO), pp. 1050–1055 (2020). https://doi.org/10.1109/ICRITO48877.2020.9197996

14. Richardson, T., Levine, J.: The Remote Framebuffer Protocol. RFC 6143, RFC Editor (2011). https://www.rfc-editor.org/rfc/rfc6143.txt

15. Richardson, T., Stafford-Fraser, Q., Wood, K., Hopper, A.: Virtual network computing. IEEE Internet Comput. **2**(1), 33–38 (1998). https://doi.org/10.1109/4236.656066

16. Rot, A., Chrobak, P.: Benefits, limitations and costs of IT infrastructure virtualization in the academic environment. Case study using VDI technology. In: Proceedings of the 13th International Conference on Software Technologies - ICSOFT, pp. 704–711. INSTICC, SciTePress, Porto (2018). https://doi.org/10.5220/0006934707380745

17. Smirnov, V.A., Korolev, E.V., Poddaeva, O.I.: Cloud environments with GPU virtualization: problems and solutions. In: International Conference on Data Mining, Electronics and Information Technology (DMEIT), pp. 147–154 (2015)

18. Su, K., Wang, Z., Lu, X., Chen, W.: An original-stream based solution for smoothly replaying high-definition videos in desktop virtualization systems. J. Vis. Lang. Comput. **25**(6), 676–683 (2014). https://doi.org/10.1016/j.jvlc.2014.09.009

19. von Suchodoletz, D., Rechert, K., Valizada, I.: Towards emulation-as-a-service: cloud services for versatile digital object access. Int. J. Digit. Curation **8**(1), 131–142 (2013). https://doi.org/10.2218/ijdc.v8i1.250

20. Sullivan, G.J., Ohm, J.R., Han, W.J., Wiegand, T.: Overview of the high efficiency video coding (HEVC) standard. IEEE Trans. Circ. Syst. Video Technol. **22**(12), 1649–1668 (2012). https://doi.org/10.1109/TCSVT.2012.2221191

21. Taylor, C., Pasquale, J.: Improving video performance in VNC under high latency conditions. In: 2010 International Symposium on Collaborative Technologies and Systems, pp. 26–35 (2010). https://doi.org/10.1109/CTS.2010.5478527

22. Tian, K., Dong, Y., Cowperthwaite, D.: A full GPU virtualization solution with mediated pass-through. In: Proceedings of the 2014 USENIX Conference on USENIX Annual Technical Conference, USENIX ATC 2014, pp. 121–132. USENIX Association (2014). https://www.usenix.org/conference/atc14/technical-sessions/presentation/tian

23. Wang, Z.: An Introduction to Intel GVT-g (2017). https://01.org/sites/default/files/documentation/an_introduction_to_intel_gvt-g_for_external.pdf
24. Wei, W., Zhang, Y., Lu, Y., Gao, P., Mu, K.: A VDI system based on cloud stack and active directory. In: 2015 14th International Symposium on Distributed Computing and Applications for Business Engineering and Science (DCABES), Guiyang, China, pp. 151–154 (2015). https://doi.org/10.1109/DCABES.2015.45
25. Wu, J., Wang, J., Qi, Z., Guan, H.: SRIDesk: a streaming based remote interactivity architecture for desktop virtualization system. In: 2013 IEEE Symposium on Computers and Communications (ISCC), pp. 281–286 (2013). https://doi.org/10.1109/ISCC.2013.6754960

Security in Cloud/Edge Platforms

Trustworthy IoT Computing Environment Based on Layered Blockchain Consensus Framework

Yueyu Dong, Fei Dai$^{(\boxtimes)}$, and Mingming Qin

Southwest Forestry University, Kunming, China
{dongyueyu,daifei,swfuqmm}@swfu.edu.cn

Abstract. The Internet of Things is widely used and has far-reaching significance. It is essential to ensure the trustworthiness of the IoT computing environment. Using blockchain technology to store and manage the data traces in the IoT is feasible to implement the trustworthy IoT. In a "Cloud-Edge-End" structure, the difference in the degree of energy constraint between various parts makes the use of the same consensus algorithm a compromise between overall performance degradation and energy constraints on terminal devices. We take advantage of the high modularity of the chained consensus algorithm to build a layered consensus mechanism framework, running a two-phase consensus algorithm in the local environment of the terminal devices, and a three-phase consensus algorithm with better overall performance. Preliminary evaluation shows that this scheme is feasible.

Keywords: Trustworthy IoT · Blockchain · Consensus framework

1 Introduction

The Internet of Things (IoT), which realizes the Internet of Everything, connects the information network and the real world. The IoT has unprecedentedly expanded the reach of the Internet, and has spawned many new applications, such as smart homes, smart cities, smart healthcare, and industrial Internet of Things. It is considered the key technology of the fourth industrial revolution. Under the data-driven paradigm, the IoT is not only an important data information source, but also an important infrastructure for data processing and application.

On the other hand, IoT devices are generally exposed and lack environmental safety guarantees. The wireless communication technology is widely used in the IoT, which is vulnerable to interference, data theft, and network attacks. The security and credibility of IoT devices and data has received great attention [3, 6]. The transactions in the IoT, especially whether the relevant data is trustworthy, are critical to the application of the IoT [2, 7]. For scenarios such as smart transportation and smart medical care, it is even directly related to human life safety.

To achieve a trustworthy IoT, it is necessary to ensure that the IoT obtains information and provides feedback based on credible data. Blockchain is a new computing model

M. R. Khosravi et al. (Eds.): CloudComp 2021, LNICST 430, pp. 167–180, 2022.
https://doi.org/10.1007/978-3-030-99191-3_13

that integrates distributed storage, consensus mechanism, and encryption algorithm. The decentralization and anti-tampering characteristics of the blockchain can ensure the security and trustworthiness of data in the IoT system. Use blockchain to store complete data traces, including who, when, where and how to obtain or generate, how processed, what kind of derivatives were generated, what kind of applications were used, and so on. It can ensure that the data is tamper-proof, complete, and traceable.

The IoT is a heterogeneous system. In a typical "Cloud-Edge-End" three-tier environment, there are huge differences in computing power, storage capacity, network bandwidth, and energy supply among cloud computing centers, edge servers at the edge of the network, and numerous terminal devices. Especially, energy constraints are most representative. It can be clearly divided into two parts: resources-unconstrained part and resources-constrained part. The consensus mechanism is the core foundation for the realization of functions of the blockchain. One single consensus mechanism can adapt to the huge differences in such a heterogeneous system is a major challenge of the integration blockchain with the IoT, which can run on the cloud with sufficient resources, and can also work on resource-constrained terminal devices.

The Byzantine Fault Tolerant (BFT) algorithm based on State Machine Replica (SMR) is an important type of blockchain consensus mechanism, such as PBFT [10]. These algorithms are derived from early distributed systems and required blockchain-oriented improvements. HotStuff [11] is representative work in this series of improvements. This algorithm implements the so-called chained SMR protocol. The process of consensus can be accomplished by a chain of identical structured consensus phases in a manner similar to the chain of blocks in blockchains. It archives the separation of safety rules and liveness rules. The liveness mechanism can be implemented independently. The high modularity of the identical structured consensus phases makes it possible to build a unified blockchain consensus framework in the IoT heterogeneous environment based on this algorithm. This framework is promising to meet the demands of the trustworthy IoT.

Specifically, the main contributions of this article include:

- Proposed a general consensus framework suitable for heterogeneous IoT environments based on a common algorithm foundation;
- Designed the voting phase and view changing algorithm to adapt to different layers in the framework;
- Proposed the deployment plan of the consensus framework based on microservices.

2   Related Works

Blockchain originated from encrypted electronic currency, and with further research, its unique value has become increasingly visible. In the field of IoT, using blockchain to ensure the trustworthiness of transactions is the most typical application. Huang et al. [4] proposed a blockchain system that can run in the resource-constrained environment of IoT terminal devices, which ensures that the transactions on these devices are tamper-proof and non-repudiation. Liu et al. [5] used blockchain in a heterogeneous IoT environment to ensure data security and credibility. It also emphasizes that the blockchain consensus mechanism must not only be able to adapt to "brawny" nodes with abundant resources, but also be able to adapt to "wimpy" nodes with limited resources. The work of Bai et al. [2] focuses on the trustworthiness of computing service scheduling and edge data sharing in the heterogeneous environment of the industrial energy Internet of things.

Traditional IoT applications run on the infrastructure composed of cloud servers and terminal devices. Due to their own characteristics, IoT terminal devices lack sufficient capabilities and need to transmit data to the cloud for computing and storage. Therefore the industry proposes a new computing model that provides data processing capabilities at the edge of the network, that is, Edge Computing. The IoT system infrastructure that introduces edge computing has changed from the traditional two layers to three layers composed of "Cloud-Edge-End". The introduction of edge gateways, edge servers and other devices has enabled the computing and storage capabilities of the traditional cloud to be deployed closer to IoT terminal devices. Under the offloading of computing tasks, data analysis and processing can be performed at nearby locations, which greatly avoids the huge communication overhead with the cloud. To achieve blockchain consensus in the IoT environment, the role of edge servers is unique and critical. Terminal devices usually lack sufficient resources and cannot afford the calculation and communication costs of the consensus process. Terminal devices are energy-constrained, and cannot always stay online. Works such as DPoS [7] also shows that in the blockchain, it is not the best choice for all nodes to directly participate in the consensus process. It is a common solution to use the edge server as the agent instead of the terminal node to participate in the consensus. In Edgence [9], the blockchain is used to implement self-management and self-supervision of decentralized applications. The core function of the proposed platform is to be deployed on edge servers. The literature PoQF [1] applies blockchain in the vehicular network environment. Its work shows that without the support of edge servers, the blockchain consensus mechanism is difficult to implement in the vehicular network environment.

In the heterogeneous environment of the IoT, the blockchain consensus algorithm needs to adapt to the resource-constrained terminal devices. The literatures Liu, Huang, and PoQF all proposed new consensus algorithms for this demand. Among them, the literature Huang and PoQF independently designed new algorithms, and the literature Liu used their new strategies to improve the classic GHOST algorithm. Entirely new algorithms are not fully tested. Improved existing algorithms, especially those that have been verified by practical applications, is mature and reliable. It is usually without too many compromises. The HotStuff algorithm has Byzantine fault tolerance comparable to classic algorithms such as PBFT. And it has been applied in Facebook's electronic currency Libra [8].

3   Trustworthy IoT Model with Integrated Blockchain

The key to achieve a trustworthy IoT is to ensure that the data in the IoT system is credible. The blockchain has the characteristics of decentralization and tamper-proof. Integrating the blockchain into the IoT and recording data traces with the blockchain can ensure the data credibility (Fig. 1). In this model, all participating nodes should be verified and trustworthy.

3.1 System Model Overview

In the typical "Cloud-Edge-End" three-tier structure of the IoT, the whole system can be clearly divided into two parts according to the degree of energy constraint. Cloud and edge servers belong to the part with less resource constraints; the part mainly composed of terminal devices, which is the narrowly defined the Internet of Things, is the part with generally constrained energy supply. For a blockchain consensus algorithm to be able to run in a "Cloud-Edge-End" environment, it must adapt to this difference. The blockchain integrated into the IoT also needs to be composed of two various parts. The part running on the terminal devices ensures that the data in the local network is credible. The part that runs on the cloud and edge servers records the data traces on the cloud and edge servers. The edge server has a unique position. The two parts can be connected through the edge servers, so as to implement the global trustworthiness of data.

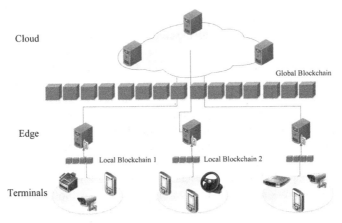

Fig. 1. A synergistic framework for the integration of IoT and blockchain

3.2 Build a Two-Layer Blockchain for the IoT

The blockchain integrated into the IoT needs to adapt to the two different components in the IoT. The blockchain on the energy-constrained part collects the data traces in this part, and packs a series of data transactions into blocks under consensus. The process of packaging and consensus can be performed on the edge server by task offloading. In fact, edge servers also act as participants in this layer of blockchain consensus. Therefore, whether when the edge server is selected as the leader to dominates the consensus and to pack data traces into blocks, or when other nodes offload packing tasks to the edge server, there will always be blocks copies of trusted data traces of the energy-constrained part on the edge server. These data traces blocks will be placed onto a local blockchain. The local blockchain does not need to record all the blocks, and just keep a sufficient amount of recent blocks to meet the needs of the consensus process. By participating in the consensus process of the energy-unconstrained part by the edge server, these data traces record blocks can be finally added to the global blockchain and stored in the energy-unconstrained part. Shown in Fig. 2.

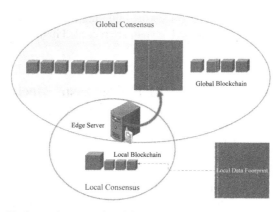

Fig. 2. Exchange between the global consensus and the local consensus

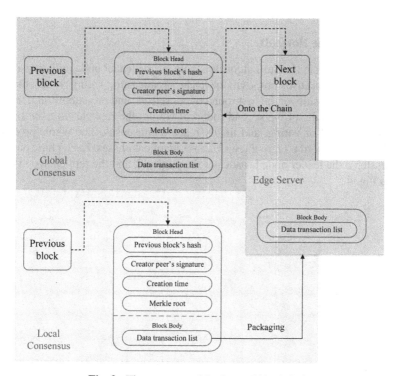

Fig. 3. The structure of the layered blockchain

The structure and operations of the global blockchain running on the energy-unconstrained part are more similar to the ordinary blockchain. The edge servers and the clouds record the data traces in the energy-unstrained part, pack the data traces into blocks, and join blocks into the global blockchain by consensus. The latest confirmed block in the local blockchain is added to the global blockchain under consensus by the edge server serving as the consensus initiating node. In this way, as shown in Fig. 3, the data traces in the entire IoT system are recorded in the blockchain to achieve trustworthiness.

4   Layered Chained BFT (LCBFT) Consensus Mechanism

The most important contribution of HotStuff is a byzantine fault tolerant consensus framework for blockchain. Under this framework, the consensus process can be regarded as a series of successive phases and phases are identical structured. This denoted as chained consensus in its document. And it achieves the separation of safety rules and liveness rules. Consensus voting with different "chain lengths" company with different view change mechanisms. Such a consensus framework has high modularity and has the ability to adapt to different scenarios. Based on this idea, the LCBFT consensus mechanism is proposed to implement the aforementioned two-layer blockchain.

4.1   Overview of the HotStuff

The process of the basic HotStuff algorithm includes the leader node initiating a consensus; voting on the consensus proposal; the leader broadcasting voting results, the replica node voting on the results of the first round of consensus, and pre-submitting; the leader broadcasting the results of the second round of voting; the replicas vote on the results of the second round of voting, and finally reach a consensus. The whole process can be simplified and described into three structure-identical phases. Each phase consists of two main steps: the leader node broadcasts the proposal, and the replica node votes. As shown in Fig. 4.

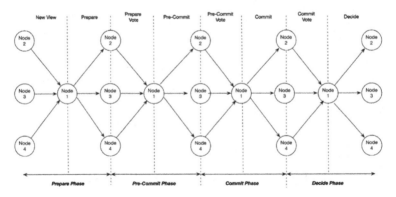

Fig. 4. HotStuff consensus process includes several identical-structured phases

After the completion of the three phases, this round of consensus was reached. To change the view to ensure the quality of the chain. Because the three phases of one round are identical-structured, and the content voted to be confirmed in each phase is successive, consensus process can form a pipeline. The second phase on the first block can be used as the first phase on the second block. When the consensus on the fourth block is started, the three phases on the first block have been completed, and the first block has been confirmed and cannot be tampered with ever. At this time, the so-called "Three-Chain" is formed.

The above description is mainly about the security rules in the consensus mechanism. The liveness rules corresponding to safety rules are also required. HotStuff itself is a Three-Chain consensus protocol. The consensus on the current proposal also means the confirmation of the location of the unmodifiable block in the blockchain. The cost of view changing is linear, therefore leader replacement can be performed in each round. Under the HotStuff framework, the Two-Chain consensus protocol can also be constructed. Explicit corresponding liveness rules are needed, which is similar as the view changing algorithm in PBFT, or the mandatory delay in Casper, and so on.

4.2   Consensus and Block Generation in Energy-Constrained Part

Due to limited resources, the blockchain consensus mechanism in this part requires lower computational overhead. The use of two-phase consensus can effectively reduce computational overhead. In this part, the key issue is the credible record of data traces, not a complete blockchain for persistent storage. All need to do is to keep the "chain of necessary length" to meet the needs of the consensus process.

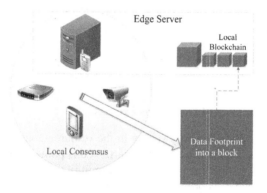

Fig. 5. Data footprints collected and recorded trustworthily in local consensus process

The edge server participates the consensus progress in this part. After the consensus is reached, the data transactions are packed into blocks, and the edge server records the data traces of this part and submits them to the global blockchain, then these blocks will be stored onto the chain under consensus. Shown in Fig. 5. The edge server is naturally suitable as the leader of the consensus in the energy-constrained part. When other nodes act as leaders, they also can offload computing tasks such as collecting votes to the edge server.

4.3 Global Blockchain Consensus and Joining Blocks onto the Chain

The consensus of global block chain is reached with the participation of clouds and edge servers, and data traces occurring on cloud and edge servers are stored on the global blocks chain (Fig. 6). Among them, the blocks that the edge server submitted includes data traces in the energy-constrained part. The global consensus of block chain adopts a three-phase process to improve data throughput, and changes view every round to ensure the quality of the blockchain.

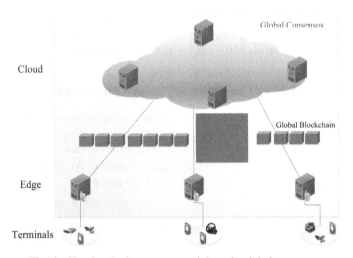

Fig. 6. Cloud and edge servers participate in global consensus

4.4 Liveness Mechanism of Consensus Process

Considering the constrained energy supply in the resource-constrained part, the Two-Chain consensus mechanism is used in this part. At this point, the consensus process is similar to classic algorithms such as PBFT, and multiple rounds of voting are required to determine a new leader according to the view changing protocol to complete the view change. This process is costly in calculation and network communication. But in this scenario, the view changing is not performed every round, and it is only performed when the leader node is faulty or not trusted. Therefore, the frequency of view change can be reduced by optimizing the leader selecting. thereby the overall cost of the consensus mechanism can be reduced. In the "Cloud-Edge-End" IoT environment, determining leader mainly by stable online time can ensure that stable nodes such as edge servers act as leader to dominate the consensus process, and can reduce the overhead caused by view change. Algorithm 1 and 2 describes the whole process systematically.

Algorithm 1 Local Consensus

1: **begin**

2: Two phases voting for safety

3: Choose new leader node

4: Several voting to confirm new leader and the check point for liveness

5: **end**

Algorithm 2 Choose new leader node

1: **begin**

2: **for** every terminal t_i (including the edge server) in the same local consensus domain **do**

3:     Check accumulative available time ta_i of t_i

4:     **if** ta_i is the max **then**

5:         Choose t_i as new leader node

6:     **end if**

7: **end for**

8: **end**

Three-Chain consensus can be carried out in the resource-unconstrained part composed of cloud servers and edge servers, and the view can be switched every round to improve the quality of the blockchain. The cost of each round is linear, but it is still necessary to select the leader node for a new round of consensus. In this part, because there are no constraints in capability and energy, a new leader node can be determined in a round-robin manner. As shown in Algorithm 3.

Algorithm 3 Get leader in global consensus

1: **begin**

2:     Check the identifying number i of the current leader node p_i

3:     **if** $(i + 1)$ % n (amount of the peers) $== j$ **then**

4:         Choose p_j as the leader node of next round

5:     **end if**

6: **end**

---

5   Microservice-Based Consensus Protocol Deployment Plan

In the chained consensus protocol, each phase of the consensus process is identical-structured, that is, collecting votes and publishing voting results or launching the next round of voting. In the HotStuff protocol, voting is achieved with the help of Threshold Digital Signature. From the perspective of application deployment, one phase of the consensus process can be deployed as a reusable software module in the computing environment, and the consensus process can be implemented through multiple reuses. The three-phase mechanism and the two-phase mechanism used in different parts of the system can be achieved by reusing corresponding times. The view changing process to ensure liveness in the two-phase consensus mechanism is also a series of voting phases. It also can be implemented by running reusable software modules, which can be brought about by threshold signatures.

Algorithm 4 One basic phase of the consensus

1: **begin**

2:     **as a leader**:

3:         collect votes with Threshold Digital Signature

4:         broadcast the vote result

5:     **as a replica**:

6:         wait for message from leader, and vote after message received

7:     **as the next leader**:

8:         wait for messages until there are n-f votes, then start to act as the leader
            node

6: **end**

Microservices are a feasible way to deploy reusable software modules. Reusable modules can be deployed on cloud servers and edge servers in the form of microservices. In the global consensus process, the cloud server and the edge server reach consensus through three rounds of reuse the reusable module, and record the data traces on the chain. In the local consensus process, poor energy supply constrains replica nodes to run the consensus algorithm. At this time, the related computing tasks can be migrated to the edge server by offloading. A consensus can be achieved by reusing of the aforementioned reusable modules certain times. In the consensus process, the edge server may be a malicious node, but this does not affect its use as a destination for tasks offloading in the edge computing mode. If a view changing occurs, it can also execute the tasks offloaded from those energy-constrained nodes, which cannot afford the execution cost. So as to perform the view change and start the next round of consensus. The microservices Si provides a basic phase computing of the chained consensus algorithm, which is deployed in the part consisting of the cloud servers CSi and the edge servers ESi. The microservices also can be deployed on energy-unconstrained terminal devices (Fig. 7).

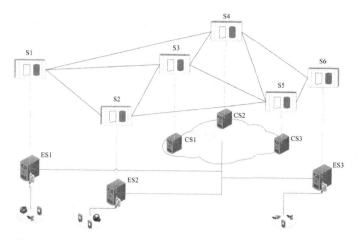

Fig. 7. Deployment of the consensus protocol based on microservice

6   Evaluation

The energy consumption of the consensus process is proportional to the calculation amount. By analyzing the calculation amount of the consensus process, the energy consumption of the consensus process can be judged.

6.1   Computational Structure of the Two Consensus Mechanisms

As mentioned earlier, each round of global consensus is a three-phase process, and thus achieves linear cost of the view change. Because no additional complex liveness rule is needed, the view is changed every round. The calculation of the global consensus is mainly composed of three basic consensus phases (Algorithm 4), as shown in Fig. 8(a).

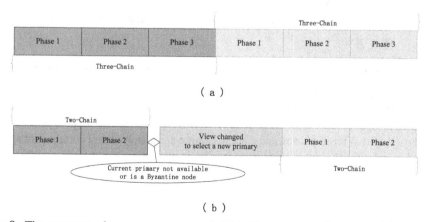

Fig. 8. The structure of one consensus round (a) is the structure of one round in 3-Phase consensus (b) is the structure of one round in 2-Phase consensus

Local consensus is carried out in a two-phase manner per round, as shown in Fig. 8(b). Different from the three-phase method of global consensus, an additional special view changing protocol needs to be run as main body of the liveness rules. For example, in the typical two-phase BFT consensus algorithm PBFT, after the view change is initiated, a consensus on the current stable checkpoint and the willingness to change to new view needs to be voted on, and then a reliable view change can be implemented to ensure the liveness of the consensus (Algorithm 5). Drawing on the thinking behind the chained consensus algorithm, this process can be described as a form composed of two basic phases, see Algorithm 6.

Algorithm 5 View change in PBFT

1: **begin**

2:     Replica i collected $2f+1$ votes for the current stable checkpoint, then broadcast
        view-change message with greater sequence number

3:     Replica nodes vote to confirm new view $v+1$ to new leader node selected ac-
        cording to *Algorithm 2*

4:     New leader node collected $2f+1$ votes for the view $v+1$, then broadcast
        new-view message with vote result

5: **end**

Algorithm 6 Description of view change based on the basic phases

---

1: **begin**

2:     The basic phase to confirm the current stable checkpoint and propose changing
        to new view $v+1$

3:     The basic phase to confirm the new view $v+1$ and announce the begin of the
        new view

4: **end**

It should be noted that the view change in the local consensus is only performed when the current leader node is faulty or malicious. The view changing protocol will only be executed in these cases. On the whole, each round of the local consensus process is mainly composed of two basic phases and a view change appearing with a certain probability whose calculation amount equivalent to two basic phases.

6.2   Energy Consumption Analysis of Two Consensus Mechanism

Based on the above analysis of the calculation amount, a basic consensus phase can be used as the measurement unit of the calculation amount. Then, based on the measurements of calculation amount, the energy consumption of the consensus process can be analyzed.

The calculation amount of each round of global consensus is recorded as 3 basic phases. Let CM_g represent the calculation amount of the global consensus, and CM_s represent the calculation amount of a basic phase, then the calculation amount of each round of the global consensus can be recorded as:

$$CM_g = 3 * CM_s \tag{1}$$

In the calculation of each round of local consensus, it is certain that there will be two basic consensus phases. There is also a view change that appears with a certain probability p, and the calculation amount of the view change is equivalent to the two basic phases. The calculation amount of each round of local consensus CM_l can be recorded as:

$$CM_l = 2 * CM_s + p * 2 * CM_s \tag{2}$$

With reference to relevant literature and analysis based on the actual situation of the IoT, p is usually much less than 0.5. Therefore, CM_l is less than $3CM_s$ and less than CM_g, and our proposed two-layer consensus framework can meet the energy consumption constraints of the IoT, and can implement a trustworthy computing environment in the IoT.

7   Conclusion

After preliminary evaluation, the overall cost of the two-phase consensus is lower than that of the three-phase consensus, which is suitable for energy-constrained terminal devices. The consensus framework we propose can build a trustworthy IoT computing environment. The structure of the chained consensus facilitates deployment in a "Cloud-Edge-End" environment with microservices.

Acknowledgements. This work has been supported by the Project of National Natural Science Foundation of China under Grant No. 61702442 and 61862065, the Application Basic Research Project in Yunnan Province Grant No. 2018FB105, the Major Project of Science and Technology of Yunnan Province under Grant No. 202002AD080002 and No. 2019ZE005, the Project of Scientific Research Foundation of Yunnan Department of Education under Grant No.2017ZZX212.

References

1. Ayaz, F., Sheng, Z., Tian, D., Guan, Y.L.: A Proof-of-Quality-Factor (PoQF)-based blockchain and edge computing for vehicular message dissemination. IEEE Internet Things J. **8**, 2468–2482 (2021). https://doi.org/10.1109/JIOT.2020.3026731

2. Bai, F., Shen, T., Yu, Z., Zeng, K., Gong, B.: Trustworthy blockchain-empowered collaborative edge computing-as-a-service scheduling and data sharing in the IIoE. IEEE Internet Things J. X (2021). https://doi.org/10.1109/JIOT.2021.3058125

3. Guo, S., Hu, X., Guo, S., Qiu, X., Qi, F.: Blockchain meets edge computing: a distributed and trusted authentication system. IEEE Trans. Ind. Inf. **16**, 1972–1983 (2020). https://doi.org/10.1109/TII.2019.2938001

4. Huang, Z., Mi, Z., Hua, Z.: HCloud: a trusted JointCloud serverless platform for IoT systems with blockchain. China Commun. **17**, 1 (2020). https://doi.org/10.23919/JCC.2020.09.001

5. Liu, Y., Wang, K., Qian, K., Du, M., Guo, S.: Tornado: enabling blockchain in heterogeneous internet of things through a space-structured approach. IEEE Internet Things J. **7**, 1273–1286 (2020). https://doi.org/10.1109/JIOT.2019.2954128

6. Mendki, P.: Blockchain enabled IoT edge computing. ACM Int. Conf. Proc. Ser. Part **F1481**, 66–69 (2019). https://doi.org/10.1145/3320/15433/20166

7. Sun, W., Liu, J., Yue, Y., Wang, P.: Joint Resource allocation and incentive design for blockchain-based mobile edge computing. IEEE Trans. Wirel. Commun. **19**, 6050–6064 (2020). https://doi.org/10.1109/TWC.2020.2999721

8. Team, T.L.: State Machine Replication in the Libra Blockchain, pp. 1–21 (2020)

9. Xu, J., Wang, S., Zhou, A., Yang, F.: Edgence: a Blockchain-enabled edge-computing platform for intelligent IoT-based dApps. China Commun. **17**(4), 78–87 (2020)

10. Xu, X., Zhu, D., Yang, X., Wang, S., Qi, L., Dou, W.: Concurrent practical byzantine fault tolerance for integration of blockchain and supply chain. ACM Trans Internet Technol. **21** (2021). https://doi.org/10.1145/3395331

11. Yin, M., Malkhi, D., Reiter, M.K., Gueta, G.G., Abraham, I.: HotStuff: BFT consensus in the lens of blockchain, 1–23 (2018). (arXiv)

Heuristic Network Security Risk Assessment Based on Attack Graph

Wei Sun[1], Qianmu Li[1,2(✉)], Pengchuan Wang[1], and Jun Hou[3]

[1] Nanjing University of Science and Technology, Nanjing, China
{sw24816,qianmu,wangpc}@njust.edu.cn
[2] Intelligent Manufacturing Department, Wuyi University, Nanping, China
[3] School of Social Science, Nanjing Vocational University of Industry Technology, Nanjing, China

Abstract. With the development of attack technology, attackers prefer to exploit multiple vulnerabilities with a combination of several attacks instead of simply using violent cracking and botnets. In addition, enterprises tend to adopt microservices architectures and multi-cloud environments to obtain high efficiency, high reliability and high scalability. It makes modeling attack scenarios and mapping the actions of potential adversaries an urgent and difficult task. There have been many improvements that can automatically generate attack graphs for complex networks. However, extracting enough effective information from such complex attack graphs is still a problem to be solved. Traditional algorithms can't always accomplish this task because of variable and complex attack graph inputs. In contrast, heuristic algorithms have the advantages of adaptability, self-learning ability, robustness and high efficiency. In this paper, we present heuristic algorithms to complete the analysis of attack graphs, including fusion algorithm of particle swarm optimization (PSO) algorithm and grey wolf optimization (GWO) algorithm for finding the spanning arborescence of maximum weight and improved genetic simulated annealing (GA-SA) algorithm for finding attack path with the biggest risk. Also, we present a method for node importance evaluation based on the interpretive structural modeling (ISM) method. We test our methods on a multi-cloud enterprise network, and the result shows that our methods perform well.

Keywords: Attack graph · Attack paths · Heuristic algorithm · CVE · Cyber security

1 Introduction

The report on major global cyber attacks and data breaches in the first half of 2021 pointed out that cyber attacks, hacking organizations, and data breaches have always existed in the cyber world. For example, 30 TB data in a Brazilian database was destroyed in January, 220 million people were affected. In February,

M. R. Khosravi et al. (Eds.): CloudComp 2021, LNICST 430, pp. 181–194, 2022.
https://doi.org/10.1007/978-3-030-99191-3_14

the user data of Clubhouse was stolen by malicious hackers or spies and published on the third-party website. In March, 8 million COVID-19 nucleic acid test results leaked in India, and the information contained sensitive personal information such as name, age, marital status, test time, residential address, etc. Therefore, grasping the current network security situation in real-time in a complex and changeable network environment, providing early warning and protection against the security situation, and reducing the harm of network attacks is the primary task of network security work.

Attack graph technology displays possible attack paths in the network in a graphical form, helping defenders to understand the relationship between vulnerabilities in the target network intuitively so that the defenders can take corresponding defensive measures. Phillips and Swiler [16] proposed the concept of attack graph and applied it to network vulnerability analysis. With the development of attack graph technology, it is used in alert information correlation analysis, network security risk assessment, network intrusion intent identification, etc. Unlike traditional passive defense technology, attack graph models attack scenarios from attackers' perspective, showing the relationship between the exploitation of vulnerabilities. By analyzing the attack graph, defenders can prepare for possible cyber attacks in advance and reduce security risks.

In recent decades, many heuristic algorithms have been proposed to solve complex optimization problems in engineering technology. Swarm intelligence algorithm is a new bionic evolutionary algorithm, mainly including ACO and PSO algorithms. Swarm intelligence algorithm has strong robustness and is easy to implement. Distributed computer system makes it effective enough to be applied to many fields, such as function optimization, multi-objective optimization, solving integer constraints and mixed integer constraint optimization, neural network training, signal processing, routing algorithms, etc. The practical results have proved the feasibility and efficiency of these algorithms [7]. Genetic algorithm is also a classic heuristic algorithm used in many fields. However, it is easy to fall into local optimization and precocity. In advantages of the simulated annealing algorithm complement the shortcomings of the genetic algorithm [9]. Different heuristic algorithms perform great differently when facing the same problem, so it is necessary to choose the proper algorithm and improve it according to the actual situation.

2   Related Work

After Phillips and Swiler [16] proposed the concept of attack graph, attack graph generation technology has always been a hot research topic. Sheyner et al. [13] created state enumeration attack graphs. Each node of the state enumeration attack graph represents one state of the entire system, and edges mean attacks lead to state transitions. They used finite automata to get the attack path in the graph, but it didn't play well when the graph size became bigger. Ammann et al. [1] made each node a system condition instead of the entire system state and made edges the relationships between nodes. This type of attack graph can reflect the dependencies between system conditions. In their analysis method, attackers will always hold the permissions that have been obtained, which is closer to the real situation.

Ou et al. [11] groundbreakingly proposed the MulVal framework. MulVal is an end-to-end framework and reasoning system that can perform multi-host, multi-stage vulnerability analysis on the network. MulVal has two different nodes: derivation nodes and fact nodes. Ingols et al. [6] developed a system called NetSPA to build multiple-prerequisite graphs from massive source data, and this kind of attack graph has greater expressive power. Ibrahim et al. [5] presented a method to generate attack graphs for microservice architecture by relating microservices to network nodes. Liu et al. [8] combined the attack graph and evidence graph. This combination of refined attack graphs and evidence graphs can help defenders compute or refine potential attack success probabilities.

As important as generating attack graphs, many scholars are also concerned about how to analyze attack graphs. Dai et al. [2] used the fuzzy comprehensive evaluation method to quantify the number and the length of attack paths, combined with attack paths to discover threats to the network and analyze the riskiest attack paths in the network system to predict the risks of potential attacks to network security. Abraham et al. [14] judged the value of the network security situation by analyzing the variation of the vulnerability life cycle with the release event and the relationship between the attack path and the vulnerability life cycle. Musa et al. [10] presented an effective model of depicting the devices and the data flow that efficiently identifies the weakest nodes along with the concerned vulnerability's origin, making attack graphs easier for the users to interpret and reducing the time taken to identify the attack paths. Stergiopoulos et al. [15] split the analysis of complex attack graphs into multiple steps. The core idea was to use Edmonds' algorithm, graph centrality metrics and clustering on attack graphs weighted with risk assessment calculations. It provided automated prioritization of systems and detected vulnerabilities.

3 Heuristic Network Security Risk Assessment Based on Attack Graph

3.1 Attack Graph

Common Vulnerabilities and Exposures (CVE) is like a dictionary table, giving a common name for widely recognized vulnerabilities or vulnerabilities that have been exposed. Using a common name can help users share data in various independent vulnerability databases and vulnerability assessment tools. Suppose a vulnerability is specified in a vulnerability report and has a CVE name. In that case, you can quickly find the corresponding patch information in any other CVE-compatible database to solve the security problem. Common Vulnerability Scoring System (CVSS) is an industry open standard designed to measure the severity of vulnerabilities and help determine the urgency and importance of the required response. CVE and CVSS are both published and updated by the U.S. government repository of standards based vulnerability management data (NVD).

This paper utilizes tools and methods from [5,8] to generate attack graphs. This kind of attack graph is similar to the attack graph introduced in [6], whose nodes correspond to states and edges to vulnerability instances. CVSS provides a way to score vulnerability instances [12] so that we can determine the weight of each edge.

Between two nodes in our attack graph, there could be several edges that indicate different vulnerabilities. To simplify the initial attack graph, We only keep one edge with the most prominent weight between two nodes, in which case we can get the worst scenario of the target network. When conducting network security risk assessments, it is critical to consider the worst scenario.

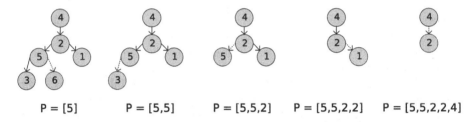

Fig. 1. An example of the encoding process of a directed tree.

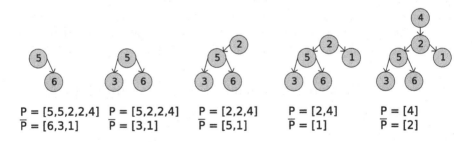

Fig. 2. An example of the encoding process of the code string P.

3.2 Heuristic Graph Arborescences of Maximum Weight Generation Algorithm

Attack graphs are directed acyclic graphs, and it is applicable to utilize Edmonds' algorithm to find spanning arborescence of minimum weight. After a simple adjustment, it can be used to find spanning arborescence of maximum weight. Edmonds' algorithm is based on the idea of greed and shrinkage, and it can deal with directed graphs with an actual minimum spanning tree, which means

Edmonds' algorithm requires input that meets certain conditions. The problem of finding minimum weight arborescence is similar to the degree-constrained minimum spanning tree problem for undirected graphs. Usually, we employ algorithms to find approximate solutions. Heuristic algorithms have an excellent performance in solving such issues [3].

Coding Design of Directed Graph Spanning Tree. As the root node in our attack graph indicates the end goal of attacks, the spanning arborescence T of maximum weight can reveal the potential attack surfaces. T has several characteristics: 1) The in-degree of all nodes in T except the root is 1. 2) There is only one directed path from the root to any other node. According to those characteristics, we learn from the Prüfer coding. There are n^{n-2} different spanning trees in an undirected graph complete graph with n nodes. Prüfer coding can uniquely express every tree by using the arrangement of $n - 2$ numbers between 1 and n. Learned from Prüfer, we encode the directed graph spanning tree. Suppose that T is a directed tree that has n nodes, and u is its root. We need $n - 1$ numbers between 1 and n to express it.

There are four steps when we encode a directed tree:

Step1: Let j be the biggest label among leaves' labels, if i is the starting node of the directed edge $<i, j>$ adjacent to j, add i to the rightmost side of the code string P.
Step2: Delete j and edge $<i, j>$.
Step3: When the number of nodes left in the tree T is greater than 1, go to the first step and repeat the above steps; when there is only one node left in the tree T, go to step 4.
Step4: Output the code string P with $n - 1$ numbers.

When decoding code string P, we need three steps:

Step1: Let $\overline{P}$ contain node labels do not appear in P, and arrange the labels in $\overline{P}$ in descending order from left to right.
Step2: Suppose that i is the leftmost label in P and j is the leftmost label in $\overline{P}$, add edge $<i, j>$ to the tree T and then delete the chosen labels from P and $\overline{P}$. If i no longer appears in the remaining part of p, then add i to $\overline{P}$ (keep in descending order).
Step3: Repeat the above steps until there are no labels in P and $\overline{P}$.

Figure 1 shows an example of the encoding process of a directed tree, and Fig. 2 shows an example of the decoding process of the code string obtained in Fig. 1.

Fusion Algorithm of PSO Algorithm and GWO Algorithm. Suppose we have a processed attack graph $G = \{V, E\}$, $V = \{v_1, v_2, ..., v_n\}$ is a set of nodes, $E = \{w_{1,2}, ..., w_{i,j}, ..., w_{n-1,n}\}$ is a set of edges. If it exists a directed edge from i to j, $w_{i,j}$ represents the weight of the edge. Otherwise, we make $w_{i,j} = -1$. When finding the spanning arborescence T of maximum weight, we select $n - 1$

edges each time. In this case, the encoding and decoding algorithms are used to verify whether the selected edges can form a tree. If the selected edges meet the requirements, the encoding algorithm can output a code string with $n-1$ numbers, and the decoding algorithm uses the code string to rebuild the tree while the tree may not exist in G at the very beginning. With the iteration of the fusion algorithm, the tree will meet the requirements more and more, and the algorithm will do its best to find the spanning arborescence T of maximum weight. Suppose that $X = \{x_{1,2}, x_{1,3}, ..., x_{i,j}, ..., x_{n-1,n}\}$ indicates the tree rebuilt by decoding algorithm, $x_{i,j} = 1$ means edge $w_{i,j}$ is selected, otherwise $x_{i,j} = 0$. The mathematical model of the maximum spanning tree problem for weighted directed graphs is as follows, and it can be the fitness function of our fusion algorithm:

$$\max \quad f(x) = \sum_{i=1}^{n} \sum_{\substack{j=1, \\ j \neq i}}^{n} w_{i,j} x_{i,j}$$
$$\text{s.t.} \quad \begin{cases} 0 \leq \sum_{i=1}^{n} x_{i,j} \leq 1, \quad j = 1, 2, \dots, n, \\ x \in X, \end{cases} \tag{1}$$

The fusion algorithm has the advantages of both PSO algorithm and GWO algorithm. GWO algorithm simulates grey wolf social class and grey wolf hunting process. The leadership levels of wolves are divided into four categories: α, β, δ, ω wolves, among which α, β wolves are responsible for leading the entire wolf pack. α wolf has the largest fitness value, wolves have the second and third fitness values are marked as β and δ. The optimization process of GWO algorithm is mainly guided by the α, β, δ. Assuming that the number of wolves is N and the search area is d-dimensional, the position of the i-th wolf can be represented as $X_i = \{x_{i1}, x_{i2}, ..., x_{id}\}$. When the grey wolves search for prey, they will gradually approach the prey and surround it. The mathematical model of this behavior is as follows:

$$D = C \circ X_p(t) - X(t)$$
$$X(t+1) = X_p(t) - A \circ D$$
$$A = 2a \circ r_1 - a \tag{2}$$
$$C = 2r_2$$
$$a = 2\left(1 - \frac{t}{T_{\max}}\right)$$

Where t represents the current iteration number, $\circ$ is hadamard product, A and C are the vector of synergy coefficients, X_p indicates the position of prey, X_t is the current position of the wolf. a is the convergence factor, which decreases linearly from 2 to 0 as t increases. r_1 and r_2 are two random numbers in $[0, 1)$.

Grey wolves have the ability to identify the position of potential prey (optimal solution). The search process is mainly completed by the guidance of α, β, and δ. In each iteration, keep the positions of α, β and δ, and then update the positions of other search agent wolves (including ω) based on their position information. The mathematical model of this process is as follows:

$$D_\alpha = |C_1 \circ X_\alpha - X|, D_\beta = |C_2 \circ X_\beta - X|, D_\delta = |C_3 \circ X_\delta - X|$$
$$X_1 = X_\alpha - A_1 \circ D_\alpha, X_2 = X_\beta - A_2 \circ D_\beta, X_3 = X_\delta - A_3 \circ D_\delta \tag{3}$$
$$X(t+1) = \frac{X_1 + X_2 + X_3}{3}$$

Where X_α, X_β, X_δ represent the positions of α, β, and δ grey wolves, D_α, D_β, D_δ are the distances from the position of the agent wolf X_t to α, β and δ.

However, when finding the spanning arborescence T of maximum weight, GWO algorithm doesn't play well because the GWO algorithm only considers the position information of α, β and δ, and ignores the information exchange between grey wolf individuals and their own experience. So the idea of PSO algorithm is introduced to improve the position update process. The new mathematical model is as follows:

$$
\begin{aligned}
X_i(t+1) &= c_1 r_3 \left(w_1 X_1(t) + w_2 X_2(t) + w_3 X_3(t) \right) \\
&\quad + c_2 r_4 \left(X_{ibest} - X_i(t) \right) \\
w_i &= \frac{|X_i|}{|X_1 + X_2 + X_3|}, i = 1, 2, 3
\end{aligned}
\tag{4}
$$

Where c_1 is the social learning factor that controls the influence of the optimal value of population, c_2 is the cognitive learning factor that controls the influence of the optimal value of the individual. w_1, w_2 and w_3 are inertia weights that affect the strength of global optimization capability. r_3 and r_4 are two random numbers in $[0, 1)$.

The process of the fusion algorithm is divided into six steps:

Step1: Set the size of the population N, the dimension d, which equals the number of edges, and initialize the values of A, C, and a.

Step2: Randomly generate population individuals $\{X_i, i = 1, 2, 3 \ldots N\}$.

Step3: Use Eq. 1 to calculate the fitness of each individual, and then choose top-3 individuals as α, β and δ. Use Eq. 3 to get X_α, X_β and X_δ.

Step4: Use Eq. 2 to calculate the parameter a, and then update the values of A and C.

Step5: Use Eq. 4 to update the position of each individual, and then calculate the fitness again to update α, β and δ.

Step6: If the number of iterations reaches the maximum, output α; else go back to step3.

Table 1. Node ID and description of the corresponding system state

ID	Discription of state	ID	Discription of state
S1	Start	S10	VMGroupsATL (root access privilege)
S2	Admin (root access privilege)	S11	VMGroupsC lib (root access privilege)
S3	DBServer (execCode [user])	S12	VMGroupsLICQ (user access privilege)
S4	DBServer (netAccess [tcp, 1434])	S13	WebServer (execCode)
S5	MailServerACLs (root access privilege)	S14	WebServer (netaccess [tcp, 80])
S6	MailServerSMTP (root access privilege)	S15	WebServer (user access privilege)
S7	NatServerOpenSSH1 (user access privilege)	S16	WorkStation (execCode)
S8	NatServerOpenSSH2 (root access privilege)	S17	WorkStation (access Malicious input [secretary, 'IE'])
S9	Root access to VMs	S18	End

3.3   Heuristic Attack Path Finding Algorithm for Maximum Risk

Coding Design of Path in Directed Graph. The most significant improvement of our method is the choice of coding method. When looking for paths between two nodes, the conventional coding method may use a binary code string of length N, and the value of 1 indicates that the node is selected. Set the value at the position of the start node and the end node as 1, then take other points at random. However, there are too many possibilities for the method, and most of them are useless because the attack graph is directed. Under these circumstances, we designed a new coding method that codes nodes with priority. To obtain a feasible path, the adjacent nodes connected by directed edges need to be put into the alternative list L from the start node to the end node. Each time along the path, there may be multiple nodes as the next choice. The priority of nodes determines which next node to choose to put into the alternative list L. The steps of the method are as follows:

Step1: Generate sets of adjacent nodes for each node.
Step2: Select the next node from the set of adjacent nodes of the current node as the next current node.
Step3: Until the selected current node is the end node, otherwise repeat Step2.

GA-SA Algorithm. Genetic algorithm is an iterative process. Its global search capability is better than local search capability, while simulated annealing algorithm's local search capability is better than global search capability. GA-SA algorithm gets the advantages of both GA and SA, and becomes a comprehensive algorithm. In this algorithm, the fitness function is set as follows:

$$\max \quad f(x) = \sum w_{node_i, node_{i+1}} \quad (node_i, node_{i+1}) \in L \qquad (5)$$

To ensure the diversity of the population, the crossover probability P_c is set to a relatively large value in the early evolution and a relatively small value in the later evolution. It makes the algorithm converge to the optimal result faster. The mathematical model is as follows:

$$P_c = \begin{cases} e^{P_{c1} \times (1-t/T)}, & P_{c1} \times (1-t/T) > P_{c2} \\ e^{P_{c2}}, & P_{c1} \times (1-t/T) < P_{c2} \end{cases} \qquad (6)$$

Where t represents the current iteration number, T is the max iteration number. P_{c1} and P_{c2} are two numbers in $(0,1)$.

In the mutation operation, in order to ensure the optimization of alternative list L, the principle adopted is: robust individuals try to reduce the mutation rate, and inferior individuals increase the mutation rate, which can be reflected in the following equation:

$$P_m = \begin{cases} \frac{k_1(F_{max}-F)}{F_{max}-F_{avg}}, & F > F_{avg} \\ k_2, & F < F_{avg} . \end{cases} \qquad (7)$$

Where $F_{\max}$ indicates the maximum fitness of the population, F_{avg} indicates the average fitness of the population. k_1 and k_2 are adjustment constants and $k_1 < k_2$.

The process of the GA-SA algorithm is divided into six steps:

Step1: Initialize the population. Set the simulated annealing temperature as t_0.

Step2: Calculate fitness function $f(x)$.

Step3: Use the roulette wheel selection algorithm for selection operation.

Step4: Select the crossover method, and perform crossover operation on the selected two individuals according to the probability P_c.

Step5: Evaluate each individual after the crossover operation and perform mutation operation with probability P_m. In the mutation operation, the probability of child generation varies according to the temperature T_R.

Step6: If the number of iterations reaches the maximum, output the optimal result; else go back to step2.

Table 2. Edge ID and CVE reference

ID	CVE reference	Risk	ID	CVE reference	Risk
E1	Browse malicious websites	8	E14	CVE-2018-7841	6
E2	–	0	E15	CVE-2004-0840	10
E3	CVE-2010-3847	7	E16	CVE-2009-1918	8
E4	CVE-2010-3847	7	E17	CVE-2008-5416	4.8
E5	CVE-2003-0693	10	E18	CVE-2018-7841	6
E6	CVE-2003-0693	10	E19	CVE-2008-5416	6
E7	CVE-2007-4752	6	E20	CVE-2010-3847	7
E8	CVE-2001-0439	8	E21	CVE-2008-0015	9
E9	CVE-2008-4050	9	E22	CVE-2008-0015	9
E10	CVE-2008-4050	9	E23	CVE-2008-0015	9
E11	CVE-2008-0015	9	E24	CVE-2001-1030	8
E12	CVE-2008-0015	9	E25	CVE-2009-1535	8
E13	CVE-2009-1918	8			

3.4   Node Importance Evaluation Based on ISM

The importance of state nodes is one of the core indicators we can extract from attack graphs. Before calculating the importance, we should reverse the direction of each edge because the root node is the target of attackers, and ISM needs to get the reachability of the graph. The simple method of node importance evaluation is to use the degree value of the node to express the importance of the node. This method is easy to operate, but it is one-sided. The interpretive structure model (ISM) is widely used in various fields. It is used for attribute recognition, analysis, and investigation in the software development process. We can use ISM methods to identify the superior-subordinate relationship between attributes and establish a structural hierarchy model [4].

Using ISM can divide the attack graph into layers. Nodes at a higher level are more important in the attack graph. Also, the results of ISM and graph arborescences of maximum weight generation can confirm each other. Then, we assign weight information to each layer. The formula to define the weight is as follows:

$$Q_i = \frac{1/L_i}{\sum_1^N (1/L_i)} \tag{8}$$

In the process of analyzing the importance of attack graph nodes, it is necessary to consider not only the level of the node to be evaluated but also the level of other nodes connected to the node. Suppose the coefficient of the in-degree node is I, and the coefficient of the out-degree node is O. I is always greater than O. Using an example to illustrate the reason, the importance of the paper is reflected in the number of citations by others. Finally, the formula for node importance evaluation is as follows:

$$T_i = Q_i \left(I \sum_k Q_{k \to i} W_{k \to i} + O \sum_j Q_{i \to j} W_{i \to j} \right) \tag{9}$$

Where Q_i represents the layer weight of node i, $Q_{k \to i}$ represents the layer weight of node k which points to node i, $Q_{i \to j}$ represents the layer weight of

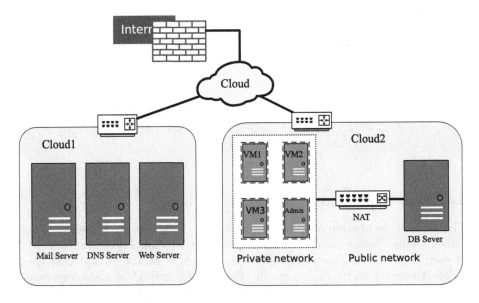

Fig. 3. Web application framework.

node j which is pointed by node i. $W_{k\to i}$ is the weight of $<k, i>$ and $W_{i\to j}$ is the weight of $<i, j>$. We set $I + O = 1$, and $I = 0.75$, $O = 0.25$ (Fig. 3).

4 Experimental Settings and Results

4.1 Experimental Environment

To verify our method, we built a client-server web application that contains two cloud infrastructures connected to the Internet through an external firewall [15]. The framework is shown in Fig. 2. After scoring the edges and making edge reduction, we got the attack graph given in Fig. 4(a). It reveals attackers' attack ways aimed at VMs in the private network and the DB server in the public network. The details of the attack graph are contained in Table 1 and Table 2.

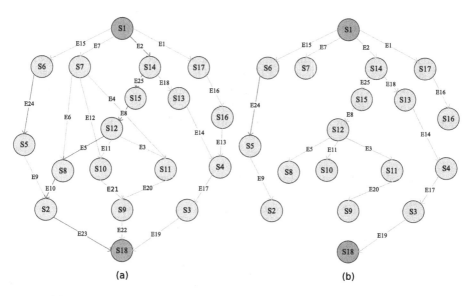

Fig. 4. (a) Attack graph of the framework. (b) The spanning arborescence of maximum weight. (Color figure online)

4.2 Experimental Results

Firstly, for the purpose of assessing the overall risk of the network, we use the fusion algorithm of PSO and GWO to find the spanning arborescence T of maximum weight. We set the size of the population as 30 and set the maximum number of iterations as 300. In the limited number of iterations, it can always find the target spanning arborescence T, which is shown in Fig. 4(b). In addition, the change of its fitness function value can be seen in Fig. 5(a), which shows the process of the algorithm to obtain the optimal result.

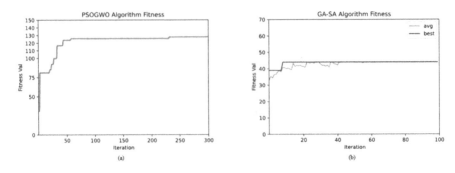

Fig. 5. (a) Fitness for PSOGWP. (b) Fitness for GA-SA.

Then, to find the path with maximum risk, we set the size of the population as 15 and set the max number of iterations as 100. The path found in the attack graph is marked red in Fig. 4(a). Its best and average fitness function values are shown in Fig. 5(b).

Finally, measuring the importance of each state node in the attack graph is also a significant job. The result of ISM shows that the graph is divided into four layers. From the first layer to the fourth layer are $\{S1, S6, S7, S14, S15, S17\}$, $\{S5, S12, S13, S16\}$, $\{S4, S8, S10, S11\}$, $\{S2, S3, S9, S18\}$. This result can be mutually confirmed by the spanning arborescence T. Table 3 shows the ranking list of node importance.

Table 3. Statistical table of importance degree of each node

ID	Q	Importance	ID	Q	Importance
S1	0.48	4.320	S8	0.16	0.418
S14	0.48	1.958	S10	0.16	0.389
S7	0.48	1.843	S13	0.24	0.346
S6	0.48	1.267	S11	0.16	0.302
S15	0.48	1.520	S2	0.12	0.205
S17	0.48	1.520	S4	0.16	0.204
S12	0.24	0.979	S9	0.12	0.174
S16	0.24	0.461	S3	0.12	0.088
S5	0.24	0.425	S18	0.12	0.086

5 Conclusion

This paper proposes two heuristic algorithms and a node importance evaluation method for extracting messages from attack graphs, and they get excellent performance in the test environment. Compared to traditional algorithms, their advantage is not obvious when the input scale is small, and the input is specific. However, the attack graph scale is growing with the development of network technology, and the attack graph situation becomes variable. Traditional algorithms are no longer applicable. Heuristic algorithms have natural advantages in dealing with such complex problems. No matter what the input attack graph looks like, heuristic algorithms can always find the optimal result within a fixed time to complete the iteration.

This paper analyzes the attack graph from three levels: entire attack graph, single attack path, single state node and extracts as much information as possible that may be contained in the attack graph. The results generated by algorithms are related to each other, and they can be used to complete a comprehensive network risk assessment.

Acknowledgement. This work is supported by the National Key R&D Program of China (Funding No. 2020YFB1805503). The 2020 Industrial Internet Innovation and Development Project from Ministry of Industry and Information Technology of China, the Fundamental Research Fund for the Central Universities (30918012204, 30920041112), Jiangsu Province Modern Education Technology Research Project (84365); National Vocational Education Teacher Enterprise Practice Base "Integration of Industry and Education" Special Project (Study on Evaluation Standard of Artificial Intelligence Vocational Skilled Level); Scientific research project of Nanjing Vocational University of Industry Technology (2020SKYJ03).

References

1. Ammann, P., Wijesekera, D., Kaushik, S.: Scalable, graph-based network vulnerability analysis. In: Proceedings of the ACM Conference on Computer and Communications Security, pp. 217–224 (2002). https://doi.org/10.1145/586110.586140
2. Dai, F., Hu, Y., Zheng, K., Wu, B.: Exploring risk flow attack graph for security risk assessment. IET Inf. Secur. **9**(6), 344–353 (2015)
3. Ghoshal, S., Sundar, S.: Two approaches for the min-degree constrained minimum spanning tree problem. Applied Soft Computing **111**, 107715 (2021). https://doi.org/10.1016/j.asoc.2021.107715
4. Hasteer, N., Bansal, A., Murthy, B.K.: Assessment of cloud application development attributes through interpretive structural modeling. Int. J. Syst. Assur. Eng. Manag. **8**, 1069–1078 (2017). https://doi.org/10.1007/s13198-017-0571-2
5. Ibrahim, A., Bozhinoski, S., Pretschner, A.: Attack graph generation for microservice architecture. In: Proceedings of the ACM Symposium on Applied Computing, vol. Part F147772, pp. 1235–1242 (2019). https://doi.org/10.1145/3297280.3297401
6. Ingols, K., Lippmann, R., Piwowarski, K.: Practical attack graph generation for network defense. In: Proceedings - Annual Computer Security Applications Conference, ACSAC, pp. 121–130 (2006). https://doi.org/10.1109/ACSAC.2006.39
7. Kar, A.K.: Bio inspired computing - a review of algorithms and scope of applications. Expert Syst. Appl. **59**, 20–32 (2016). https://doi.org/10.1016/j.eswa.2016.04.018
8. Liu, C., Singhal, A., Wijesekera, D.: Mapping evidence graphs to attack graphs. In: WIFS 2012 - Proceedings of the 2012 IEEE International Workshop on Information

Forensics and Security, pp. 121–126 (2012). https://doi.org/10.1109/WIFS.2012. 6412636

9. Mann, M., Sangwan, O.P., Tomar, P., Singh, S.: Automatic goal-oriented test data generation using a genetic algorithm and simulated annealing. In: Proceedings of the 2016 6th International Conference - Cloud System and Big Data Engineering, Confluence 2016, pp. 83–87 (2016). https://doi.org/10.1109/CONFLUENCE.2016. 7508052

10. Musa, T., et al.: Analysis of complex networks for security issues using attack graph. In: 2019 International Conference on Computer Communication and Informatics, ICCCI 2019 (2019). https://doi.org/10.1109/ICCCI.2019.8822179

11. Ou, X., Govindavajhala, S., Appel, A.W.: MulVAL: a logic-based network security analyzer. In: 14th USENIX Security Symposium, pp. 113–128 (2005)

12. Blank, R.M., Gallagher, P.D.: NIST Special Publication 800-30 Revision 1 - Guide for Conducting Risk Assessments, p. 95. NIST Special Publication, September 2012

13. Sheyner, O., Haines, J., Jha, S., Lippmann, R., Wing, J.: Automated generation and analysis of attack graphs. In: IEEE Symposium on Security and Privacy, p. 273, May 2002

14. Sing, A.N.U., Raphs, A.T.G.: A predictive framework for cyber security analytics using attack graphs. Int. J. Comput. Netw. Commun. **7**(1), 1–17 (2015)

15. Stergiopoulos, G., Dedousis, P., Gritzalis, D.: Automatic analysis of attack graphs for risk mitigation and prioritization on large-scale and complex networks in Industry 4.0. Int. J. Inf. Secur. **21**, 37–59 (2021). https://doi.org/10.1007/s10207-020-00533-4

16. Swiler, L.P., Phillips, C.: A graph-based system for network-vulnerability analysis. In: The 1998 Workshop (1998)

Research on Network Security Automation and Orchestration Oriented to Electric Power Monitoring System

Xiaobo Ling[1], Longyun Qi[2], Man Li[3], and Jun Yan[2,4,5(✉)]

[1] State Grid Shanghai Municipal Electric Power Company, Shanghai 200122, China
[2] State Grid Electric Power Research Institute, Nanjing 210003, China
qilongyun@sgepri.sgcc.com.cn, yanjun_2021@163.com
[3] State Grid Shanghai Municipal Electric Power Company Songjiang Power Supply Company, Shanghai 201699, China
[4] Intelligent Manufacturing Department, Wuyi University, Jiangmen 529020, China
[5] School of Cyber Science and Engineering, Nanjing University of Science and Technology, Nanjing 210094, China

Abstract. Nowadays, an electric power monitoring system may cause great damage due to security incidents happened. Furthermore, traditional active defense technologies no longer guarantee the safety and reliability of an electric power monitoring system. Thus, it is urgent to develop a new security defense technology suitable for the electric power monitoring system, the new security defense technology can take precautions against the destructive attacks occurring in the electric power monitoring system. According to the analysis of the network security demands of the electric power monitoring system, we propose an active defense system framework based on security automation and orchestration technology (i.e., SAOT). The active defense system framework with multi-layer architecture and functional modules integrates modules such as the behavioral feature extraction of typical network security events, the security disposal strategy generation of typical network security events, and the automation orchestration of security disposal strategies. Furthermore, the SAOT active defense system framework simultaneously solves the aspects of the vulnerability and security problems in the electric power monitoring system. Finally, a case study is adopted to further describe and explain the SAOT active defense system framework. Results indicate that the SAOT active defense system framework can ensure the information security of the national power system in cyberspace.

Keywords: Network security · Security automation and orchestration technology · Electric power monitoring system · Active defense system

1 Introduction

Currently, computer, network and communication technologies are popular in modern power systems; furthermore, the electric power monitoring system is a piece of intelligent

M. R. Khosravi et al. (Eds.): CloudComp 2021, LNICST 430, pp. 195–206, 2022.
https://doi.org/10.1007/978-3-030-99191-3_15

equipment that monitors and controls the process of power production and supply based on computer and network technology, supported by communication and data networks. In fact, the electric power monitoring system makes sense to ensure the safe and stable operation of the modern power system [1]. Moreover, according to the neural network and control center of the whole power system, i.e., the electric power monitoring system, the countries and the governments can provide reliable electricity to industries efficiently and residents to enhance economic and social development in a further step.

However, computer, network and communication attacks against the electric power monitoring system have broken out frequently, and these computer, network and communication attacks have the characteristics of specialization, high hazard and high persistent threat [2, 3]. Thus, the security defense of the electric power monitoring system has already been emphasized at the national security level. Furthermore, as computer, network and communication security incidents may cause great damage to the electric power monitoring system, the power grid company needs to establish and improve a comprehensive security protection system of the electric power monitoring system continuously.

In the electric power monitoring system, the appropriate and rapid response to computer, network and communication attacks is crucial to minimize and avoid attack as it is hard to prevent all attack incidents before it comes out. To this end, it is now becoming significant to construct a quick and proper network security response in the electric power monitoring system. The network security response can minimize and avoid attacks to the electric power monitoring system caused by attack incidents; meanwhile, the network security response can reduce the possibility of data damage.

Drawing on mature security defense theories at home and abroad [4], and according to the analysis of the network security demands of the electric power monitoring system, we propose an active defense system framework based on the security automation and orchestration technology (i.e., SAOT). Furthermore, the SAOT active defense system framework consists of multi-layer architecture and functional modules. This framework mainly integrates modules such as the behavioral feature extraction of typical network security events, the security disposal strategy generation of typical network security events, and the automation orchestration of security disposal strategies. In fact, the active defense system framework simultaneously solves the aspects of the vulnerability and security problems in the electric power monitoring system to ensure the safe, stable, and economic operation of the modern power system and the electric power monitoring system; furthermore, the set of active defense system framework further ensures the information security of the national power system in cyberspace.

Contributions of this paper can be summarized as follows:

(1) To minimize and avoid attacks to the electric power monitoring system caused by computer, network and communication attack incidents, we propose an active defense system framework based on security automation and orchestration technology (i.e., SAOT). The SAOT active defense system framework can simultaneously address the vulnerability and security problems in the electric power monitoring system.

(2) The SAOT active defense system framework consists of multi-layer architecture and functional modules. This framework mainly integrates modules such as the

behavioral feature extraction of typical network security events, the security disposal strategy generation of typical network security events, and the automation orchestration of security disposal strategies.

(3) Finally, we employ a case study to further verify the effectiveness and feasibility of the SAOT active defense system framework. Meanwhile, the SAOT active defense system framework can ensure the safe, stable, and economic operation of the modern power system and the information security of the national power system in cyberspace.

The rest of this paper is organized as follows. Section 2 refers to related work. Section 3 presents the research motivation of the electric power monitoring system security defense. Section 4 presents an active defense system framework based on security automation and orchestration technology (i.e., SAOT). In Sect. 5, a case study verifies the effectiveness and feasibility of the SAOT active defense system framework. Finally, Sect. 6 summarizes the research content and future direction of the paper.

2 Related Work

2.1 Anomaly Detection

Anomaly detection is an active research topic and plays an important role in more and more fields. Currently, the role of anomaly detection in different scenarios has been explored and researched in many aspects [5]. For example, the work of [6] proposed a probability model of the mentioning behavior of a social network user, and the probability model detected the emergence of a new topic from the anomalies. For electric power data, Pang et al. [7] taken advantage of data mining correlation analysis, anomaly detection, hypothesis testing and sequence analysis methods in responding to the challenges faced by the information security protection system. Based on the deep learning algorithm, Hinami et al. [8] integrated a generic CNN model and anomaly detection based on environment to solve the problem of joint detection and recounting of abnormal events in videos; in practice, their first learned CNN with multiple visual tasks to separate object features and action attributes, and then recounted and detected anomalous activity by plugging the model into anomaly detectors. Furthermore, Luo et al. [9] were inspired by the capability of sparse coding-based anomaly detection, and presented a Temporally-coherent Sparse Coding (TSC) approach; the TSC approach mapped a temporally coherent sparse coding for stack RNN to enhance the reconstruction coefficient and executed identification based on reconstruction error. In fact, as smaller amounts of anomalous instances are combined with the dictionary, the TSC approach failed to detect similar types of anomalous activities. In addition, the log-based anomaly detection research was classified into two broad categories, i.e., online anomaly detection system and offline anomaly detection system [10]: for online anomaly detection system, as the events are recorded, the system performs anomaly detection in real-time; for offline anomaly detection system, the system is mainly used to debug or detect anomalies when they occur.

2.2 Active Defense

Traditional active defense methods mainly contain the fire-wall, honeypot techniques and so on. At present, academia and industry have made progress in active defense. For example, many defensive measures have been taken by the cybersecurity community to solve the adversarial intrusion problems in industrial control networks. Wang et al. [3] proposed an active defense system framework based on the analysis of the network security demands of the electric power monitoring system. The active defense system framework contained multiple modules (i.e., data collection, threat analysis and identification, active defense strategy library, etc.), and these modules were independent of each other. Furthermore, the security attacks of the industrial Internet have become more covert and diversified. Traditional active defense approaches only defended a single attack, so Sun et al. [11] showed a three-dimensional defense architecture depended on deception defense and active defense. The model can deal with the complex and diversified security protection requirements of the industrial Internet. In addition, Zhang et al. [12] presented an active DDoS defense model based on packet marking to address the problem of DDoS attacks. The model mainly contained two parts: the subsystem for tracking the attacks and the subsystem for filtering the attack flows. Meanwhile, the model used an authenticated packet marking scheme for IP trace-back to reconstruct the attack path efficiently. Ma et al. [13] proposed a malicious code intrusion active defense technology and the defense technology structure in solving the low defense efficiency and poor stability problems of the traditional LAN networks. Meanwhile, the system structure mainly contained three parts: executive layer, kernel layer and hardware layer, and the work-flow contained four parts, i.e., file display, file processing, file judgment and file compression.

In this section, we mainly show various existing anomaly detection and active defend methods. According to the above research analysis, we propose an active defense system framework based on security automation and orchestration technology (i.e., SAOT). SAOT can simultaneously solve the vulnerability and security problems in the electric power monitoring system. Next, we will describe the research motivation of the electric power monitoring system security defense in Sect. 3.

3   Research Motivation

In Fig. 1, the main structure of the electric power monitoring system is a multi-layer star network. Specifically, the electric power monitoring system adopts the double star structure between the backbone layer and the core layer; meanwhile, the upper point of the backbone layer and the core layer is regarded as the network node. As the network structure characteristics of the electric power monitoring system are multi-layer and distributed, the power monitoring system needs to realize self-defense within the node domain of the local level and cross-domain cooperation defense between different levels. In addition, existing security technologies have static superposition characteristics, and some existing defense methods have single and solidified characteristics. According to the above analysis, the existing security defense approaches fail to satisfy the demand of the electric power monitoring system with dynamic, active, and cross-domain defenses under the background of new threats. Therefore, we will encounter and address some problems in the process of active defense, as follow:

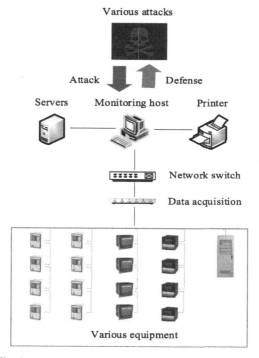

Fig. 1. An intuitive example of our research motivation.

(1) At present, all kinds of security facilities deployed on the electric power monitoring system mainly depend on the equipment's solidification strategy. Thus, the coordination among these security facilities is facing different safety defense objectives.

(2) Furthermore, various types of security operation information, equipment operation information and data log information data of these security facilities fail to collect, fuse, process and distribute rapidly, so the security facilities do not share security threat information among themselves in time and further increase the case of missing and misinformation of threat warning information.

(3) In the electric power monitoring system, the decentralized detection and response mechanisms need to be integrated to adaptively implement diverse security disposal strategies that support the master station layer, network layer, plant station layer, and various equipment (i.e., cross-network equipment, security equipment and host equipment). Thus, the electric power monitoring system can achieve the blocking and isolation of network security risks more reliably, accurately, and faster.

In short, according to the network structure of the electric power monitoring system and the existing security defense technologies, how to design a multi-level and cross-domain automation orchestration technology of security disposal strategies is the key and difficult point of this paper. Next, this paper proposes a new active defense system framework based on security automation and orchestration technology (i.e., SAOT), introduced in detail in Sect. 4.

4   An Active Defense System Framework Design

According to the above analysis, we propose an active defense system framework based on the security automation and orchestration technology (i.e., SAOT). As shown in Fig. 2, our active defense system framework follows a task sequence, and the task sequence mainly contains the following three activities: (1) the behavioral feature extraction of typical network security events, (2) the security disposal strategy generation of typical network security events, (3) and the automation orchestration of security disposal strategies.

4.1   The Behavioral Feature Extraction of Typical Network Security Events

As shown in Fig. 2, there are three diverse data source feature extraction technologies, i.e., data source feature extraction and analysis based on Agent acquisition, data source feature extraction and analysis based on network flow acquisition, and the behavioral feature extraction and analysis of ATT&CK attack.

Data Source Feature Extraction and Analysis Based on Agent Acquisition. The research of the data source feature extraction and analysis based on Agent acquisition focuses on log files collection, files integrity collection and command monitoring. For log files collection, the Agent log analysis module catches security issues such as system errors, configuration errors, intrusion attempts, and strategy conflicts by monitoring the log files on the server. As the built-in basic analysis rules of Agent can be issued uniformly through the network security management platform, we can identify the remote login of violent cracking, Web attack detection, database violent cracking, system abnormal errors, Web application anomalies and database error information. Furthermore, the Agent log analysis module has the self-adaptive ability, can automatically scan the log directory, and complete the automatic configuration.

For files integrity collection, the Agent files integrity monitoring module can monitor specific files, trigger logging when modifying these files and report to the network security management platform. In addition, the monitoring contents mainly include important Linux system files and Windows registry entries, executable programs, SSH keys and other custom attributes. The files and paths of the built-in Agent basic file integrity monitoring can be uniformly distributed through the network security management platform.

For command monitoring, the Agent command monitoring module can execute system commands, information queries, script predefined operations on the operating system, and then further realize process monitoring, port opening monitoring, network connection monitoring, resource performance monitoring, historical record monitoring, process monitoring, and other custom commands.

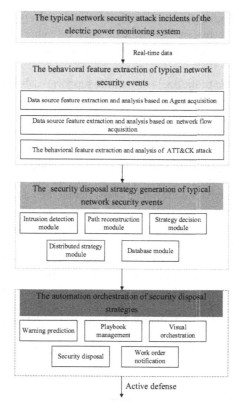

Fig. 2. An active defense system framework based on the security automation and orchestration technology.

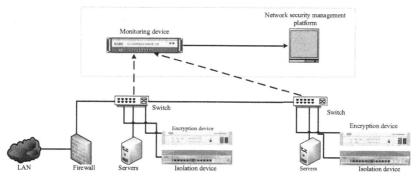

Fig. 3. An intuitive example of data source feature extraction and analysis based on network flow acquisition.

Data Source Feature Extraction and Analysis Based on Network Flow Acquisition.
As shown in Fig. 3, the research of the data source feature extraction and analysis
based on network flow acquisition concentrates on traffic storage, protocol analysis, and
abnormal behavior collection.

For traffic storage, the traffic analysis module supports real-time collection and storage of 100M, Gigabit, and 10G network traffic, and has a certain length of flow data
storage capacity and storage expansion capacity. Furthermore, the traffic analysis module
can save various statistical data such as captured raw data packets, data streams, network
sessions, and application logs in real-time. For protocol analysis, the protocol analysis
module supports the recording of communication logs and connection information of
common network protocols and industrial control protocols. For abnormal behavior collection, the abnormal behavior collection module detects and analyzes the network flow
of the electric power monitoring system to detect abnormal information in the network
in time and alarm. The classification of abnormal alarm includes worm, attack, Trojan,
abnormal traffic, sensitive information, and so on. Furthermore, the parameter threshold detected by anomalies can be adjusted according to the electric power monitoring
system's requirements, and the triggered anomaly information can be uploaded to the
network security management platform.

The Behavioral Feature Extraction and Analysis of ATT&CK Attack. The research
of the behavioral feature extraction and analysis of ATT&CK attack mainly contains
two databases (i.e., threat intelligence database and ATT&CK model database) and four
layers (i.e., data layer, analysis layer, recognition layer, and application layer).

In fact, the data layer mainly carries out data collection, normalization processing
and data management of network events in the electric power monitoring system. The
analysis layer includes two parts: feature analysis and correlation analysis. Furthermore,
the analysis layer ascertains the APT attack clues, Trojan viruses, and violent password
cracking from the algorithm model based on features. According to the APT attack
clues obtained by the analysis layer, the recognition layer identifies and correlates the
APT attack from the dimension of attack technology and attack tactics respectively, and
finally generates the full picture of the APT attack from the perspective of the attacking
team. The application layer mainly performs the visual presentation of the APT attack,
the presentation of the global security situation, and the security early warning.

According to the above analysis, three diverse data source behavioral feature extraction technologies can realize the perception, discovery, and root tracing of network attack
events in the electric power monitoring system.

4.2 The Security Disposal Strategy Generation of Typical Network Security Events

As shown in Fig. 2, the proposed security disposal strategy generation technology mainly
includes five modules: intrusion detection module, path reconstruction module, strategy
decision module, distributed strategy module and the database module. The whole security disposal strategy generation technology adopts the centralized control way, and the
deployment process adopts the distributed implementation way.

As shown in Fig. 4, the intrusion detection module will respond timely when it detects the intrusion attack. At the same time, the intrusion alarm and attack data are transmitted to the path reconstruction module. Once receiving the intrusion alarm and attack data information, the path reconstruction module will analyze the attack event and reconstruct the path, and send the reconstructed attack path information (i.e., attack topology information) to the strategy decision module. After receiving the attack topology information, the strategy detection module starts to analyze the attack topology information and formulate the corresponding security strategy. After that, the prepared security strategy information is edited into strategy request information and sent to the distributed strategy module. Then, the distributed strategy module generates the corresponding security strategy rules and the deployment information. The distributed strategy module integrates the generated security strategy rules and deployment information, edits the strategy request response information, and sends it to the strategy decision module. At last, when the strategy request-reply is received from the distributed strategy module, the strategy decision module sends a strategy reply message to the intrusion detection module to complete the strategy generation process. Meanwhile, all generated entire strategies are stored in the database module.

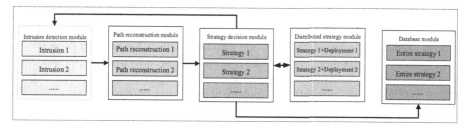

Fig. 4. The process of the security disposal strategy generation technology.

Based on the behavioral feature extraction of typical network security events, the response and generation of the security disposal strategy can be completed by evaluating the impact factors comprehensively such as event type, event frequency, response time, scope, and risk.

4.3 The Automation Orchestration of Security Disposal Strategies

As shown in Fig. 2 and Fig. 5, the proposed automation orchestration of security disposal strategies mainly includes five parts: warning prediction, playbook management, visual orchestration, security disposal, and work order notification. Additionally, the process of the automation orchestration of security disposal strategies can achieve the blocking and isolation of network security risks reliably, accurately, and faster.

The warning prediction is mainly made up of trigger conditions and response actions. In fact, the warning prediction is a continuous analysis and response to a group of related log events. Furthermore, the warning prediction can assign different Playbook scripts to different types of cases with the case processing function, and supervise the execution. For playbook management, Playbook is a "script" that records the security engineer's workflow. Common Playbooks include investigation and forensics, global blocking, host isolation, work order, email warning, etc. In fact, Playbook can be created and saved through visual orchestration and can be referenced by rules. Meanwhile, the Playbook is triggered when the conditions are met, and the response device is called to perform the response action.

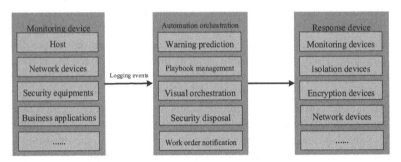

Fig. 5. The process of the automation orchestration of security disposal strategies.

The visual orchestration charges for generating strategies and Playbooks. The visual orchestration simplifies the security operational disposal process by the drag-and-drop way. In addition, the visual orchestration provides context for security disposal and reduces the complexity of security incident disposal. For security disposal, the automatic orchestration ban is generally implemented by devices performing response disposal actions, and Playbook calls different triggered devices to perform disposal action. For work order notification, the manager will carry out relevant security disposals after receiving the work orders.

5 A Case Study

In this section, a case study is discussed to demonstrate the process of the active defense system framework based on the security automation and orchestration technology (i.e., SAOT).

In Fig. 6, we use the data information provided by NARI Information & Communication Technology CO., LTD to implement the execution process of the SAOT method. First, we use three diverse data source feature extraction technologies (i.e., data source feature extraction and analysis based on Agent acquisition, data source feature extraction and analysis based on network flow acquisition, and the behavioral feature extraction and analysis of ATT&CK attack) to process existing data. Thus, the behavioral feature extraction of typical network security events approach can realize the perception, discovery, and root tracing of network attack events in the electric power monitoring system. Next, according to the behavioral feature extraction of typical network security events, the response and generation of the security disposal strategy can be completed by comprehensively evaluating the impact factors such as event type, event frequency, response time, scope, and risk. Finally, based on the behavioral feature extraction of typical network security events and the security disposal strategy generation, we take advantage

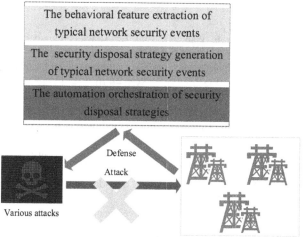

The electric power monitoring system

Fig. 6. A case study of the electric power monitoring system attack and defense.

of the automation orchestration mothed to adaptively implement and perform diverse security disposal strategies that support the master station layer, network layer, and plant station layer. Thus, the electric power monitoring system can achieve the blocking and isolation of network security risks more reliably, accurately, and faster.

6   Conclusion and Future Work

In this paper, we put forward a novel active defense system framework based on security automation and orchestration technology (i.e., SAOT). The SAOT mainly integrates modules such as the behavioral feature extraction of typical network security events, the security disposal strategy generation of typical network security events, and the automation orchestration of security disposal strategies. Furthermore, the SAOT simultaneously solves the vulnerability and security problems in the electric power monitoring system to ensure the safe, stable, and economic operation of the modern power system and the electric power monitoring system.

In the follow-up work, the real-world experiments are designed and performed to further validate the feasibility and effectiveness of the SAOT approach. Meanwhile, we will continue to verify the field test work of the security automation and orchestration technology suitable for the electric power monitoring system.

Acknowledgment. This work was supported in part by 2021 Science and Technology Project of State Grid Corporation: Research on Vulnerability Analysis and Threat Detection Key Technology of Power Monitoring System in Cyberspace. No. 5108-202117055A-0-0-00. The 4th project "Research on the Key Technology of Endogenous Security Switches" (2020YFB1804604) of the National Key R&D Program, the 2020 Industrial Internet Innovation and Development Project from Ministry of Industry and Information Technology of China, the Fundamental Research Fund for the Central Universities (30918012204, 30920041112).

References

1. Li, T., Su, S., Yang, H., Wen, F., Wang, D., Zhu, L.: Attacks and cyber security defense in cyber-physical power system. Autom. Electric Power Syst. **41**(22), 162–167 (2017)
2. Liu, N., Yu, X., Zhang, J.: Coordinated cyber-attack: inference and thinking of incident on Ukrainian power grid. Autom. Electric Power Syst. **40**(6), 144–147 (2016)
3. Wang, Z., Zhu, S., Huang, T., Zhu, J., Fang, H.: Research on network security active defense system oriented to electric power monitoring system. In: 2020 IEEE International Conference on Information Technology, Big Data and Artificial Intelligence (ICIBA), Chongqing, China, pp. 883–887. IEEE (2020)
4. Xu, R., Chen, J.: Collaborative defense architecture of cyberspace security. Commun. Technol. **49**(01), 92–96 (2016)
5. Qi, L., Zhang, X., Li, S., et al.: Spatial-temporal data-driven service recommendation with privacy-preservation. Inf. Sci. **515**, 91–102 (2020)
6. Takahashi, T., Tomioka, R., Yamanishi, K.: Discovering emerging topics in social streams via link anomaly detection. IEEE Trans. Knowl. Data Eng. **26**(1), 120–130 (2013)
7. Kim, H., Kim, I., Chung, T.-M.: Abnormal behavior detection technique based on big data. In: Park, J., Zomaya, A., Jeong, H.-Y., Obaidat, M. (eds.) Frontier and Innovation in Future Computing and Communications. LNEE, vol. 301, pp. 553–563. Springer, Dordrecht (2014). https://doi.org/10.1007/978-94-017-8798-7_66
8. Hinami, R., Mei, T., Satoh, S.: Joint detection and recounting of abnormal events by learning deep generic knowledge. In: 2017 IEEE International Conference on Computer Vision (ICCV), Venice, Italy, pp. 3639–3647. IEEE (2017)
9. Luo, W., Liu, W., Gao, S.: A revisit of sparse coding based anomaly detection in stacked RNN framework. In: 2017 IEEE International Conference on Computer Vision (ICCV), Venice, Italy, pp. 341–349. IEEE (2017)
10. Vannel, Z., Donghyun, K., Daehee, S., Ahyoung, L.: An unsupervised anomaly detection framework for detecting anomalies in real time through network system's log files analysis. High-Confidence Comput. **1**(2), 100030 (2021)
11. Sun, Y., Peng, X., Tian, Z., Guo, S.: A deception defense and active defense based three-dimensional defense architecture: DA-3DD design and implementation plan. In: 2019 15th International Conference on Mobile Ad-Hoc and Sensor Networks (MSN), Shenzhen, China, pp. 422–427. IEEE (2019)
12. Zhang, Y., Wan, Z., Wu, M.: An active DDoS defense model based on packet marking. In: 2009 Second International Workshop on Computer Science and Engineering, Qingdao, China, pp. 435–438. IEEE (2009)
13. Ma, L., Kang, Y.-J., Han, H.: Research on LAN network malicious code intrusion active defense technology. In: Gui, G., Yun, L. (eds.) ADHIP 2019. LNICSSITE, vol. 301, pp. 57–64. Springer, Cham (2019). https://doi.org/10.1007/978-3-030-36402-1_6

Energy- and Reliability-Aware Computation Offloading with Security Constraints in MEC-Enabled Smart Cities

Bohai Zhao[1], Kai Peng[1(✉)], Fangyuan Zhu[2], and Shengjun Xue[3]

[1] College of Engineering, Huaqiao University, Quanzhou, China
`kai.peng@hqu.edu.cn`
[2] School of Electronic Science and Engineering, Xiamen University, Xiamen, China
[3] School of Computer Science and Technology, Silicon Lake College,
Suzhou, China

Abstract. Smart city is a fast-growing system that provides a large number of collaborative services enabled by emerging technologies such as wireless sensor networks and radio frequency identification. Generally, massive heterogeneous smart devices in smart cities are served by limited resources, resulting in low processing efficiency and even insufficient reliability of applications. In this regard, people invented mobile edge computing (MEC) to provide smart devices with more processing capacity. Unfortunately, the computing resources of edge servers in MEC are limited. Consequently, it is of great importance to improve the resource management efficiency of the MEC system. In view of this, we construct a four-layer edge-enabled smart cities model in this paper. Technically, we propose an energy- and reliability-aware multi-objective optimization method which can jointly optimize the energy consumption of smart devices, the resource utilization of edge servers and improve the system's reliability while meeting the privacy constraints. Experimental results prove that our proposed method has good benefits to meet the needs of computation offloading in smart cities.

Keywords: Mobile edge computing · Multi-objective · Energy consumption · Reliability · Privacy protection

1 Introduction

In recent years, with the continuous improvement of city intelligence and the continuous upgrading of mobile device performance, the types of applications show a diversification trend, at the same time, the requirements of mobile users are also becoming more and more widespread [1–3]. The urgency of making the city a more suitable place for quality communication is triggering many initiatives from academia and industry. Benefiting the development of various core

M. R. Khosravi et al. (Eds.): CloudComp 2021, LNICST 430, pp. 207–220, 2022.
https://doi.org/10.1007/978-3-030-99191-3_16

technologies in the Internet of Things (IoT), a new concept came into existence, called smart city [4].

Smart cities contain countless smart devices (SDs), and the number of these SDs continues to grow at a fairly good clip. According to a study by the Cisco Visual Networking Index, the national network traffic network will grow nearly sevenfold from 2017 to 2022, to around 77 exabytes per month, which will undoubtedly be a major challenge for smart cities [5]. Nevertheless, the resources of SDs are often limited, resulting in limited computing speed, massive energy consumption and even inevitable faults, which may affect the further development of smart cities [6,7].

Fortunately, the emergence of mobile edge computing (MEC) brings hope to deal with the above problem [8–11]. The most straightforward idea is offloading the workflow applications to the edge servers for execution [12,13]. At the same time, the edge servers are generally placed close to the edges of the SDs, thus the energy consumption generated during computation migration can also be optimized to some extent.

However, the computing resources of edge servers are also limited, which means the workflow applications can not be offloaded arbitrarily, and proper offloading strategies must be devised for them. Otherwise, unreliable scenarios such as server downtime may occur. Furthermore, the edge servers in smart cities are heterogeneous, and even for the same edge server, the state of resources is set to dynamic for energy-efficient. Furthermore, compared with general applications, workflow applications in smart cities are not so easy to handle because of their complex structure. Besides, the security of tasks served by external servers is also one of the critical concerns in smart cities [14–16].

In view of the above analysis, we investigate the offloading strategy formulation problem for SDs in smart cities. The main contributions of this paper can be summarized as follows.

(1) In order to improve the reliability of the system, we build a four-layer edge-enabled smart city model based on the traditional three-layer MEC structure. Specifically, we combine the lazy shadow scheme with the MEC architecture and add a shadow server layer between the edge servers and core network. Besides, the workflow applications generated by SDs and the edge servers are defined as heterogeneous.

(2) We propose an energy- and reliability-aware multi-objective optimization method with security constraint based on the Non-dominated Sorting Genetic Algorithm II (ERMOS). Both the energy consumption of SDs, the resource utilization of edge servers, as well as the reliability of the edge servers are optimized jointly with security constraints.

(3) We carry on sufficient experiments and analysis to show the advantages of ERMOS.

The rest sections of this paper are described as follows. Section 2 introduces the related work in two directions, i.e., computing offloading for workflow application and computing offloading in smart cities. Then, the system model, workflow applications model, as well as mathematical model of the optimization goals are described in Sect. 3. Section 4 introduces the details of the proposed method. Then, the comparative experiments and experimental results are described in Sect. 5. Finally, we conclude our work and describe our future work.

2   Related Work

Computation Offloading for Workflow Applications. Xu et al. [17] studied the computation offloading issue in wireless metropolitan area network. They set the computing power of edge servers as a fixed value. Then, they proposed a novel method to optimize the energy consumption and the time consumption of the system. Aiming to reduce the algorithm overhead during offloading strategy formulation, Fan et al. [18] investigated the computation offloading problem by using a DAG-based model, and proposed a shortest-path-based algorithm offloading strategy for mobile-edge workflow applications. Similarly, Zhu et al. [19] devised a network resource allocation algorithm on the basis of deep Q-learning, which effectively reduced the completion time and energy consumption of service workflow applications.

Computation Offloading for Smart City. In order to minimize the energy consumption and execution latency of SDs while improving the quality of service for users in smart cities, Mazza et al. proposed a cluster-based computing offloading method in [20]. Qian et al. [21] focused on the computation offloading in IoT-Based smart cities. They proposed a scalable and sustainable IoT framework, which can reduce the end-to-end offloading time and energy consumption. Esposito et al. [22] propose a new method to cope with data privacy security issues during data packet transmission in cloud-enabled smart cities.

At present, most of the research on edge-enabled systems mainly focuses on multi-objective optimization for SDs. However, the unreliability of the edge server, such as downtime, may lead to workflow execution failure. Especially for smart cities, when facing massive data to be processed, the edge servers may get into a state of collapse at any time, resulting in a remarkable decline in the service benefit. In view of this, inspired by the lazy shadow scheme [23], we built a four-layer edge-enabled smart city model to explore the computation offloading problem for workflow applications generated by SDs. The energy consumption of SDs, the resource utilization of edge servers, the reliability of the system as well as the security of workflow applications during task processing are all taken into consideration.

3   System Model

In this section, the edge-enabled smart city mode is constructed firstly. Next, the computation model of the total energy consumption of SDs, the resource utilization, the reliability of the edge servers as well as the constraint model of privacy protection are described respectively. Finally, the problem formulation and our optimization goals are proposed. Some key variables are described in Table 1.

Table 1. Variables and explanations

Meaning	Notation
Workflow applications generated by SDs	SD
The maximum number of workflow applications	W
The data need to be calculated	S
The relationship between tasks	D
The power of SDs	P
Offloading strategy of tasks	OF
Propagation latency	PE
The maximum number of edge servers	ES
The maximum number of shadow servers	SS
Error probability of servers	RP

3.1 Network System Model

As Fig. 1 shows, the four-layer edge-enabled smart city model is constructed. This model is composed of four layers (i.e., SDs, edge servers, shadow servers and core network). Lower-layer terminals can request upper-layer services through corresponding wireless access nodes. Specifically, SDs in layer 1 will generate a certain number of workflow applications firstly. These workflow applications can directly obtain the services of SDs, but when faced with a huge amount of data, computation offloading, namely, to request upper-layer services, which is undoubtedly a better choice.

As the infrastructure of the second layer, edge servers can provide SDs with high-quality services through local area network (LAN). Specifically, edge servers can also communicate with the core network through wide area network (WAN) directly to ensure the workflow applications can be served by enough computing resources. Namely, the same as the traditional three-layer MEC model.

Particularly, based on the lazy shadow scheme [23], we construct a new layer between edge servers and the core network, defined as the shadow servers layer. Shadow servers are used to undertake some specific tasks from edge servers layer, so as to improve the reliability of workflow applications processing. The principle of shadow servers will be elaborated in Sect. 3.5.

Finally, the core network with almost infinite resources will serve as the uppermost terminal to ensure that the entire architecture has sufficient resources. All lower-layer servers can directly exchange data with it through the WAN.

3.2 Workflow Applications Model

The workflow applications are donated as $SD_w = (S_w, D_w)$ where $S_w = \{s_{1,w}, s_{2,w}, \ldots, s_{m,w}\}$ represents the data need to be calculated in the w-th workflow application while the number of the tasks are denoted as $m \in \{1, 2, \ldots, M\}$,

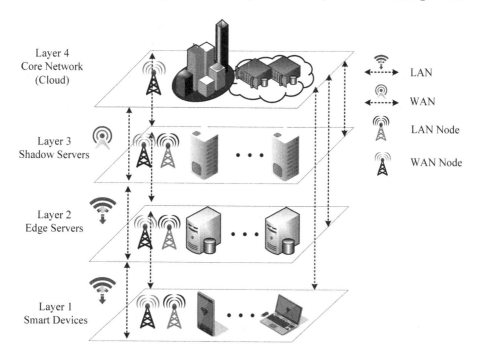

Fig. 1. Four-layer MEC-enabled smart city mode

and $w \in \{1, 2, \ldots, W\}$. Then, D_w represents the relationship between tasks and can be further denoted by a binary array, namely, $D_w = \{R(s_{m,w}, s_{m',w}), E_{m,m'}\}$ where $R(s_{m,w}, s_{m',w})$ represents the relationship between task $s_{m,w}$ and task $s_{m',w}$. In addition, $E_{m,m'}$ represents the transmission data between $s_{m,w}$ and $s_{m',w}$.

3.3   Energy Consumption Model

The total energy consumption mainly consists of three parts, namely, transmission energy, queue waiting energy and computation energy.

Layer 1. First of all, since SDs has certain computing resources, so the workflow applications can still obtain services directly, the energy consumption at this could be calculated and it is given by Eq. (1)

$$E_1(s_{m,w}) = \frac{S_w}{G_{local}} \times P_{work}, \tag{1}$$

where G_{local} indicates the computing resources of the SDs, and P_{work} represents the power cost when SDs work properly.

Layer 2. Then, when task requests for upper service, transmission energy is generated first.

$$E_2^{\alpha}(s_{m,w}, s_{m',w}) = \frac{E_{m,m'}}{W_{m,m'}} \times P_{cors}. \tag{2}$$

As Eq. (2) shows, there is a sequence constraint between two tasks $s_{m,w}$ and $s_{m',w}$, it is necessary to transfer some data to $s_{m',w}$ after the precursor task $s_{m,w}$ has been completed.

Besides, $W_{n,n'}$ represents the bandwidth for transmission. Specially, for layer 2, when two tasks are offloaded to the same edge server (i.e., $OF_{m,w} = OF_{m',w}$), we define $QC = 1$, and the bandwidth $W_{n,n'} = \infty$. However, when $OF_{m,w} \neq OF_{m',w}$, but both $OF_{m',w}$ and $OF_{m',w} \in \{1, 2, \ldots, ES\}$, $QC = 2$. $W_{n,n'}$ is defined as W_{sa}. When one of $OF_{m,w}$ and $OF_{m',w} \in \{1, 2, \ldots, ES\}$ and the other equals 0, at this time, $QC = 3$ and $W_{n,n'} = W_{df}$.

$$W_{n,n'} = \begin{cases} \infty & QC = 1 \\ W_{sa} & QC = 2 \\ W_{df} & QC = 3 \end{cases} \tag{3}$$

Similarly, when QC gets different values, SDs have two optional states, namely, working state and idle state. The power P_{cor} of SDs in different states follows the principle shown in Eq. (4)

$$P_{cor} = \begin{cases} P_{idle} & QC = 1 \\ P_{idle} & QC = 2 \\ P_{work} & QC = 3 \end{cases} \tag{4}$$

Similar to our previous work [24], the queue waiting energy consumption E_2^β is obtained based on queuing theory [25].

As shown in Eq. (5), the average queue length, the time interval of task arrival and the service time are denoted as L_{ave}, V_{task}, T_{sev}, respectively.

$$E_2^\beta = (\frac{L_{ave}}{V_{task}} - \frac{1}{T_{sev}}) \times P_{idle}. \tag{5}$$

Finally, the energy consumption can be obtained by Eq. (6) in which G_{es} represents the processing power of the es-th edge server ($es \in \{1, 2, \ldots, ES\}$). Then, PE_{es} represents the propagation delay during the offloading of $d_{n,a}$ to edge server es.

$$E_2^\gamma(s_{m,w}) = (\frac{S_w}{G_{es}} + PE_{es}) \times P_{idle}. \tag{6}$$

Layer 3. In this layer, the energy consumption is mainly generated in the stage of processing the copy of tasks and can be calculated by Eq. (7)

$$E_3 = \begin{cases} (\frac{SF_w}{V^{low}} \times P_{idle}) & FM = 0 \\ (\frac{S_w - SF_w}{V^{fast}} + \frac{SF_w}{V^{low}}) \times P_{idle} & FM = 1 \end{cases}, \tag{7}$$

where SF_w represents the amount of data that has been computed before the shadow server status changes, and FM represents the system status. When the value of FM is equal to 0, it means that no fault occurs. After SD_w^τ has been processed by es, its corresponding copy will also be discarded. But when $FM = 1$, which means a failure has occurred. Then, the shadow server ss will replace es to complete the subsequent processing for SD_w^τ. The specific model and related parameters of the lazy shadow scheme will be described in Sect. 3.5.

Layer 4. Different from the edge servers layer, the core network has nearly infinite computing resources, thus we will not consider the queuing waiting energy and the transmission energy caused by the inherent relationship of workflow applications. However, due to the long physical distance between core network and SDs, it is necessary to consider the energy consumption TE_c caused by network latency during offloading. At the same time, the propagation latency PE_c of the workflow application on the core network is also not negligible. In summary, the total energy consumption in layer 4 can be expressed as follows.

$$E_4(s_{m,w}) = TE_c + \left(\frac{S_w}{G_c} + PE_c\right) \times P_{idle}. \tag{8}$$

3.4   Resource Utilization Model

Edge servers are often defined as heterogeneous in smart cities, and their resources are extremely precious. The full use of resources also affects the level of the quality of service.

The resource utilization of es can be expressed by Eqs. (9) and (10). Generally, the number of virtual machines that can be accommodated in an edge server determines its resource capacity, namely, VM_{es}.

$$R_{es} = \begin{cases} \frac{K_{es}}{VM_{es}} & K_{es} < VM_{es} \\ 1 & K_{es} \geq VM_{es} \end{cases}, \tag{9}$$

$$K_{es} \in \{0, 1, \ldots, A \times Q\}, \tag{10}$$

where K_{es} represents the number of tasks offloaded to es, and $A \times Q$ represents the capacity of es.

3.5   Reliability Model

When an edge server es provides services for SD_w, it cannot guarantee to be completely accurate. On the contrary, a fatal error may occur in that edge server at any time. Therefore, in this paper, we allocated several shadow servers on the upper layer above edge servers, denoted as $ss \in \{1, 2, \ldots, SS\}$. Then, some tasks with reliability constraints are defined as SD_w^τ. When SD_w^τ is determined need to be offloaded to es, they will be copied to the corresponding ss. Next, when an error occurs while SD_w^τ is being calculated, ss will replace es in charge of processing workflow application SD_w^τ. When there is no error occurs, ss will discard the copy of SD_w^τ. Technically, ss has two states, namely, low-speed V_{low}

and high-speed V_{fast}, to perform the copy tasks. The state switching depends on whether an error occurs in es [23].

As a hardware infrastructure, the error probability of edge servers is very low, i.e. the typical rate is 4%. As a similar facility, shadow server also can not guarantee 100% reliability. Therefore, in this article, we use RP_{es} and RP_{ss} to represent the error probability of edge servers and shadow servers, respectively. Then the possibility that SD_w^τ can be successfully processed in an architecture equipped with n shadow servers can be expressed as

$$PO(s_{m,w}) = 1 - RP_{es} \times RP_{ss}^n. \tag{11}$$

3.6   Privacy Preservation Model

Through computation offloading, users in smart cities can enjoy high-quality services but may also have serious privacy leakage issues. Therefore, whether the privacy of users in smart cities can be guaranteed has aroused strong concern. Fortunately, faced with massive workflow applications, hackers must obtain enough task data that they can pose a threat to user privacy. Thus, privacy constraint has been added in this paper to improve the security of the system.

Specifically, two tasks with privacy conflicts should not be serviced by a single edge server [11]. The privacy constraints between two tasks $s_{m,w}$ and $s_{m',w}$ are redefined as $CO_w(m, m')$

$$CO_w(m, m') = \begin{cases} 1 & Have\ Privacy\ Conflicts \\ 0 & No\ Privacy\ Conflicts \end{cases}. \tag{12}$$

As Eq. (12) shows, when task $s_{m,w}$ and $s_{m',w}$ have privacy conflicts, namely, $CO_w(m, m') = 1$. The corresponding offloading strategy $OF_{m,w}$ can not be equal to $OF_{m',w}$. But when $CO_w(m, m') = 0$, there is no limit. Namely, $OF_{m,w}$ and $OF_{m',w}$ must satisfy the constraint shown by

$$\begin{cases} OF_{m,w} \neq OF_{m',w} & CO_w(m, m') = 1 \\ Unlimited & CO_w(m, m') = 0 \end{cases}. \tag{13}$$

3.7   Problem Formulation

In this paper, the energy consumption of SDs, the resource utilization of edge servers, the reliability of the system and the security of workflow applications are considered. Our optimization problem can be formulated as

$$Min\ \{E_{sum}(d_{m,w})\}, \tag{14}$$

$$Max\ \{R_{es}, PO(s_{m,w})\}, \tag{15}$$

$$OF_{m,w} \neq OF_{m',w}\ \ when\ \ CO_w(m, m') = 1. \tag{16}$$

4   Energy- and Reliability-Aware Multi-objective Optimization Method with Security Constraint (ERMOS)

In this part, faced with the four-layer network model constructed above, we propose a multi-objective optimization method for workflow applications, named Energy- and Reliability-aware Multi-Objective Optimization Method with Security Constraint (ERMOS). Based on NSGA-II [26], ERMOS can be roughly divided into 6 basic steps, namely, initialization, selection, crossover, mutation, calculation of crowding distance, and population update. The details of the method are described as follows.

The pseudo code is shown in Algorithm 1. First, based on genetic algorithms, we need to construct a new parent population PC_p. The size of the parent population TN_p is equal to the total number of tasks performed in SD_w. And the processing of tasks in the population also needs to meet the relational constraints D_w (Lines 1–3).

Then, we need to calculate the energy consumption, resource utilization, and reliability of the current iteration based on Eqs. (1)–(11). Then, we can get a new offspring population PC_o through selection, crossover and mutation based on PC_p. The size of PC_o is the same as PC_p. Specifically, the selection operation will select and sort based on the crowded distance of individuals in PC_p, and the crowding distance $Dis_{m,w}$ can be expressed as Eq. (17). $Dis_{m,w}$ actually depends on our proposed optimization goals, namely, the normalized value of energy consumption, resource utilization, and reliability probability. The smaller $Dis_{m,w}$, the higher the optimization efficiency of the individual under the current offloading strategy, and the greater the possibility that the individual will enter the next generation. In addition, the crossover and mutation operations effectively reduce the probability of local convergence (Lines 5–9).

After generating the offspring population, we need to fuse PC_p and PC_o to generate a mixed population, denoted as PC_{Mix}. Then, the parent population PC_p will be temporarily emptied. After non-dominated sorting from mixed populations, we can get several non-dominated layers NF (Lines 10–12). Finally, the best N individuals will be selected layer by layer to join the new parent population to achieve the purpose of updating the parent population. Particularly, if the last non-dominant layer cannot just fill the parent population. Then again, the better individuals in this layer will be selected to fill the parent population based on the crowding distance (Lines 13–20).

$$Dis_{m,w} = Normalized(E_{sum}, R_{es}, PO(s_{m,w})). \tag{17}$$

5   Experimental Evaluation

In this section, we conduct a detailed experimental evaluation of the method. Specifically, we construct three comparison methods in this paper. Then, the

---

Algorithm 1. ERMOS

Input: Workflow Applications SD_w, Maximum iteration times IT_{Max},
Output: Optimal offloading strategy $O_{m,w}$
1: $IT_{cur} = 1$
2: Initialize parent population PC_p
3: $TN_p = M \times W$
4: **while** $IT_{cur} \leq IT_{Max}$ **do**
5:      **for** PC_p **do**
6:          Calculate crowding distance $Dis_{m,w}$ based on (17)
7:      **end for**
8:      $PC_o =$ selection, crossover and mutation PC_p
9:      $TN_o = TN_p$
10:     $TN_{Mix} = TN_p + TN_o$
11:     $NF = fastnondominatesort(TN_{Mix})$
12:     $PC_p = \emptyset$
13:     $s = 0$
14:     **while** $len(PC_p) + len(NF[s]) < TN_p$ **do**
15:         $PC_p = PC_p \cup NF[s]$
16:         $s = s + 1$
17:     **end while**
18:     Calculate crowding distance of $(NF[s])$ based on (17)
19:     $PC_p = PC_p \cup$ select $NF[s]$
20:     $IT_{cur} = IT_{cur} + 1$
21: **end while**
22: **return** $O_{m,w}$

---

experimental results are analyzed and the effectiveness of the proposed method
is verified accordingly.

5.1   Experimental Setting

First, we construct three comparison methods. Their specific descriptions are
shown as follows.

Random Offloading Method (RO): All workflow applications will be
offloaded randomly.
Sequential Offloading Method (SO): All workflow applications will be
offloaded sequentially.
All Random Offloading to Edge Servers Method (ROE): All workflow
applications will be offloaded randomly, but they only consider edge servers
and will not be offloaded to other locations.
Our Method (ERMOS): The proposed method. All workflow applications
are offloaded based on ERMOS.

We implement these methods by MATLAB on a physical machine with 2
Intel Core i7-7700U 2.80 GHz processors and 16 GB RAM and the operating
system is Win10 64.

5.2   Experimental Result and Discussion

In this paper, the number of workflow applications and the maximum available edge servers are selected as experimental variables. Besides, considering that not all tasks require reliability guarantees. Therefore, only half of the edge servers have the ability to communicate with the shadow servers, which can obtain further reliability guarantee services. We have conducted 50 convergence experiments for each target.

The comparison among the four methods in terms of energy consumption are shown in Fig. 2 and Fig. 3. Due to a large number of workflow applications being offloaded to the local or core network, RO and SO will consume more energy than ROE and ERMOS. For ROE, while workflow applications are all offloaded to seemingly superior edge servers, there is a high probability that this random offloading strategy will still face challenges such as tasks exceed the maximum capacity of edge servers resulting in an energy-intensive wait in the queue. In contrast, the proposed method ERMOS can maintain good performance in energy consumption optimization, whether the number of workflow applications or edge servers changes.

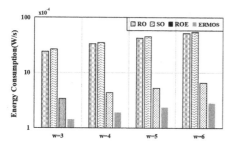

Fig. 2. Comparison of energy consumption when ES = 3

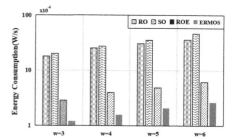

Fig. 3. Comparison of energy consumption when ES = 4

In terms of resource utilization, as shown in Fig. 4 and Fig. 5, whether the number of workflow applications or the number of edge servers changes, ERMOS can still maintain a high resource utilization. At the same time, combined with the above analysis of energy consumption, ERMOS can make a suitable computing offloading strategy to optimize energy consumption and reduce the waste of resources jointly.

Finally, as Fig. 6 shows, by adding several shadow servers to MEC structure, the reliability of the workflow application processing can be effectively improved. At the same time, the comparison between ERMOS and ROE can also prove that ERMOS has a practical optimization results in terms of reliability.

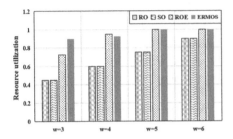

Fig. 4. Comparison of resource utilization when ES = 3

Fig. 5. Comparison of resource utilization when ES = 4

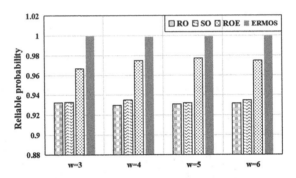

Fig. 6. Comparison of reliability when ES = 5

6 Conclusion

In this study, we investigate computation offloading for SDs in smart city. In particular, considering the reliability requirements of smart cities, we construct a four-layer MEC-enabled smart city model. The model of energy consumption, resource utilization and the reliability guarantee scheme are all described in details. Correspondingly, we propose a multi-objective optimization method, called ERMOS. The energy consumption of SDs, the resource utilization of edge servers, the system's reliability, and the security of workflow applications are taken into consideration jointly. Finally, extensive experiments and detailed discussion have proved the effectiveness and efficiency of our proposed solution.

In the future, we intend to combine the proposed method with blockchain, machine learning and other promising technologies in practical scenarios, such as intelligent warehousing.

Acknowledgment. The authors thank for the National Science Foundation of China (Grant No. 61902133), the Fundamental Research Funds for the Central Universities (ZQN-817), Quanzhou Science and Technology Project (No. 2020C050R) and College Students Innovation and Entrepreneurship Project (202010385011), Huaqiao University 2021 Teacher Teaching Development Reform Project (No. HQJG202120).

References

1. Giang, N.K., et al.: CityFlow: exploiting edge computing for large scale smart city applications, p. 8679234 (2019)
2. Khan, L.U., Yaqoob, I., Tran, N.H., Kazmi, S.M.A., Dang, T.N., Hong, C.S.: Edge computing enabled smart cities: a comprehensive survey. Networking and Internet Architecture (2019). arXiv:1909.08747
3. Mora, O.B., Rivera, R., Larios, V.M., Beltrán-Ramírez, J.R., Maciel, R., Ochoa, A.: A use case in cybersecurity based in blockchain to deal with the security and privacy of citizens and smart cities cyberinfrastructures. In: 2018 IEEE International Smart Cities Conference (ISC2), pp. 1–4. IEEE (2018)
4. Camero, A., Alba, E.: Smart city and information technology: a review. Cities **93**, 84–94 (2019)
5. Cisco Visual Networking Index. Cisco visual networking index: global mobile data traffic forecast update, 2017–2022. Technical report, Cisco, San Jose, CA, USA (2019)
6. Deng, S., Huang, L., Taheri, J., Zomaya, A.Y.: Computation offloading for service workflow in mobile cloud computing. IEEE Trans. Parallel Distrib. Syst. **26**(12), 3317–3329 (2014)
7. Abbas, N., Zhang, Y., Taherkordi, A., Skeie, T.: Mobile edge computing: a survey. IEEE Internet Things J. **5**(1), 450–465 (2017)
8. Peng, Kai, et al.: An energy- and cost-aware computation offloading method for workflow applications in mobile edge computing. EURASIP J. Wirel. Commun. Netw. **2019**(1) (2019). Article number: 207. https://doi.org/10.1186/s13638-019-1526-x
9. Wu, H., Sun, Y., Wolter, K.: Energy-efficient decision making for mobile cloud offloading. IEEE Trans. Cloud Comput. **8**(2), 570–584 (2018)
10. Hu, Y.C., Patel, M., Sabella, D., Sprecher, N., Young, V.: Mobile edge computing-a key technology towards 5G. ETSI White Paper **11**(11), 1–16 (2015)
11. Xu, X., Liu, X., Xu, Z., Wang, C., Wan, S., Yang, X.: Joint optimization of resource utilization and load balance with privacy preservation for edge services in 5G networks. Mob. Netw. Appl. **25**(2), 713–724 (2019). https://doi.org/10.1007/s11036-019-01448-8
12. Meng, T., Wolter, K., Huaming, W., Wang, Q.: A secure and cost-efficient offloading policy for mobile cloud computing against timing attacks. Pervasive Mob. Comput. **45**, 4–18 (2018)
13. Cheng, J., Shi, Y., Bai, B., Chen, W.: Computation offloading in cloud-RAN based mobile cloud computing system. In: 2016 IEEE International Conference on Communications (ICC), pp. 1–6. IEEE (2016)
14. Peng, K., Zhang, Y., Wang, X., Xu, X., Li, X., Leung, V.C.M.: Computation offloading in mobile edge computing. In: Shen, X., Lin, X., Zhang, K. (eds.) Encyclopedia of Wireless Networks, pp. 1–5. Springer, Cham (2019). https://doi.org/10.1007/978-3-319-78262-1_331
15. Shi, W., Cao, J., Zhang, Q., Li, Y., Lanyu, X.: Edge computing: vision and challenges. IEEE Internet Things J. **3**(5), 637–646 (2016)
16. Zhang, W.-L., Guo, B., Shen, Y., Wang, Y., Xiong, W., Duan, L.T.: Computation offloading on intelligent mobile terminal. Chin. J. Comput. **39**(5), 1021–1038 (2016)
17. Xu, X., et al.: An energy-aware computation offloading method for smart edge computing in wireless metropolitan area networks. J. Netw. Comput. Appl. **133**, 75–85 (2019)

18. Fan, L., Liu, X., Li, X., Yuan, D., Xu, J.: Graph4Edge: a graph-based computation offloading strategy for mobile-edge workflow applications. In: 2020 IEEE International Conference on Pervasive Computing and Communications Workshops (PerCom Workshops), pp. 1–4. IEEE (2020)

19. Zhu, A., et al.: Computation offloading for workflow in mobile edge computing based on deep Q-learning. In: 2019 28th Wireless and Optical Communications Conference (WOCC), pp. 1–5. IEEE (2019)

20. Mazza, D., Tarchi, D., Corazza, G.E.: A cluster based computation offloading technique for mobile cloud computing in smart cities. In: 2016 IEEE International Conference on Communications (ICC), pp. 1–6. IEEE (2016)

21. Qian, L.P., Wu, Y., Ji, B., Huang, L., Tsang, D.H.K.: HybridIoT: integration of hierarchical multiple access and computation offloading for IoT-based smart cities. IEEE Netw. **33**(2), 6–13 (2019)

22. Esposito, C., Castiglione, A., Frattini, F., Cinque, M., Yang, Y., Choo, K.-K.R.: On data sovereignty in cloud-based computation offloading for smart cities applications. IEEE Internet Things J. **6**(3), 4521–4535 (2018)

23. Cui, X., Znati, T., Melhem, R.: Adaptive and power-aware resilience for extreme-scale computing. In: 2016 International IEEE Conferences on Ubiquitous Intelligence & Computing, Advanced and Trusted Computing, Scalable Computing and Communications, Cloud and Big Data Computing, Internet of People, and Smart World Congress (UIC/ATC/ScalCom/CBDCom/IoP/SmartWorld), pp. 671–679. IEEE (2016)

24. Peng, K., Zhao, B., Xue, S., Huang, Q.: Energy- and resource-aware computation offloading for complex tasks in edge environment. Complexity **2020**, 1–4 (2020). https://doi.org/10.1155/2020/9548262

25. Xu, X., et al.: Multiobjective computation offloading for workflow management in cloudlet-based mobile cloud using NSGA-II. Comput. Intell. **35**, 12 (2018)

26. Deb, K., Pratap, A., Agarwal, S., Meyarivan, T.: A fast and elitist multiobjective genetic algorithm: NSGA-II. IEEE Trans. Evol. Comput. **6**(2), 182–197 (2002)

A Review of Cross-Blockchain Solutions

YuXuan Zuo[1] , Miao Yang[2], ZhenPing Qiang[1](✉) , Dai Fei[1] ,
XiaoFeng Shao[1] , ShiQi Su[1] , Qi Mo[3], and ZhiHong Liang[1]

[1] School of Big Data and Intelligent Engineering, Southwest Forestry University,
Kunming 650224, China
{scarlet,qzp}@swfu.edu.cn
[2] Yunnan Institute of Product Quality Supervision and Inspection, Kunming, China
[3] School of Software, Yunnan University, Kunming 650091, China

Abstract. With the development of distributed ledgers, a variety of blockchain projects, with different characteristics, are emerging and working in a broad range of application scenarios. Cross-Blockchain Solutions are designed to solve the issue of interoperability between different blockchains that are usually impossible with existing protocols and standards, those solutions are growing massively which have different properties. However, it is difficult for technicians to weigh the pros and cons and choose the optimal solution. In this paper, to understand the available solutions thoroughly, the protocol mechanisms of three mature cross-blockchain solutions are discussed. Then, four innovative solutions and their new capabilities are introduced, the pros and cons of above solution are identified. Finally, available industrial solutions in the market are discussed.

Keywords: Cross-blockchain · Distributed ledger · Interoperability

1 Introduction

Blockchain [1] is a kind of decentralized, tamper-proof, and traceability distributed database that can integrate the traditional single-party maintenance of multiple isolated databases only related to their own business. In this way, the information sharing and supervision between multiple parties can be realized, the tedious manual account checking can be avoided, the business processing efficiency can be improved, and the transaction cost can be reduced [2]. Therefore, blockchains have the potential for widespread application in many areas. These areas range from industry [3], finance [4], medicine [5], encryption [6], privacy protection [7] and so on. In short, blockchain can be applied to any tamper-proof and fully decentralized scenario of executing transactions and storing data without relying on a centralized third party.

The application demands of different fields of blockchain have promoted the generation of various blockchain projects. Since the birth of blockchain technology in 2008, thousands of blockchain projects have been gradually developed, they have formed numerous independent infrastructures and business systems [8]. However, on the one hand, all solutions are unable to exchange information and asset transfer, they are just

M. R. Khosravi et al. (Eds.): CloudComp 2021, LNICST 430, pp. 221–233, 2022.
https://doi.org/10.1007/978-3-030-99191-3_17

like "islands of information" that are isolated from each other. On the other hand, one of the core issues to be solved by blockchain technology is to improve transaction efficiency, but compared with the traditional centralized system, there is still a big gap [9]. Due to the development of the blockchain industry has been severely constrained by these restrictions, researchers have started to focus on the concept of cross-blockchain [10].

Cross-blockchain solutions allow value to cross the barriers between Blockchains, thus the circulation of value and the improvement of transaction efficiency are realized. Over the past few years, the number of proposed cross-blockchain solutions has been increasing. These solutions explore unique cross-blockchain technologies, each with its advantages and disadvantages. On the one hand, innovative cross-blockchain solutions enable developers to take advantage of new features and technologies, but this often means less security and more vulnerabilities. On the other hand, choosing mature and well-known cross-blockchain solutions can reduce the risk of losses, but innovative features are still unusable. For the above reasons, these problems need to be addressed urgently: how to grasp the current research status of cross-blockchain, understand various cross-blockchain technologies quickly, and select applications according to the development needs.

To solve these problems, the main contribution of this paper is as follow:

1) We have described the protocol mechanisms of three mature cross-blockchain solutions in detail.
2) We have Retrieved and introduced innovative cross-blockchain solutions and their new capabilities.
3) We have discussed the available industrial solutions on the market.

2   Mature Cross-Blockchain Solutions

Due to the complex problems faced by cross-blockchain technology, cross-blockchain solutions is still in the research and discussion stage, it has not been popularized and applied on a large scale. Because of the lack of interoperability at the beginning of the blockchain technology, the design and implementation of cross-chain technology should not only consider the blockchain system adapted to different architectures, but also ensure the high efficiency and security of cross-chain operation. At present, the mature cross-chain technology includes Notary Schemes, Sidechain/relay, and Hash-locking [11]. This section analyzes the principles and characteristics of the above three technologies. Table 2 shows the advantage and weaknesses of the above solutions.

2.1   Notary Schemes

In 2012, Ripple [12] proposed the Interledger [13] protocol, the purpose is to achieve mutual collaboration and communication between different blockchain ledgers, through this agreement to open up different information islands around the world, to realize the self-owned circulation and transmission of information in the whole Internet. Notary Schemes are improved technical framework based on Interledger protocol.

When different blockchain users do not trust each other when transacting, the easiest way is to find a trusted notary to conduct the transaction. The Notary Schemes are that the two parties of the transaction elect one or a group of nodes with high credibility to prove and verify the transaction transactions on different blockchains. The specific process is as follows: User N on the chain A transfers the assets to the notary, and the notary locks and confirms the assets and then transfers the corresponding assets to User M on the chain B. The greatest advantage of the Notary Schemes is that it is simple to implement and does not require complex proof of work.

The classification of Notary Schemes is shown in Fig. 1. If the notary is a trusted third party or an exchange, it is a single-signature notary scheme, which is responsible for the collection, verification, and transaction confirmation of the data. When a notary is a union of several agencies, it is called multi-signature notary scheme. Obviously, the above two models are relatively centralized, contrary to the decentralization of blockchain. Then it was born with distributed-signature notary schemes, the specific process based on generating the secret key cryptography, split into multiple parts, distributed to the random notary, allowing a percentage of the notary signature after together. Distributed-signature notary schemes can piece together a complete secret key, to complete a more decentralized transaction process.

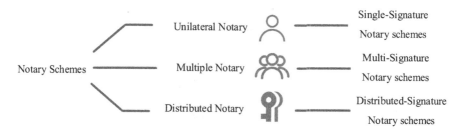

Fig. 1. Classification of notary mechanism

In 2015, the Ripple team released the Interledger Protocol (ILP) [14, 15] project based on Interledger protocol, which is currently the most representative scheme using the notary schemes. ILP allows two different blockchain systems to exchange value, information, and assets through third-party "connector". The ledger system does not need to trust the "connector", because the project uses cryptographic algorithm to create fund custody for the two ledger systems and the connector. When all the nodes involved in the cross-chain transaction have no objection to the transaction content, the transfer of the assets between different chains will be formally carried out with the assistance of the "connector".

2.2 Sidechain/Relay

Blockstream, a company founded in 2014 by bitcoin's core developers, is dedicated to developing a sidechain extension mechanism. That same year, Blockstream published its paper [16], in which the sidechain/relay was first proposed. They note that the technical architecture of Bitcoin is born with a lack of extensibility, such as long transaction latency, low throughput, and lack of support for Turing-complete smart contracts, which must be addressed by refactoring infrastructure and algorithms. However, as Bitcoin is the largest, most liquid, and most widely recognized digital currency, modifying its infrastructure may cause huge risks. Therefore, sidechain/relay is proposed and has many representative projects such as BTC Relay [17].

Sidechain. A sidechain is a concept as opposed to a mainchain. Blockstream's formal definition of "sidechain" is that "a sidechain is a blockchain that validates data from other blockchains." Solution of sidechain starts a blockchain to transfer the assets on the mainchain to the sidechain, and conversely, assets on the sidechain can be transferred back to the mainchain, to share the pressure on the mainchain and expand the performance and function of the mainchain. The bidirectional transfer of assets on the mainchain and sidechain is called Two-way Peg [18] of assets which is the core principle of sidechain implementation. The security of Two-Way Peg implementation depends on the incentives on the blockchain to enable the key parties involved in Two-Way Peg to perform what Two-Way Peg is supposed to do. Two-Way Peg can be achieved through the following modes: Single Custodian, Federated peg, Simplified Payment Verification (SPV) Proof [16], Drivechain [19], and Hybrid Models. Table 1 shows a comparison between the different technologies of the sidechain.

Table 1. Comparative analysis of sidechains

Category	Centralization	Security	Fork	Applicability
Single Custodian	High	Low, depending on the escrow	No	Low
Federated peg	High	Low, depending on the federation	No	Low
SPV Proof	Low	High	Soft fork of mainchain	High
Drivechain	Middle	Low, depending on the participation of the miners	Soft fork of mainchain	Middle
Hybrid Model	–	–	–	–

Relay. A sidechain is a relationship expression of chains, yet a relay-chain is more like a dispatch center for multiple chains. When the "sidechain" links many mainchains, it becomes a relay-chain. The relay mode is suitable for linking two heterogeneous or homogeneous blockchains and is a more direct way to achieve blockchain interoperability. This model does not completely rely on the verification and judgment of the trusted third party, but only performs self-verification by the middleman collecting the data status of the two chains. The verification methods vary significantly according to their own structure. Whether sidechain or relay, the most basic requirement is to collect the mainchain information.

The differences between sidechain and relay are:

1) In terms of dependency relationship, the sidechain is subordinate to the mainchain, and the transaction is limited between the mainchain and the sidechain. The relay is not subordinate to a mainchain but is more like a "dispatch center", only responsible for data transmission, but not for the maintenance of blockchain.
2) In terms of execution, the sidechain needs to synchronize all the block headers to verify whether the blockchain network recognizes the transaction; Relay does not need to download all the headers; therefore, it has superior speed.
3) In terms of security, the security of the sidechain is based on the basis that miners can be effectively verified for transaction consistency by the sidechain, while the security of the mainchain cannot play a role on the sidechain. The relay is verified by the mainchain, so the security is guaranteed.

2.3 Hash-Locking

In May 2013, The idea of Atomic Transfers [20] was proposed by Nolan on the BitcoinTalk forum, which forms the initial basic technical scheme for realizing atomic cross-blockchain digital asset transactions. In February 2015, On this basis, the Lightning network [21] is proposed and first uses Hash-Locking.

Hash-locking is a mechanism based on the one-way property and low collision of the hash function, and it takes advantage of the characteristics of the delayed execution of transactions on the blockchain. A puzzle is implemented by using hash-locking and is set up in a transaction, which is stored on the blockchain by both parties to the transaction and anyone who can solve the puzzle within a specified period can get the tokens for the transaction. Recoverable Sequence Maturity Contract (RSMC) and Hashed Timelock Contract (HTLC) are designed for the implementation of the lightning network.

RSMC. In lighting network, each party pays a certain amount of Bitcoin into a multi-address account, the token in the account must have the private keys of both sides to be withdrawn so that both sides of the transaction establish a channel. The core idea of the RSMC is that users who close the trading channel will have to wait for a period before they can use the asset, while counterparties can use the digital asset immediately. So, if one party forces the closing of the channel, it will be penalized by delaying the transaction.

HTLC. The two-way payment channel built by RSMC above can only realize secure transactions within the channel. However, it is impossible to establish a two-way payment channel between all nodes of the lightning network, which would constitute a fully connected network. Therefore, HTLC is designed to achieve secure transactions between two nodes where no two-way payment channel has been established, that is, to use a network of channels across multiple nodes to build secure transmission to the destination. The purpose of HTLC is to allow a global state to be implemented across multiple nodes by hashing. This global state is ensured by time commitments and time-based unencumbering of resources via disclosure of preimages. Suppose that between A and C without a payment channel, A wants to trade BTC to C, so it can borrow the payment channels between A, B, and B, C for the transaction.

Table 2. Advantage and weaknesses of above solutions

Category	Advantage	Weakness and limitation
Notary Schemes	• Different structures of blockchains are flexibly supported • Simple implementation	• Notaries need to be given greater trust by participants of cross-chain • There is a serious risk of centralization
Sidechain	• The more application scenarios are implemented • Simple implementation	• As the number of transactions increases, the use of smart contracts can lead to slower transactions
Relay	• The strong scalability to support interaction between a variety of different blockchains and relay-chains	• Complex implementation • Security is affected by each subchains
Hash-Locking	• The security of information exchange is ensured • An almost unlimited number of transactions were allowed • The realization of micropayments	• Hash locking can only be used for exchange, not cross-blockchain transfer of assets • Exchange rate fluctuations within the window of the hash-locking need to be considered

3 Innovative Cross-Blockchain Solutions

The number of cross-blockchain approaches which have wide availability are limited, and they primarily operate on the mechanisms mentioned above. Although these technologies do not rely on trusted third parties, at present, the following operations can only be performed within a single blockchain:

- Tokens are sent between participants.
- Execution of smart contracts.
- The storage of validity guaranteed data on the blockchain.

Due to these limitations, new cross-blockchain solutions are still being actively studied, and in this section, we will introduce a more advanced and universally applicable approach to blockchain interoperability than simple switching protocols. They not only allow asset ownership changes across blockchains but also allow actual tokens to be transferred from one blockchain to another. In this chapter, we select several emerging cross-chain solutions with good development prospects to illustrate. Table 3 shows the summary of the solutions and discuss their weakness and limitation.

3.1 DexTT

Deterministic Cross-Blockchain Token Transfers (DexTT) [22], a protocol implementing eventual consistency for cross-blockchain token transfers. DexTT reduces the dependency and risk on a single blockchain, where tokens are not locked into a single blockchain. The protocol defines a token that can be transferred over a protocol that is not a local token (such as Bitcoin), but rather a type of token that can exist concurrently on a given number of blockchains. They can transact and synchronize across all participating different blockchains. In theory, DeXTT supports the use of any number of blockchains and autonomously synchronizes its transactions across them in a fully decentralized manner. The DexTT also can effectively prevent double-spending and deal with the cross-blockchain proof problem.

3.2 Blockchain Router

Blockchain Router [23] built a network that allows blockchains to connect and communicate with each other. In this network, a blockchain plays the role of the blockchain router, which has the task to analyze and send communication requests, it also dynamically maintains a topology structure of the network. In the protocol, the blockchains that want to communicate with each other are called subchains. Subchains can send messages to other subchains through the chain router and can receive messages from the chain router, but they cannot communicate directly with each other. Subchains connect to chain routers by following cross-chain communication protocols [24].

Table 3. List of the innovative cross-blockchain solutions

Category	Architecture	Function	Consensus mechanism	Weakness and limitation
DexTT [22]	Sender, Receiver, Contestant and Observer	Implementing the cross-blockchain Token transfer protocol on multiple blockchains reduces the dependency and risk on a single blockchain and can be used for the exchange of any asset on any number of blockchains	Designing Claim - First Transactions and Witness Contest to ensure transaction propagation and consistency	• On each participation blockchain at least one claim transaction for every token transfer is required which leads to high costs • Eager execution of unconfirmed transactions can result in inconsistencies
Blockchain Router [23]	Validator, Surveillant, Nominator and Connector	Introducing a blockchain router that enable general cross-blockchain communication	Similar to Practical Byzantine Fault Tolerance (PBFT) [29]	• No actual Solution have been fully operational

(*continued*)

Table 3. (*continued*)

Category	Architecture	Function	Consensus mechanism	Weakness and limitation
Satellite Chain [25]	Subchains and Regulators	Proposing a new blockchain architecture designed to meet industry standards and allow different satellite chains to transfer assets among themselves. It can be easily integrated within existing blockchain platforms	Each satellite chain can decide to adopt any consensus protocol that does not violate the policies mandated by the regulator	• Only be used for asset transfer • The cost of participating in the satellite chain has not been estimated
HyperService [26]	DApp Clients, Verifiable Execution Systems, Network Status Blockchain and Insurance Smart Contracts	A platform that offers interoperability and programmability across heterogeneous blockchains	A unified state model is proposed, which is a neutral and extensible model for describing State transitions between different blockchains	• Designed for writing cross-chain DApps, the platform has an additional overhead in transfer-ring tokens

3.3 Satellite Chain

The concept of Satellite Chain [25] is proposed, which supports the parallel operation of heterogeneous consensus algorithms on different subchains. The architecture consists of independent subchains running different consensus algorithms and Regulators using smart contracts to manage the entire network and specific roles. The Satellite Chain is defined as a distributed private ledger maintained by stakeholders in the network. Different from the sidechain, the model has no restriction on the underlying consensus used by each Satellite Chain, and each Satellite Chain can adopt any consensus mechanism in the protocol. It also supports the transfer of assets between different Satellite chains, and the access control of the private ledger is maintained by each subchains. Therefore, this solution supports an unbounded number of active chains at any time, thereby allowing for unprecedented levels of scalability in the system. This architecture can be integrated into existing blockchain platforms such as Hyperledger Fabric and Corda.

3.4 HyperService

The HyperService [26] platform aims to extend the functionality of blockchain interoperability from asset transfer to distributed computing. HyperService is the first platform to delivers interoperability and programmability across heterogeneous blockchains and execute Cross-chain Decentralized Applications (DApps). The design of HyperService includes a developer-facing programming framework that allows developers to build cross-blockchain applications in a unified programming model. In addition, Universal InterBlockchain Protocol (UIP) is proposed, which is a secure blockchain-facing cryptography protocol designed to safely implement complex operations defined in DApps on the blockchain.

4 Industrial Solutions

The available industrial solutions of cross-blockchain are discussed in this section. Table 4 shows the summary of the industrial solutions.

4.1 Cosmos

The Cosmos [27] project aims to implement a blockchain network to create a heterogeneous cross-chain platform by transferring cross-chain information through an intermediate chain. To support cross-chain interoperability between parallel chains, Cosmos proposes an Inter-blockchain Communication Protocol (IBC) [28], the instant determinism of the Tendermint consensus algorithm is utilized to realize value and data transfer between multiple heterogeneous chains. Tendermint is an adaptation of the Proof of Stake (PoS) consensus algorithm proposed by Castro and Liskov in 2014 based on the Practical Byzantine Fault Tolerance (PBFT) [29]. The blockchain in Cosmos has its own label, called "Atom". Cosmos consists of two main parts, the shared Hub and Zone. A Hub is a relay-chain to handle cross-chain interactions, and a Zone is a parallel chain in Cosmos.

4.2 Polkadot

The Polkadot [30] is an inter-chain blockchain protocol, enabling decentralized and trust-free cross-chain interactions. Polkadot provides a relay-chain on which all the information of the other chains connected to the relay-chain is stored in the form of blockchain data. The information comes from the independently running chains connected to the relay-chain. Therefore, these parallel and structured blockchains are called parachain.

4.3 Aion

Aion [31] is an advanced third-generation blockchain. In this design, Aion, as a general blockchain, is used to connect other blockchains and manage its own large number of on-chain programs, encouraging and guaranteeing the overall operation of the network through the internal economic model. Tokens of Aion serve as fuel for the entire network that can be used to create new blockchains, monetize across chains, and secure the entire network.

4.4 Wanchain

The Wanchain [32] aims to create a public chain for cross-chain transactions, thus providing a platform for the circulation and transaction of various digital currencies and providing an infrastructure with infinite possibilities for the financial market of digital currencies. Account model and Ethereum virtual machine (EVM) [33] are adopted by Wanchain to implement the contract. For the first time, secure multi-party computing and threshold key sharing technology is adopted to realize secure cross-chain transactions.

4.5 Lisk

Lisk [34], originated in 2016, is a blockchain application platform similar to Ethereum, but it aims to design blockchain technology into the world better through the Sidechain Development Kit (SDK) written in JavaScript. The difference with Ethereum is that it mainly hopes to improve the efficiency of blockchain through sidechain and realize the landing of applications.

Table 4. Summary of the available industrial solutions

Category	Architecture	Brief description	Consensus mechanism
Cosmos [27]	Hub and Zone	An intermediate chain is used to relay cross-chain information to create a heterogeneous cross-chain platform	IBC, Tendermint
Polkadot [30]	Relay Chain, Parachain and Bridge	Establishing information channels between relay-chains and parallel chains for cross-chain communication which makes Polkadot as a scalable cross-chain platform	Byzantine Fault Tolerance (BFT) [35]
Aion [31]	Connecting Network, Interchain transaction, Bridge and Participating Network	Aion-1, at the heart of the Aion network, is an open third generation blockchain, designed to connect other blockchains and manage its own large number of on-chain programs	BFT
Wanchain [32]	Registration module, Cross chain transaction and Data transmission module	The Wanchain aims to create a public chain for cross-chain transactions, thus providing a platform for the circulation and transaction of various digital currencies and providing an infrastructure with infinite possibilities for the financial market of digital currencies	PoS

(*continued*)

Table 4. (*continued*)

Category	Architecture	Brief description	Consensus mechanism
Lisk [34]	Node.js, Swagger, PostgreSQL and Redis	Each distributed application of the Lisk runs on its own blockchain (sidechain)	Delegated Proof of Stake (DPoS) [36]
Ark [37]	Smart Bridge	The ARK enables any user to build their own blockchain in a small amount of time by creating a framework. The main feature of the project is Smart Bridge, which is used to connect incomplete and independent blockchains	DPoS
Metronome [38]	Exporting, Importing and Validation	The cross-blockchain transmission of Metronome Tokens is implemented by Metronome	Proof-of-exit receipt

4.6 Ark

Ark [37] is a blockchain project that improves on the DPoS system of Lisk. Users, developers, and startups are provided with innovative blockchain solution by Ark. The goal of the Ark is to build a complete blockchain ecosystem that is highly flexible, adaptable, and scalable. The main feature of the project is Smart Bridge, which is a mechanism that can provide any blockchain with the ability to communicate with each other.

4.7 Metronome

An approach to blockchain interoperability has been implemented by Metronome [38], which claims to enable cross-blockchain transmission of Metronome Tokens (MET). To move a MET from one blockchain A to another blockchain B, the user must first destroy and delete the MET from blockchain A and generate a certificate of destruction. This proof is provided to Metronome's smart contract, than the tokens that have been destroyed can be declared on blockchain B and the coinbase transaction can be initiated on blockchain B.

5 Conclusion

We discuss the widely recognized cross-blockchain technologies and industrial solutions, and these methods are described and compared. Each of these solutions have its own focus but also have some defects in some ways, such as system upgrade, fault tolerance and so on. It seems that some solutions have excellent usability, but their future is not assured. We can conclude that the topic of blockchain interoperability is almost a new area of research. Most solutions only show the early proof-of-concept. Thus, at present, there are no cross-blockchain solution that is mature enough to meet the business needs fully.

It can be predicted that the industry will develop distributed ledger with structures such as Directed Acyclic Graph (DAG) [39, 40] and Hashgraph [41] in the future, and cross-blockchain solutions will be faced more complex scenarios. Thus, it is difficult to develop a unified and universal cross-blockchain solution, the available way is more inclined to the standardized data interface communication technology like the Internet.

Acknowledgment. This work was funded by the National Natural Science Foundation of China (12163004), the basic applied research program of Yunnan Province (202001AT070135, 202101AS070007, 202002AD080002, 2018FB105).

References

1. Nakamoto, S.: Bitcoin: a peer-to-peer electronic cash system (2008)
2. Javarone, M.A., Wright, C.S.: From bitcoin to bitcoin cash: a network analysis. In: Proceedings of the 1st Workshop on Cryptocurrencies and Blockchains for Distributed Systems, pp. 77–81 (2018)
3. Chen, S., Shi, R., Ren, Z., et al.: A blockchain-based supply chain quality management framework. In: 2017 IEEE 14th International Conference on e-Business Engineering (ICEBE), pp. 172–176. IEEE (2017)
4. Tapscott, A., Tapscott, D.: How blockchain is changing finance. Harv. Bus. Rev. **1**(S), 2–5 (2017)
5. Sinclair, D., Shahriar, H., Zhang, C.: Security requirement prototyping with hyperledger composer for drug supply chain: a blockchain application. Presented at the Proceedings of the 3rd International Conference on Cryptography, Security and Privacy, Kuala Lumpur, Malaysia (2019). https://doi.org/10.1145/3309074.3309104
6. Rahulamathavan, Y., Phan, R.C.-W., Rajarajan, M., et al.: Privacy-preserving blockchain based IoT ecosystem using attribute-based encryption. In: 2017 IEEE International Conference on Advanced Networks and Telecommunications Systems (ANTS), pp. 1–6. IEEE (2017)
7. Feng, Q., He, D., Zeadally, S., et al.: A survey on privacy protection in blockchain system. J. Netw. Comput. Appl. **126**(S), 45–58 (2019)
8. Leible, S., Schlager, S., Schubotz, M., et al.: A review on blockchain technology and blockchain projects fostering open science. Front. Blockchain **2**(S), 16 (2019)
9. Sun, G., Dai, M., Sun, J., et al.: Voting-based decentralized consensus design for improving the efficiency and security of consortium blockchain. IEEE Internet Things J. **8**(S), 6257–6272 (2020)
10. Schulte, S., Sigwart, M., Frauenthaler, P., Borkowski, M.: Towards blockchain interoperability. In: Di Ciccio, C., et al. (eds.) BPM 2019. LNBIP, vol. 361, pp. 3–10. Springer, Cham (2019). https://doi.org/10.1007/978-3-030-30429-4_1
11. Buterin, V.: Chain interoperability. R3 Research Paper (2016)
12. Schwartz, D., Youngs, N., Britto, A.: The ripple protocol consensus algorithm. Ripple Labs Inc White Paper **5**(S), 151 (2014)
13. Hope-Bailie, A., Thomas, S.: Interledger: creating a standard for payments. Presented at the Proceedings of the 25th International Conference Companion on World Wide Web (2016). https://doi.org/10.1145/2872518.2889307

14. Schwartz, E.: A payment protocol of the web, for the web: or, finally enabling web micropayments with the interledger protocol (2016)
15. Thomas, S., Schwartz, E.: A protocol for interledger payments (2016)
16. Back, A., Corallo, M., Dashjr, L., et al.: Enabling blockchain innovations with pegged sidechains **72**(S) (2014). http://www.opensciencereview.com/papers/123/enablingblockch ain-innovations-with-pegged-sidechains
17. BTC Relay. http://btcrelay.org/. Accessed 1 Mar 2021
18. Asgaonkar, A., Krishnamachari, B.: Solving the buyer and seller's dilemma: a dual-deposit escrow smart contract for provably cheat-proof delivery and payment for a digital good without a trusted mediator (2018)
19. Sztorc, P.: Drivechain. http://www.truthcoin.info/blog/drivechain/
20. Nolan, T.: Alt chains and atomic transfers. In: Bitcoin Forum (2013)
21. Poon, J., Dryja, T.: The bitcoin lightning network: scalable off-chain instant payments (2016)
22. Borkowski, M., Sigwart, M., Frauenthaler, P., et al.: DeXTT: deterministic cross-blockchain token transfers. IEEE Access **7**(S), 111030–111042 (2019)
23. Wang, H., Cen, Y., Li, X.: Blockchain router: a cross-chain communication protocol. In: Proceedings of the 6th International Conference on Informatics, Environment, Energy and Applications, pp. 94–97 (2017)
24. Johnson, S., Robinson, P., Brainard, J.: Sidechains and interoperability. arXiv preprint arXiv: 1903.04077 (2019)
25. Li, W., Sforzin, A., Fedorov, S., et al.: Towards scalable and private industrial blockchains. In: Proceedings of the ACM Workshop on Blockchain, Cryptocurrencies and Contracts, pp. 9–14 (2017)
26. Liu, Z., Xiang, Y., Shi, J., et al.: Hyperservice: interoperability and programmability across heterogeneous blockchains. In: Proceedings of the 2019 ACM SIGSAC Conference on Computer and Communications Security, pp. 549–566 (2019)
27. Kwon, J., Buchman, E.: Cosmos: A network of distributed ledgers (2016). https://cosmos.net work/whitepaper
28. Kwon, J.: TenderMint: consensus without mining. Draft v. 0.6, fall **1**(S) (2014)
29. Castro, M., Liskov, B.: Practical Byzantine fault tolerance and proactive recovery. ACM Trans. Comput. Syst. (TOCS) **20**(S), 398–461 (2002)
30. Wood, G.: Polkadot: vision for a heterogeneous multi-chain framework. White paper (2016)
31. AION. https://aion.network. Accessed 1 Mar 2021
32. Wanchain. https://wanchain.org. Accessed 1 Mar 2021
33. Buterin, V.: A next-generation smart contract and decentralized application platform. White paper **3**(S) (2014)
34. Lisk. https://lisk.com. Accessed 1 Mar 2021
35. Eyal, I., Gencer, A.E., Sirer, E.G., et al.: Bitcoin-NG: a scalable blockchain protocol. In: 13th Symposium on Networked Systems Design and Implementation (NSDI 2016), pp. 45–59 (2016)
36. MediaWiki. Delegated Proof of State. https://en.bitcoin.it/wiki/Delegated. Accessed 1 Mar 2021
37. ARK. https://ark.io. Accessed 1 Mar 2021
38. Metronome. https://www.metronome.io. Accessed 1 Mar 2021
39. Churyumov, A.: Byteball: a decentralized system for storage and transfer of value (2016). https://byteball.org/Byteball.pdf
40. Gross, J.L., Yellen, J.: Handbook of Graph Theory. CRC Press, Boca Raton (2003)
41. Tsai, W.-T., Yu, L., Wang, R., et al.: Blockchain application development techniques. J. Softw. **28**(S), 1474–1487 (2017)

Author Index

Printed in the United States
by Baker & Taylor Publisher Services